Structural Flaws in the Middle East Peace Process

International Political Economy Series

General Editor: **Timothy M. Shaw**, Professor of Commonwealth Governance and Development, and Director of the Institute of Commonwealth Studies, School of Advanced Study, University of London.

Titles include:

Francis Adams, Satya Gupta and Kidane Mengisteab (*editors*)
GLOBALIZATION AND THE DILEMMAS OF THE STATE IN THE SOUTH

Susan Dicklitch
THE ELUSIVE PROMISE OF NGOs IN AFRICA
Lessons from Uganda

David Hulme and Michael Edwards (*editors*)
NGOs, STATES AND DONORS
Too Close for Comfort?

Staffan Lindberg and Árni Sverrisson (*editors*)
SOCIAL MOVEMENTS IN DEVELOPMENT
The Challenge of Globalization and Democratization

Laura Macdonald
SUPPORTING CIVIL SOCIETY
The Political Role of Non-Governmental Organizations in Central America

Kurt Mills
HUMAN RIGHTS IN THE EMERGING GLOBAL ORDER
A New Sovereignty

Michael G. Schechter (*editor*)
THE REVIVAL OF CIVIL SOCIETY
Global and Comparative Perspectives

J. W. Wright, Jr. (*editor*)
STRUCTURAL FLAWS IN THE MIDDLE EAST PEACE PROCESS
Historical Contexts

J.W. Wright, Jr. and Laura Drake (*editors*)
ECONOMIC AND POLITICAL IMPEDIMENTS TO MIDDLE EAST PEACE
Critical Questions and Alternative Scenarios

International Political Economy Series
Series Standing Order ISBN 0–333–71708–2 hardcover
Series Standing Order ISBN 0–333–71110–6 paperback
(*outside North America only*)

You can receive future titles in this series as they are published by placing a standing order. Please contact your bookseller or, in case of difficulty, write to us at the address below with your name and address, the title of the series and one of the ISBNs quoted above.

Customer Services Department, Macmillan Distribution Ltd, Houndmills, Basingstoke, Hampshire RG21 6XS, England

---

Structural Flaws in the Middle East Peace Process

Historical Contexts

Edited by

J.W. Wright, Jr.
American Association for the Advancement of Science Overseas Diplomacy Fellow
US Agency for International Development Mission
Cairo, Egypt

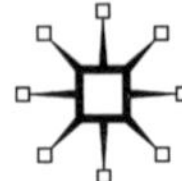

First published 2002 by
PALGRAVE
Houndmills, Basingstoke, Hampshire RG21 6XS and
175 Fifth Avenue, New York, N.Y. 10010
Companies and representatives throughout the world

PALGRAVE is the new global academic imprint of
St. Martin's Press LLC Scholarly and Reference Division and
Palgrave Publishers Ltd (formerly Macmillan Press Ltd).

ISBN 0–333–73850–0

This book is printed on paper suitable for recycling and
made from fully managed and sustained forest sources.

A catalogue record for this book is available
from the British Library.

Library of Congress Cataloging-in-Publication Data
Structural flaws in the Middle East peace process: historical
contexts / edited by J.W. Wright.
        p. cm. — (International political economy series)
    Includes bibliographical references (p.) and index.
    ISBN 0–333–73850–0
    1. Arab–Israeli conflict—1993——Peace. 2. Arab–Israeli
    conflict—1993——Economic aspects. I. Wright, J. W.,
    1962– II. Series.

    DS119.76 .S82 2001
    956.05—dc21
                                                        2001034496

10   9   8   7   6   5   4   3   2   1
11   10   09   08   07   06   05   04   03   02

Printed and bound in Great Britain by
Antony Rowe Ltd, Chippenham, Wiltshire

To my grandfathers, who if alive would have enjoyed seeing this book, and to my grandmothers and their children and grandchildren, who surely will enjoy seeing it.

You are all very important to me.

Contents

List of Tables and Figures

Prolog

J. W. Wright, Jr.

Structural Flaws in the Middle East Peace Process: Historical Contexts is the third in a series on the influences of trade and economics on the Middle East Peace Process. The chapters in these volumes contended that negligence in addressing, even considering, the economic impediments to Middle East Peace would lead to the Process's downfall. The other volumes are *The Political Economy of Middle East Peace: the Impact of Competing Trade Agendas* (Routledge, 1999), and *Economic and Political Impediments to Middle East Peace: Critical Questions and Alternative Scenarios* (with Laura Drake, Macmillan, 2000). These volumes grew from a thesis I developed during a Fulbright grant, which enabled me to study regional trade flows between the Gulf states and the Levant in order to see if they supported the Peace Process. It was a core assumption at the beginning of the Peace Process that market integration would facilitate economic and, by extension, political stability. I found that this assumption was fatally flawed and that as a result disintegration and not integration was occurring. However, I also found this situation was occurring for practical not political reasons.

The more hidden but more important conclusion that came out of this research was that the commercial and socio-economic structures that were developing out of the Peace Process's agreements and protocols were making the situation seriously worse. No attempt was being made to reduce the influence of lobbies that saw incentives for avoiding peace, few people were discussing impending financial crises in the Peace Process states, little attention was being paid to unemployment and underemployment, with a result that the risk of conflict was being raised.

In this volume we look back at the events over the last ten years and evaluate the structural and institutional mechanisms that have grown out of the Peace Process and analyze how they have led to its failures. What we find is that the inability to address commercial and economic issues, and the unwillingness to create fair trade regimes has not only disabled the process as a negotiating framework, it has created systemic and significantly weak social and economic structures that may prevent peace altogether; certainly they help to justify conflict. As we did when preparing the first two volumes, we hoped we would be proven wrong, but feared and still fear that indeed we were right.

There is no doubt that in this first decade in a new century that approaches to Middle East peace will change. As I wrote this introduction, Secretary of State Colin Powell had just left the Gulf War's 10th Anniversary ceremonies and was on his way to meet the region's leaderships. He no doubt told them all that in George W. Bush's administration a new style of diplomacy was imminent and that there should be renewed hope about the prospects for peace. Of course in the back rooms the dialog was different – some of which I was in. There, people were less reticent about expressing their concerns about havoc Sharonian diplomacy might cause, about offensives Baghdad might led, about possible perils on the 'Arab street', about the need to diffuse the situation in southern Lebanon, and about just how long Yasser Arafat can hang on to his control of Gaza. (Many felt he had already lost control.) No one expected Egypt's position to change dramatically as long as there continues to be a massive transfers of taxpayer dollars from the United States to Egypt. The same is true for Jordan, although they receive much less aid.

The point we wish to make herein is that the Peace Process itself has created economic and political structures – some formal and some informal – that have in fact become sources of conflict and instability. What the new leaderships is Amman, Beirut, Damascus, Jerusalem and Washington do now will be inconsequential over time unless they address the structural flaws that exist at the Process's very foundation, e.g. the region's trade regimes and social-economic support systems are weak and they are being made weaker by the protocols themselves. Unknowingly – we will assume – the Clinton Administration's inconsistent 'brinksmanship' approach to the Peace Process undermined all sides' positions, even the US's, the result being wasted time and power vacuums in the West Bank and Gaza, increased resistance in both areas, short-term regimes and inconsistent leadership in Israel, and a general lack of strategy.

Speculation about what will come next will therefore yield little fruit unless it is based upon serious analysis of the structural biases new leaders in the Peace Process have inherited, and unless those biases are placed into appropriate historical contexts. This is what we wish to do in this collection of essays, aptly entitled *Structural Flaws in the Middle East Peace Process: Historical Contexts*. While the chapters herein and the themes they address are free-standing, they function as volume III for the two books mentioned above. In those we evaluated the critical trade and political-economic questions that faced negotiators and we tried to identify alternative scenarios wherein peace might be achieved.

What has in fact happened was that we identified numerous regimes that put the Palestinians 'between' and not within structures that could enable them to address core issues. This 'between-ness' of the Palestinian situation makes their abilities to act as a state liminal, at best, and creates critical weaknesses in the Process that impede efforts toward peace. By evaluating historical contexts we provide the background needed to understand the real issues and begin repairing the faults.

Moreover, we review extant regional realities and compared them to current rhetoric in the Arab–Israeli Peace Process. There continues to be, of course, a great divide between the two. That said, it is from this rhetorical divide that we were able to identify incentives for maintaining the structures that keep the Peace Process weak. In this volume we try to more accurately identify these incentives and to investigate stakeholders' motives and influences for keeping prospects for peace at bay.

This approach also enabled us to correct false presumptions about events that have led to failure in the peace process. For example, literature has tended to view the Peace Process as an outcome of the Gulf War. There is no doubt that this military conflict set in motion a series of events that exposed the region's disparities and divisions more clearly than ever before. However, to see the Peace Process only as an outcome of the Gulf War is naïve. As Findley points out, the US role in peace negotiations predates the Camp David Accords, which were signed more than 20 years before the Gulf War. Furthermore, the economic and political structures in the Middle East that have changed in the 1990s find their roots in the 1970s and 1980s and would have occurred regardless of the Gulf War, albeit at a slower pace. For one thing, the fall of the Soviet block caused both leadership and funding voids throughout the region. For another thing, development achievements in the Gulf states caused dramatic shifts in the region's labor mobility and remittance structures. So, while we look at structures that developed since the Gulf War, placing them within historical contexts enables us to better discuss the real issues.

The collection is divided into two parts and contains 12 chapters. The first three chapters are commentaries that provide historical contexts by three leading figures who have been involved with the Middle East policy process for decades. Paul Findley was a US congressman who was intimately involved with US–Middle East affairs. George Wilson was an advisor to the White House during several administrations. Fadle Naquib is an academic who has worked closely with the United Nations' Conference on Trade and Development's Programme in support of the

Palestinian People. In Chapter 1, Findley discusses the US's road to opening relations with the Palestinians and setting policy in subsequent years. Wilson (Chapter 2) discusses the role the fall of the Soviet Union played in building consensus for a Middle East peace process. Lastly in this part (Chapter 3) Naqib examines the strictures of occupation alongside the structures of 'limited self-rule' and illustrates just how unbalanced the process is and how limited PA autority really is.

The chapters that follow are research based and focus on the 'betweeness' of the Palestinian situation. In Chapter 4 Stephen Zunes looks at US lobbyists' roles in developing a 'Pax Americana'. He asserts that 'US policy is working contrary to ... a comprehensive settlement of the Arab-Israeli conflict.' His point is that the incentive structures faced by special interest groups 'make it doubtful that US policy in the Middle East will change until priorities at home are similarly redirected.'

Labor-oriented trade issues are examined in three chapters. Ishaq Diwan and Michael Walton look at the triangular trade arrangement that actually confines relations among Jordan, Israel, and Palestine. The Palestinains are in neither a geographically nor a politically enviable position. Nora Colton further illustrates the complexity of labor supply issues by describing the role of and attitudes toward returnees from the Gulf in the Jordanian economy. She emphasizes that the most immediate problem is employment. I tie the issues of labor mobility and financial liquidity together by detailing labor-remittance dependencies that have bound the Gulf states and the Levant since the 1970s.

Alwyn Rouyer (Chapter 8), however, convincingly argues that water rights may be the most vital issue to be resolved. Access to water is critical to improving living standards in the West Bank and Gaza while industrial development is also dependent on adequate water supply.

In Chapter 9, Bradley Glasser explores the nexus between foreign aid and political and economic liberalization. He asserts that Egypt in particular has been able to avoid making needed reforms because of its ability to secure exogenous resources through aid. In contrast, Jordan has pursued reforms and is better off for it.

Denis Sullivan's chapter on the use and misuse of aid funds in Palestine furthers Glasser's point. He examines ways in which the Palestinian Authority (PA) has re-directed funds meant to support NGOs. The PA's active campaign to co-opt and control traditional civil society organizations has had dire consequences, including a strengthening of support for groups like Hamas. Issues related to increased dependency on Islamic organizations are addressed by Sara Roy in Chapter 11. She shows how groups like Hamas use basic services, such as the provision of food, health care, and education, as means of gaining popular political support and even membership.

In Chapter 12, Shimson Bichler chronicles reactions Israeli voters have had, since 1977, to economically threatening situations. Just as Zunes notes that lobbyists and populists influence US elections, Bichler illustrates how the same happens in Israel. Unlike most articles on Israeli voting patterns, Bichler goes beyond the assumption that security issues dominate voters' agendas and analyzes the impact of perceived economic threats on voter behavior. He identifies a cycle of voter discontent over economics that forces regime changes.

I try to set a continuing dialog for commercial and economic analysis in place in the Epilog. Indeed, most of us agree that the policy vision over the last ten years was superficial and ill informed, maybe from the beginning but certainly throughout the Clinton Administration. Press conferences and personal agendas do not lead to peace and we should not have expected that they would. As I wrote in 1999 at the beginning of *The Political Economy of Middle East Peace*:

> On October 24, 1998 the *Washington Post* called the accord 'a remarkable chapter of personal diplomacy' for Bill Clinton. President Clinton himself said that brokering the agreement was part to 'my job as a president, my mission as a Christian, and my personal journey of atonement.' On *Face the Nation*, Madeline Albright called this a 'personal political victory.' The important linkages here are that the spectacles through which the Clinton Administration is viewing the peace process are only personal and political, and not pragmatic or practical. … thus, while the rhetoric alone may save the day – or at least serve to divert attention away from the day's other problems – it will not create peace. Both the politicians and the pundits seem to have, once again, missed the point.

The point being that without adequate address of key economic issues dysfunctional structures would evolve, and so they have. (Maybe it is all about the economy – stupid.) We can only hope that the George W. Bush Administration will avoid the personal publicity trap that has been set and offer instead a policy vision that is practical and that is based on pragmatic analyses of the region's true economic and political realities.

What evolves out of the chapters in this volume and its predecessors is certainty that huge economic resources and enormous political energies have been devoted to the Middle East peace process. But to what end?

Over 30 years ago, in 1967, the occupation of additional Palestinian territories put into place new economic and political structures which would long leave the West Bank and Gaza behind in the development process. Ten years afterward, in 1977, the United States began its overt efforts toward brokering peace in the Middle East – an effort which set into place a structure of aid dependency that will not be easily changed. Ten years later, the Intifada further changed economic and political structures to the Palestinians' disadvantage. Ten years ago, the current Peace Process began without much apparent recognition of the effects the events ten, twenty, and thirty years earlier had on the region.

As a result, the Middle East Peace Process is riddled with structural flaws that are difficult but not impossible to repair. But we hope our words do not add unduly to feelings of despair about the prospects for peace. Rather, opportunities remain and we hope our contributions to the Process via these writings on its historical contexts will help facilitate the development of a fair and sustainable peace.

J. W. WRIGHT, JR.

Acknowledgements

This collection has been through many phases, and at each stage of its production there are people whose efforts need to be acknowledged. All the contributors' efforts and patience are greatly appreciated. Sara Roy and Denis Sullivan deserve an extra note of thanks for reviewing all of our chapters and editing several of them. In addition, Anne Martin Holt's help has been very valuable during the final round of editing.

I want to thank the Council for the International Exchange of Scholars, and in particular Gary Garrison and Davis Adams. Without a Fulbright grant, I would not have been able to finish this text. Similarly, the USIS-Abu Dhabi staff – especially Jonathan Rice, Nadia Ibrahim, Attullah Hoshan, and Margaret Hamoud – greatly facilitated my work during my Fulbright year. The Jordanian-American Commission staff also provided assistance while I was working on this project in Amman.

Similarly, Mr Juma Al Majid and his staff at the Juma Al Majid Centre for Culture and Heritage, especially Drs Obaid Bin Butti and Fawzi Khoury, as well as Amal Al Fahmi, Bashar Qudah and Raed Qudah all provided much-needed assistance. I remember the Centre fondly.

Numerous others supported the project over time, sometimes by reading chapters and making comments and otherwise being generally supportive. Among them are Eugene Bird, Murial Crawford, Allen Douglas, Willie Fainsan, John Sherman Gideons, Nahla Kasrawi, Clyde Leamaster, Davy Mc Call, Fedwa Malti-Douglas, Allen Omoto, John Presley, Vicky Lynne Sawyer, Joanne Shams, Jaroslav Stetkevych, Suzanne Stetkevych, Qeisi Stetkevych, Khaled Stetkevych, Michael Stevensons, Mary Willis, Rodney Wilson, Valerie Yorke, and, most importantly, my parents, J. Wayne and M. Diane Wright, my grandparents and the rest of my family.

J. W. Wright, Jr.

List of Abbreviations

AMF	Arab Monetary Fund
ACDA	Arms Control and Disarmament Agency
AHLC	Ad Hoc Liaison Committee
COPP	Committee for International Assistance to the Palestinian Police
DOP	The Declaration of Principles
ESCWA	United Nations Economic and Social Commission for Western Asia
GDP	gross domestic product
GNP	gross national product
GCC	Gulf Cooperation Council
IFC	International Finance Corporation
IMF	International Monetary Fund
ICA	Israeli Civil Administration
IMA	Israeli Military Authority
IS	Israeli Shekel
JD	Jordanian Dinar
JSET	Joint Supervision and Enforcement Team
JWC	Joint Water Commission
MENA	Middle East and North Africa region
MERIP	Middle East Research and Information Project
NDP	National Democratic Party (Egypt)
NGO	Non-governmental organizations (usually registered)
NIS	New Israeli Shekel
PA	Palestinian Authority/Palestinian National Authority
PMA	Palestinian Monetary Authority
Protocol	Protocol on Economic Relations Between the Government of Israel and the PLO, representing the Palestinian People. Also referred to as the 'Paris Protocol'
UN	United Nations
UNCTAD	United Nations Commission on Trade and Development
UNDP	United Nations Development Project
UNRWA	United Nations Relief and Works Agency
USIS	United States Information Service
VAT	value-added tax

Notes on the Contributors

Shimson Bichler is a Professor of Political Science at Hebrew University, Mount Scopus, Jerusalem, Israel, where he teaches courses on political economics. His publications range from articles on the changing electoral process in Israel to studies on the political significance of structural adjustments in Israeli industry, especially as they relate to the country's core conglomerates. He has also written on Israeli privatization, and the economic policies of Labor and Likud in the peace process.

Nora Ann Colton is an Assistant Professor of International Economics at Drew University, Madison, New Jersey. Since receiving a doctorate from Oxford University, her work has focused on labor migration in the Middle East. She has conducted extensive fieldwork in Jordan, Egypt and Yemen. She has written numerous articles on economics within the Middle East. Her publications include *Invisible Markets: The Informal Sector and Migration in Yemen.*

Ishaq Diwan earned a PhD in economics from the University of California, Berkeley and has since worked with various divisions at the World Bank, including its Middle East Department, where he supervise research projects on the region and where he wrote on issues relating to Arab economic development, trade, and international and interregional finance. He has also writes on Middle East political-economic relations and is an active figure in programs relating to aid distribution in the West Bank and Gaza.

Paul J. Findley was a US Congressman from 1961 to 1983, served for 12 years as the senior Republican on the Middle East Subcommittee, and has served in various capacities with international organizations. He is a writer and a lecturer, and the author of two books on the Arab–Israeli dispute, the best seller, *They Dare to Speak Out* and *Deliberate Deceptions.* He is Chairman of the Council for the National Interest, a Washington-based membership organization that focuses on Middle East policy. He resides in Jacksonville, Illinois.

Bradley L. Glasser, after earning in PhD International Studies from Columbia University, won the 1995 Social Science Research Council's

Ibn Khaldun prize for his dissertation, which also won the Andrew Wellington Cordier prize. Before that, he was Assistant Director of a Foundation devoted to Israeli–Palestinian Rapprochement. He teaches courses at the Columbia University Middle East Center, and continues to work on human rights issues facing people living in the West Bank and the Gaza Strip.

Fadle Naqib is a Professor of Economics at the University of Waterloo in Canada, where he specializes in research on commercial development in the Middle East. A consultant for the UN, he was the author of UNCTAD's 1995 report entitled 'Prospects for Sustained Development of the Palestinian Economy: Strategies and Policies for Reconstruction and Development'. His current research involves the development of econometric models which can be applied in Palestine.

Alwyn R. Rouyer is an Associate Professor of Political Science at the University of Idaho and specializes in Middle East politics and the politics of the Indian subcontinent. After earning an MA from Georgetown and a PhD from Tulane universities, he has been a Fulbright lecturer, a Joseph J. Malone Fellow, a Senior Fellow at the W. F. Albright Institute in Jerusalem, and a Visiting Scholar at Birzeit University in the West Bank in 1993. He is currently writing a book on the issue of water in the peace process.

Sara Roy is a research scholar at the Center for Middle Eastern Studies at Harvard University, where she received her PhD in political economics and international development studies. Dr Roy's work focuses on economic, political and social development in the Gaza Strip where she has lived and worked. She is the author of *The Gaza Strip: The Political Economy of De-Development* (Institute for Palestine Studies). Roy also acts as a consultant for various world aid organizations.

Denis J. Sullivan is Professor of Political Economy and Middle Eastern studies at Northeastern University in Boston, but has also served as the special assistant to the President, and is now a full professor. The author of numerous articles and editor of a collection published by Indiana University Press, he specializes in the analysis of the efficiency of international aid distributions programs. In addition, Dr Sullivan is a consultant to the World Bank and has worked with various NGOs.

Michael Walton is a macroeconomics specialist who is a primary author for the International Bank for Reconstruction and Development's Multilateral Working Group on Economic Development. He contributed to the writing of their report on the West Bank and Gaza for *Developing the Occupied Territory: an Investment in Peace*, and he serves in various consulting capacities for World Bank projects and has worked as well for the European Union.

George Wilson received his doctorate from Cornell University in 1955, and has since served as an economics advisor to Presidents Kennedy, Johnson, and Nixon. Wilson has 145 publications to his credit, including several books and over 100 articles, predominantly on the subjects of transportation systems and, more recently, on global business patterns. He is currently a Distinguished Emeritus Professor of Business Economics and Public Policy, and a former Academic Dean at Indiana University, Bloomington.

J.W. Wright, Jr. serves as the Chief Trade Advisor for the US Agency for International Development's mission in Egypt and as a Overseas Diplomacy Fellow for the American Association for the Advancement of Science. He was formerly Head of Business Development for the Dubai Chamber of Commerce and Industry. In addition to work on the economics of Middle East peace, he writes on *Business Development in Saudi Arabia* (Macmillan, 1996) and *Muslim Attitudes Toward Islamic Finance* (International Journal of Islamic and Arabic Studies, 2000).

Stephen Zunes is an Associate Professor of Political Science at the University of San Francisco, and, previously, at the University of Puget Sound, Whitman College and Ithaca College, and served as Executive Director of the Institute for a New Middle East Policy, and held posts with the Institute for Global Policy Studies, the Institute for Policy Studies, and the US Institute for Peace. He is currently completing books on conflicts in the Western Sahara, and on US Middle East policy.

Part I

Commentaries:
The Historical Context of the
Middle East Peace Process

1
Twenty Years After Camp David: Economic Diplomacy Gone Awry

Paul J. Findley

For nearly 40 years I have been involved in political negotiations between Americans, Israelis and Palestinians, but 25 years ago, along with Charles H. Percy, Adlai E. Stevenson III, Mark Hatfield, George McGovern and J. William Fulbright, and Representatives Paul N. 'Pete' McClosky, Nick Joe Rahall, and Walter Fauntroy, I lobbied President Jimmy Carter for a change in the US position regarding the Palestinian situation. He decided to break the 'no-talk' policy he had inherited and I supported his efforts by being an unofficial liaison with Palestinian Liberation Organization (PLO) president, Yasser Arafat, and his staff. Since official negotiations with the Palestinians were not permitted, US diplomats pursued negotiations via talks with Anwar Sadat and Menachem Begin. We hoped Egypt's recognition of Israel would soften hostilities between Arabs and Israelis.

Fortunately, others in the Carter Administration also saw advantage in changing US positions toward both Israel and the PLO. On the political side, Cyrus Vance maintained secret contacts in Beirut with PLO officials during the Iran hostage crisis, and he found Yasser Arafat's efforts to help free the hostages encouraging. On the economic side, Robert Straus, while serving as President Carter's special envoy to the Middle East, also wanted to meet with Chairman Arafat. Straus had a particularly strong interest in discussing the uses of trade as an incentive for peace. Had he been authorized to use his influence as a former chair of the National Democratic Council and his prominent positions in many powerful Jewish organizations and trade groups, he could have done much to advance the Peace Process. The result of our efforts was the Camp David Accords, an agreement which defused tensions between Egypt and Israeli, but that did not set a compete foundation for a broader regional peace.

Unfortunately, we were not able to extend our efforts to other nations in the region, following President Carter's re-election defeat. Even so, I felt fortunate as a Republican to work with both the Carter and Reagan Administrations on issues important to Middle East peace. For example, after the 1980 election, I tried to bridge gaps present among President Reagan's staff in the area of Middle East policy. In this administration, too, I was not alone in predicting the unrest and violence that was to come. If a more moderate Israeli policy structure did not develop, as well as a fairer trading regime for the Palestinians, it seemed inevitable that the Palestinians would be forced into despair and deeper conflict.

But this view was threatening to many special interests groups, and was presented at a time when pro-Israeli lobbies were testing a hard-line strategy to exert inordinate amounts of control over the US government in both the House and Senate. The net result was that in subsequent elections several key leaders who supported this view – including myself, J. William Fulbright, Adlai Stevenson, Jr., Pete McClosky, Charles Percy, and others – became the targets of negative and overt campaign tactics. At the same time, key State Department officials who shared this view – including Richard Parker, Talcott Seeley, Eugene Bird, and, earlier, William Stoltzfus – began to leave office and seek other means of affecting US Middle East policy. These departures left a void in policy vision about the region.

In fact, the Israeli position toward the Palestinians did not soften, which led to a tightening of strictures against Arab mobility and tighter control of the Palestinian economy. In the 1980s systemic plans aimed at confiscating additional land and water resources throughout the Territories were initiated. In addition, there was an almost complete closure of the Palestinian financial sector, business licensing programs became stricter, housing permits were increasingly limited, and there were significant increases in taxation. These situations served to lower Palestinian incomes and raise their anxieties about the inevitability of conflict. We believed a change in the US posture toward the Arabs – one that recognized the economic impacts of Israeli policies – could defuse many of these tensions.

In addition, the situation in Lebanon declined steadily throughout the 1980s, and the war between Iran and Iraq was accellerating. Both situations put thousands of people into refugee camps and caused billions of dollars of damage. The ensuing poverty further frustrated the situation and built support for militant groups like Hamas and Hezballah.

And then came the Gulf War, an event sparked by an intra-Arab aggression, intensified by dramatically declining Arab–Israeli relations, and ended by the entry of a US-led international military force. The fall-out was not limited to physical destruction; there was also the psychological damage suffered by its victims. The war, and ten years of economic sanctions, have not significantly eroded Iraqi leaders' authority, but they have broadened Arab poverty and increased cynicism about US intentions in the region. Thus, while politics may play the designing role in writing treaties and accords, we now realize that economic factors play an equally defining role in implementing sustainable peace.

Indeed, the political implications of negotiations aimed at facilitating commercial trade, financial solvency and labor mobility are foremost among the concerns of Arab leaders. One reason is that the Levantine economies are more fragile today than they were 25 years ago. Unemployment in the region began to increase following the fall of oil prices in the mid-1980s, and the jobless rate skyrocketed after the Gulf War. Underemployment reaches new highs each year in the West Bank and Gaza and neighbouring states. Capital adequacy declined dramatically in the 1990s throughout the Middle East, while interest rate and money supply fluctuations have been extreme.

The expense of supporting refugees first from Palestine itself, then from Lebanon, and later from Kuwait and Iraq, have pushed social services budgets way beyond their maximum sustainable levels in the 1990s. In addition, Arab regimes, to varying degrees – Egypt most conspicuously and to a lesser extent Jordan – have developed serious dependency habits that impede long-term economic or political development.

My point is that, in assessing the reasons for failures in achieving the Camp David Accords' goals, inadequate attention has been given to weakening socio-economic structures and their implications for the region's political structures. One example of this is the US government's failure to require assurances that its aid distributions to Egypt and Israel be used to support poverty alleviation programs and/or promote regional commercial alliances. Clearly, we did not fully consider the practical uses of economic diplomacy as a means for solving the problems caused by the region's glaring economic inequalities. These are mistakes that must not be repeated as new administrations in the US and Israel press forward with the Arab–Israeli Peace Process.

Moreover, US diplomats must realize that the current tragic events are part of the price being paid for our inappropriate economic interventions. In the face of a growing block of American and European voters who feel aid packages are not an efficient use of tax dollars, it is imperative that current funds should be spent on projects leading to sustainable economic development. In sum, the new administration's diplomats must realize the implications of their predecessor's attempts to use purely political models. It is difficult to see how peace can be sustained unless better policy apparati are developed and unless equitable resource distribution schemes are part of an enhanced diplomatic dialog with the Middle East. The current situation make the essays in this collection particularly important and timely.

2

From Cold War to a Cold Peace: the Past and Future of the Middle East Peace Process

George Wilson

I will confine my analysis to an examination of two concepts. The first addresses: the impact of the demise of the Cold War and its effect on the Middle East. The second considers how the economic restructuring of global markets could impact the region's attempts at for peace and its bid for prosperity. My perspectives are those of a Cold War-era economist who has also taken an active interest in the political and economic phenomena associated with what is loosely known as the Middle East.

In my opinion, the Middle East Peace Process would not have been conceivable without the demise of the USSR in December 1991. The termination of the Cold War allowed Gorbachev to deny the US and Europe an enemy, thus restraining the West's refusal to talk with a host of nations we had formerly seen as opposites. For example, Paul Findley (Chapter 1) is correct to note that President Carter inherited a 'no-talk' policy when it came to the PLO and that this lack of communication hampered his ability to broker peace in the region. However, what was also unnerving to too many Americans was the US alignment with Egypt, remembered for Nasser's brand of Soviet-styled rhetoric. One major concern was whether the Camp David Accords might weaken Israel's position in the region. The implicit question was, weaken their position against whom? The answer was against the Soviet-backed Arab states like Egypt and Syria.

This focus of concerns about the region changed considerably in the late 1980s and early 1990s. For one thing, with ex-USSR assistance to the Middle East cut off, many Arab governments faced bankruptcy and began to chase after international aid funding. For another thing, when Iraq's army invaded Kuwait the major rifts that exist between Arab states were revealed; with the new Commonwealth of Independent

States supporting the Allied effort (including the Gulf states, Egypt, and Syria) against Iraq, relationships among the Arab states were more thoroughly divisive than ever before. What persisted was the commonality of anti-Israeli feelings. But while it may be that Benjamin Netanyahu's aggressive stands restored a façade of unity to the Arab world, looking back it is clear that the triple set of events from 1989 through 1991, the détente between the ex-USSR and the US that ended the Cold War, the collapse of the Soviet empire, and the Gulf War so mixed up the previous relationships that the way was paved for alternative approaches to resolving the Arab–Israeli struggle. Indeed, all sides were induced to take new initiatives and to face risks hitherto deemed unfeasible and even unlikely.

The major result of the long-running confrontation and containment policies of both the US and USSR from 1945 to 1991 was the great non-event: no atomic war occurred. The other critical result of the ending of the Cold War was the overwhelming victory of political and economic liberalism over autocracy in its varied forms (fascism, communism à la Russe, feudalism, and so on.) and over detailed central planning in its modern communist forms. (Adam Smith doubtless smiles while Karl Marx is surely upset with the Russians, whom he hated anyway, for so completely mucking up his ideas.) So complete was the collapse of communism and its dictators both in the USSR and its satellites of the Warsaw Pact in Eastern Europe that some were led, like Francis Fukuyama, to define the characteristics of an imminent

> end of history [because] ... The struggle for recognition, the willingness to risk one's life for a purely abstract goal, the worldwide ideological struggle that called forth daring, courage, imagination and idealism, will be replaced by economic calculation, the endless solving of technical problems, environmental concerns, and the satisfaction of sophisticated consumer demands.[1]

This nonsense was based on a misinterpretation of Hegelianism which maintained that the two remaining opposites were communism and capitalism, and that the victory of the latter led to the end of the dialectic process and hence of history. We need not dwell on this, but the truth is that the events of 1989–91 represent a global upheaval, the significance of which may exceed anything that has happened in the last 500 years, at least in terms of making such a sudden impact on so large a proportion of the world.

Unfortunately, not all world leaders learned what they should have from this circumstance, including some from the US. Indeed, greater understandings of oil resource requirements (that of the real post-1989 geopolitical dynamics) led the Bush, Sr. and Clinton administrations to forge not-so-new visions of the Middle East. These views were not necessarily consistent with traditional American goals such as building free markets with few government subsidies or promoting democratization and ending dictatorship.

Another example is the persistence of overly-centralized planning in most Arab states, which has impeded the region's ability to attain significant levels of commercial cooperation and integration. In addition, the unwillingness of the PA to delegate decision-making authority to managers below cabinet level has proven disastrous, much like when the Kremlin realized it was bankrupt because too much centralization had distorted microeconomics and market mechanisms. The lack of delegation also has financial as well as political implications in the territories. This unfortunate situation leaves too many people looking for help wherever they can find it.

Both the imbalances created by international aid, in Israel and in Arab countries, and the persistence of poor administrative structures for distributing what could be positive about foreign sources of funding, inhibit regional abilities to develop competitive advantages needed to participate in global market expansion. This has made the Middle East a region with little inter-state commerce and falling behind in global market penetration. This situation contrasts with experiences in much of the rest of the world. The ability of market-oriented approaches to engender rapid growth has been demonstrated by Japan beginning about the mid-1950s and followed about a decade later by the so-called Asian Tigers, Hong Kong, Singapore, South Korea and Taiwan, all of whom raised their economic levels from among the very lowest in the world to rank among the top 20 within two or three decades. Malaysia, Thailand and more recently Indonesia formed the second wave of Asian tigers. The common strategic link for each of these countries has been a heavy reliance upon private enterprise. The focus was on quality production of manufactured goods and, above all, the removal of administrative barriers which impeded exports to wealthy US and EU buyers.

Is such growth possible in the newly envisioned Middle East? On the one hand, like Israel and its contiguous Arab neighbors, the Asian tigers had few real natural resources, largely because they were geographically small. As examples, Hong Kong and Singapore were city states and had nothing but human talent with which to work. It is therefore conceivable that in a peaceful era the Arab countries could move aggressively to exploit their skilled human resources and strategic geo-political positions. On the other hand, the high-growth Asian economies had plenty of government help in the form of subsidies that allowed or sometimes encouraged domestic market cartels. They also received large infusions of foreign aid. This, too, is similar to the situation faced by nations in the Levant. However, the difference seems to be that Asian regimes or in Hong Kong's case, its colonial administrative authority, expected the firms they subsidized to generate profit and spur employment. Corruption in subsidy distribution was also relatively rare in most of the fastest-growing economies, at least compared to other parts of the developing world.

The economic successes of the market- and export-oriented capitalistic approaches of so many Asian countries contrast sharply with the economic failures starkly revealed by the collapse of communism, and that seem to persist in many parts of the Arab world. Indeed, it may be that the critical turning point in the Peace Process would be to remove barriers which currently impede wider regional and global trade. If Palestine and the Arab countries, especially the non-oil Arab countries, are to overcome their dependency on foreign aid and reduce the burdens of persistent poverty, there are few realistic alternatives other than to implement policies supporting a freer and more honest economic sphere. Some trade-offs will have to be made, which is implicit in any set of policies designed to stimulate production. In fact, however, the globalization and integration of the world economy provides a special opportunity at this time, especially if the peace process negotiators legitimately seek to strip away certain political and religious barriers to trade not only within the Middle East and Israel, but beyond.

There is less unanimity in the political sphere concerning the economic necessity of democratic arrangements such as free elections, more than one party, and so on. As Shimson Bichler's chapter aptly illustrates, voters do not always act logically. Recent elections in both Israel and Palestine seem to have been based more on misinformation generating economic fears than on clear consideration of economic opportunities. But it is not unusual for prejudices to dominate real issues and, at any rate, the successful market economies in Asia did not begin with much in the way of democracy. It is certainly not true that capitalist-type successes require incipient democracy. Singapore retains its Confucian capitalism under a system of one-party rule and successfully developing Arab areas like Dubai support what some call Emirate capitalism. This is likely to persist in most of the Middle East's Gulf states.

Nor does democracy require successful capitalism, as India and the Philippines illustrate.

Similar observations can be made about the comparative support religion offers the development process. Although some religions may be more compatible than others with the emergence of certain capitalistic institutions such as self-interest (for instance, some early forms of Calvinism[2]), the sanctioning of the profit motive, private property, consumer awareness, and the reliance upon competitive markets. Individuals respond to choices such as these when they are free to do so. This is evident with respect to the Confucian-dominated Asian countries, the many capitalist Catholic-majority countries, and also in several Muslim-majority countries. For example, the richest 23 nations in the world, ranging from what the World Bank refers to as high-income economies from \$12 210 (Ireland) to \$36 080 (Switzerland) in terms of GNP per capita in 1992, contain one or more countries whose dominant religion is Protestant, Catholic, Muslim, Judaic, Buddhist-Shinto, or Confucian. The message here is that highly successful market systems can develop and thrive more or less independently of the form of religious belief predominant in any given nation. Thus, in the present context, it is fair to say that neither religion nor political systems have a decisive influence upon the creation of an effectively functioning market system unless authorities in either sphere actively seek to stifle it. That said, however, it is also true that Iran's theocracy and Iraq's dictatorship illustrate the types of gratuitous costs that can be foisted upon citizens. But this is the effect of cruel leaders, not religion.

With these background notes in mind, I feel the economic dimensions of the peace process are fairly straightforward. After Arab hostility toward Israel got beyond pretending that it did not exist, or that the country could and would be driven into the sea, the Arabs and Israelis began to discuss matters of peace, or at least a mere absence of war, and perhaps to even agree to more or less permanent boundaries. What is needed now is not only a cease-fire but a long-lasting peace. This requires a process to ensure its continuance and to attract long-term capital or even public capital from outside the region. More economic ties between Arabs and Israelis will be helpful because, once established and mutually profitable, commercial ties require the more or less free and continuous movement of goods, people, capital, resources, and communications across borders. This is not possible in today's Middle East, but, if it were, a good deal of private global capital is available for the kinds of investment that should prove viable in the Arab world and

Israel, if the region can reduce risks that now persist on ethnic, religious and historical grounds.

Sometimes, of course, economic matters may themselves lead to conflict. Indeed, two common threads binding the chapters in this collection are that (i) the agreements reached in the Protocol are unduly tilted toward an Israeli economic and resource advantage, and (ii) that, even so, the honest administration of aid funds, remittances from the Gulf, and government revenues has not taken place. These two factors create significant economic barriers to regional peace.

In essence, the 'trade-for-peace' theorem is apparently too subtle for Arab and Israeli diplomats to consider fully. The obvious reason for this situation is that economic conversion challenges leaders' short-term authorities. Moreover, huge differences in economic levels exist between most Arab countries discussed in this volume – Jordan, Lebanon, Syria, Egypt and the Palestinian entity – where GDP per head varies from a low of barely US $550 for Egypt to a high of $1300 for Syria, to Israel with almost $12 000. The extreme poverty of Israel's neighbors gives them little scope for experimentation with free trade or much else without substantial assistance to tie them over, perhaps for many years.

Fear of the potential economic dominance of Israel in a regime of fair trade is an impediment almost as large as the fundamental mistrust between the Arabs and Jews that has continued since the creation of the state of Israel. Knowing this is the case, it is understandable that as Arab countries develop democratic institutions, Arab voters will support candidates who allow Israeli integration into their economies. It is more likely that the free trade route to a lasting peace will be a hard sell to the poorer Arab states, and will require numerous modifications before it gains wide acceptance. Even free trade between Canada and the US took years of negotiation, while NAFTA that included Mexico was more difficult still. These were agreements between friendly neighbors. What can we expect from Arabs and Israelis?

Yet ultimately this is the only way to improve the economies of the poorest countries and regions and achieve a valid peace or more permanent ceasefire. When using the phrase, 'the only way' in the present context, I mean the general thrust toward market orientation, freer trade across highly sensitive borders, and as much cooperation among Syria, Lebanon, Jordan, Egypt, Israel and others as is needed to make some tangible progress toward economic integration. If this is a realistic scenario, then the existing Peace Process may work out if global markets keep driving regional groupings, including the Middle East. This assumes that the Middle East's regional blocs do not behave like their former components and act like greedy mercantilists operating under a cloak of communist alliance. More importantly, it also assumes that Israel will be accepted among its neighbors almost like any other state in the region, and that Arab business persons will be accepted and treated fairly in Israel. Unfortunately, these situations cannot develop as long as the structural flaws that exist at the very base of the Peace Process are recognized, and reconstructed, and until the crucial failures we have seen are repaired.

Notes

1. F. Fukuyama, 'The End of History', *The National Interest* (Summer 1989) 18.
2. R. H. Tawney, *Religion and the Rise of Capitalism* (New York: Harcourt Brace, 1926); and M. Weber, *The Protestant Ethic and the Spirit of Capitalism*, translated by Talcott Parsons (London: Allen & Unwin, 1930).

3

The Limiting Structure of Palestinian Limited Self-Rule: Recent Historical Perspective

Fadle Naqib

It has been more than five years since I completed my report for the United Nations Commission on Trade and Development (UNCTAD) entitled 'Prospects for Sustained Development of the Palestinian Economy: Strategies and Policies for Reconstruction and Development'. One of the points made in that report was that the establishment of self-rule in the West Bank and Gaza, which has taken place in stages since May 1994, brought euphoria to Palestinians concerned about the economic situation. It was widely felt that peace and stability would encourage domestic commercial activities, increase the level of local employment, attract foreign investment, and open the door to regional trade cooperation among the Arab countries. In addition, the benefits of the international community's commitment to underwrite large portions of the cost of infrastructure construction and reconstruction was seen as the foundation for real development and economic expansion in the Palestinian-controlled territories.

Let me begin by quoting from the UNCTAD report what we considered to be the foremost tasks facing the Palestinians:[1]

At present the PA [Palestinian Authority] faces two challenges that require immediate action. First, building new institutions for Palestinian civil administration, and the rejuvenation of old ones. Second, dealing with the unemployment problem. In tackling these two tasks, the PA needs to resist the temptation to which many governments of newly independent countries have succumbed; to embark on a programme of creating institutions that employ people directly, so ensuring their loyalties. Instead, the two problems should be dealt with in terms of the imperatives inherent in the reconstruction program. Building institutions, and alleviating the problem of unemployment, should both be directed toward expanding the capacity of the private productive sectors of the economy. Priority should be given to activities that satisfy the double requirements of generating productive employment, and expanding the infrastructure supporting the private sector. Accordingly, the most important projects will be those which increase sector resources. These include programs of land reclamation, aimed at augmenting the area suitable for cultivation, and increasing the supply of water by renovating artesian wells, drilling new wells, and constructing reservoirs. Stimulating industrial activities require increasing the supply of electricity, the improvement of transport facilities, and large investments to enhance communications. Finally, improving and modernizing the education and health systems will have a direct bearing on economic performance in the medium and long term.

In the years that have passed the development community has been continually confounded in its efforts to achieve these goals in Palestine. As the chapters in this collection illustrate, there are many problems with the systems at work in Palestine and the concept of 'limited self-rule' is the heart of the problem.

Historically, legal restrictions were used as a basis for constraining development. Under Israeli occupation all economic activities were placed under the scrutiny of the Israeli Military Authority (IMA). Every commercial undertaking had to be approved, a process that too often meant endless delays in the granting of permits and licenses. Another important restriction related to the control of technological advancement, because the IMA did not permit Palestinian firms to import new machines and tools, preferring to force these businesses to purchase second-hand equipment from Israeli distributors. In other cases, heavily subsidized Israeli products were allowed free entry into the territories, or they were leased under biased subcontracting arrangements. Extraordinary taxation of Arab business activities was equally detrimental to economic growth.

Unfortunately, the years of Palestinian Authority (PA) control have not led to many of the expected improvements. To the contrary, the general economic scenarios faced by the Palestinians, especially the local unemployment situation, have steadily deteriorated. Moreover, the PA has been unable to control its own funds, leaving it near bankruptcy, having even exhausted emergency program funding from the United Nations Reliefs and Works Agency (UNRWA). As a result, public and social services agencies are functioning at dangerously low capacity, while simultaneously the donor community is pressuring the PA to make sizable reductions in its civil service payrolls so that it can meet its budgets (see Sullivan, Chapter 10). For the Palestinians, this new turn of administration is disturbing on a psychological level and disruptive for both daily personal and business activities.[2] As frustration levels have risen, so has the amount of Palestinian civil disobedience. And, as the tenor of response turned increasingly violent under the Netanyahu regime, a cycle developed wherein security concerns led Israel to close its borders for long periods of time. This leaves more people in the territories unemployed and caused further declines in the Arab-side economy, leading to more discontent. The impact of this cycle of events was illustrated by the fact that by the end of 1992 approximately 33 percent of the Palestinian labor force worked in Israel, that 90 percent of Palestinian imports came from Israel, and that 75 percent of its exports were sold inside the green line. Estimates show that less than 10 percent of employed Palestinians worked inside Israel and that both import and export trade between Arabs and Israelis declined by approximately 75 percent. The result has been abject poverty in many of the areas under PA control.

These difficulties reflect the extent to which the PA has been unable to manage its economy under limited self-rule. On the one hand, the current state of affairs shows that the former territories have not altered their dependency on the Israeli economy. Nor has trade with Egypt, Jordan or the Gulf Arab countries replaced this dependency on Israel. On the other hand, the 1995 UNCTAD report revealed that not much had changed since the writing of the World Bank's 1993 volume on *Developing the Occupied Territories: An Investment in Peace*, which described the pre-self-rule policy environment as riddled with regulations that restricted entrepreneurial production and industrial growth, sustained asymmetric market relations with Israel, and maintained private sector financial illiquidity and fiscal policy compression. In addition, extraordinary taxation on Palestinian exports and imports reduced cash flow, caused general capital shortages, and resulted in an annual estimated financial loss of between 8 and 12 percent of the value of finished products.[3]

The limited transfer of control over economic affairs from the Israeli Civil Administration to the PA removed many direct Israeli restrictions on Palestinian business activities, at least those which cannot be asserted by border closures and transportation policies. However, notwithstanding the importance of such transfers of authority to the PA, there remain numerous indirect restrictions Israelis can implement under the terms of the governing Protocol. These restrictions include, but are not limited to, the collection of taxes on Palestinian exports and tariffs on the importation of consumer durable goods from neighboring Arab countries. Stanley Fischer estimates that half of the taxes paid by Palestinians in the former territories actually accrue to the Israeli economy through these charges.[4] This is in addition to the income and social security taxes paid by Palestinians working in Israel.

The total loss of these funds is large, estimated to be as much as 25 percent of Palestinian GNP. It is true that the Protocol requires Israel to refund to the PA 75 percent of income taxes collected from Palestinians and 100 percent from those working in the Jewish settlements. But these refunds have not been made on schedule, if ever, and more importantly the larger burden has not been lifted since, without its own port, most Palestinian imports pass through Israeli-controlled territories and are therefore subject to tariffs and taxes which generate revenues equal to customs duties charged under the old regime. These transfers have been dubbed the 'occupation tax', mainly because they continue to sustain the Israeli economy instead of being used to fund the PA's public sector expenses. A 1992 study estimated the loss of revenues under occupation as between US $88 and $195 million, or 4 to 9 percent of GDP. A 1995 study claimed a low-end estimate of lost tax revenues in excess of US $156 million, an amount roughly half of the PA's total budget deficit.[5] This clearly establishes what can only be considered a 'One Sided Customs and Monetary Union'.[6]

As a result, public infrastructure and the quality of social service provision remain poor and continually decline in both the West Bank and Gaza. It should be emphasized that the state of affairs would be even worse, were it not for the transfer of resources from the international donor community. As Sara Roy points out, it is estimated that 80 percent of annual health care expenditures and more than half of education program costs in the West Bank and Gaza are funded from external sources. But as she and Sullivan illustrate, much of these funds have not been appropriately released and many of these organizations have become dependent on radical groups for budget support.

Another key example of the limiting nature of the agreed-upon terms of self-rule comes from monetary agreements that have been signed. Indeed, the arrangements reached that establish the Palestinian Monetary Authority (PMA), which is supposed to function as the PA's central bank, combine some of the worst possible aspects of two polar-type exchange rate regimes. First, the Israeli shekel and the Jordanian dinar will be used as legal tender in the West Bank and Gaza, which sets in place a fixed exchange rate regime wherein PMA monetary policy cannot be effective. The existence of a two-currency standard has the potential for increasing the costs associated with exchange rate fluctuations. A dual currency system also tends to reduce a commercial bank's ability to set interest rates or transform debt maturities, leaving it unable to create balanced loan portfolios. These situations will surely discourage long-term lending which is essential to fostering investment and industrial growth.

Secondly, broad limitations are placed on the PMA's ability to trade in currencies or to hold foreign exchange. As J. W. Wright, Jr. explains:

> Unfortunately, in terms of creating comparative advantages the PMA has not set itself up well for supporting local competition. For example, when it was formed the Palestinian Monetary Authority (PMA) was supposed to be structured in ways that would encourage financial deepening in the former territories. However, the agreements actually signed only allow the PMA to 'predict its supervision' and work within a 'home authority and host authority' approval process. When the PMA collects the reserve requirements, it must hold those reserves in Israeli shekels. 'The liquidity requirements on the various kinds of NIS deposits in banks operating in the area will not be less than 4% to 8%;' and 'the amount of convertible NIS during a calendar year' will be decided annually by Israel. The PMA must 'supply temporary finance for banks operating in the region,' including Israeli banks. 'The clearing of money orders and transaction between banks operating in Israeli will be done between Israeli and the Palestinian clearing houses on a same working day basis,' but there is no reciprocal agreement forcing Israeli banks to process funds on a daily basis. 'The exchange of foreign currency for NIS and vice-versa by the PMA will be carried through the Bank of Israel Dealing Room,' but, 'The BOI will not be obliged to convert in any single month more than 1/5 of the semi-annual amount.'[7]

Several problems with these arrangements are obvious, primarily that they ensure the PMA's inability to set money supply policies or to regulate interest rates. The PMA also becomes unable to reinvest its entire portfolio in Arab-owned institutions and because it is forced to deal with the BOI dealing room and only then in limited amounts, the PMA has neither emergency conversion facilities nor the capability of making trading profits. Because it must deliver Arab inter-bank funds in one day without Israeli reciprocity, the PMA may have outstanding funds on which it cannot earn interest. In sum, without control of interest rates; without the ability to run market operations or plan its own investment policies; without the means for creating trading and processing profits; and without the ability to even offer licenses without prior approval, the new Palestinian Monetary Authority will not have the tools to compete with Israeli and Gulf Arab firms in bids for foreign direct investment.

While I will not discuss the real impact of implementation, or lack thereof, of agreements concerning water (even Taba), because Alwyn Rouyer (Chapter 8) analyzes this subject in detail, suffice it to say that water restrictions are as constricted for the Palestinians now as they were before the peace process began. In fact, in the declaration of principles it was agreed that there would be no change in sovereignty over water and settlements during the transition period.[8] In the case of water, for example, this means the Palestinians continue to have access to only about 15 to 20 percent of the annually available water originating in their local areas. Similarly, it means that as much as 60 percent of the land in the West Bank and Gaza will continue to be inaccessible to Palestinian farmers or developers, a situation which places severe impediments on the expansion of agricultural production for either internal consumption or for export, and serves to limit industrial and residential construction growth.

It is worth noting that some formal trade barriers remain intact for agricultural products under the Protocol. For example, there are formal trade barriers still placed on key Palestinian products, including poultry, eggs, potatoes, cucumbers, and melons. There are also two lists of goods, one relating most specifically to goods produced in Egypt and Jordan, a second relating to goods from Arab and Islamic countries, upon which the two sides must meet to agree on quantities needed by Palestinians. This part of the Israeli–Palestinian agreement claims: 'Palestinian market needs will be based on the best available data regarding past consumption, production, investment and external trade of the territories.'[9] Where this information will come from or who will produce it is not clear. This type of system presents small business with special supply problems since their needs often are not accounted for even in sophisticated reports.[10]

The most contentious part of the resources problem is land distribution. New Jewish settlements are still being built on land that has been removed from Palestinian use, providing housing for settler populations of more than 250 000 people. This is not, as many believe, a contentious issue for the Palestinians based on prejudices exemplified in housing.

Rather, Israeli policies toward land, water, and settlements create an atmosphere of strife which is both profound and demoralizing. These policies are also negative in an economic sense because they divert land use from agricultural development and intensify drainage of water resources. The scarcities caused by additional settlements raise prices which, combined with the refusal of Israel to establish clearing zones, result in high building costs for manufacturing facilities and present barriers to industrial expansion.

An example of this is that between the time the Paris Protocol was signed and 1998, an additional 166m 543 dunums of Palestinian land have been formally confiscated, 17 860 have been bulldozed by settlers without permission, and 8993 dunums have been taken for the direct expansion of existing settlements. Settlement expansion uprooted nearly 30 000 trees while road construction between settlements that do not connect Arab towns and population centers claimed approximately 12 000 dunums (a dunum measures roughly one-quarter of an acre) during this period. Such acquisitions constrain(ed) even basic attempts at economic development and continue to do so because they restrict distribution.[11]

Moreover, continuing support for these policies leaves the West Bank and Gaza's private sectors fragmented and dominated by small-scale workshops. Sixty-two percent of industrial establishment in the West Bank and 64 percent of those in Gaza employed less than four workers. Those employing more than 20 workers accounted for just 4 percent and 1 percent in the two areas respectively. The total number of establishments never exceeded 4000. In the same year, manufacturing employed just 9.2 percent of the total labor force in the West Bank and 11 percent in Gaza.[12]

The present economic difficulties in the Palestinian territories, therefore, reflect the extent to which constraints from limited self-rule place on the PA's real authority. The indications are that the most important features of the declining economic situation during the past 28 years have not been altered to a great degree, and may not be altered under the guise of limited self-rule. Of course, the accusations of corruption in the distribution of aid funds made against both Israelis and Palestinians, do not build confidence that fair markets will develop as a means of overcoming economic obstacles to the peace process. Thus, one is faced with an obvious question. To what extent are economics under the Palestinian limited self-rule era simply a continuation of economics under the Israeli occupation era?

Notes

1. F. Naqib, 'Prospects for Sustained Development of the Palestinian Economy: Strategies and Policies for Reconstruction and Development', A Report prepared for UNCTAD (November 1995) 6.
2. See 'The Peace Process so far', *Economist*, 1 June 1996, 42.
3. The World Bank, 'Developing the Occupied Territories: An Investment in Peace', Vol. 2 (Washington, DC: The World Bank, 1993); see discussion starting on p. 25; on taxation see discussion starting on p. 116.
4. S. Fischer, 'Securing Peace in the Middle East', in Stanley Fischer, D. Rodrik, and Elias Toma (eds), *The Economics of Middle East Peace* (Cambridge, MA: The MIT Press, 1993), beginning on p. 127.
5. For a discussion of both studies see M. Jawhary, 'The Palestinian Israeli Trade Agreements: Searching for Fair Revenue-Sharing' (Palestinian Economic Policy Research Institute, 1995).
6. O. Hamed and R. Shaban, 'One Sided Custom and Monetary Union: The Case of the West Bank and Gaza Strip Under Israeli Occupation', in Fischer et al., *The Economics of Middle East Peace*.
7. See Wright's Chapter in Volume I (*The Political Economy of Middle East Peace: the Impact of Competing Trade Agendas*. Routledge, 1999) entitled 'Should the US Promote an Islamic Economics Agenda in Palestine?' The quotes in this section come from 'Special Supplement to Annex V: Protocol on Economic Relations, Israeli-Palestinian Interim Agreement', reprinted by the *Palestine Report* (December 1995) 15–25.
8. The first agreement is the Declaration of Principles signed in Washington, DC on 13 September 1993. The second is the Agreement on the Gaza Strip and Jericho Area, signed in Cairo on 4 May 1994. The agreement governing economic affairs during the transitional period was signed on 29 April 1994 in Paris under the title 'Protocol on Economic Relations between the Government of Israel and the PLO, representing the Palestinian People' (Referred to in most dockets and publications simply as 'The Protocol'). For texts of these agreements see: UN A/49/80, S/1994/727, 20 June 1994.
9. Naqib, 'Prospects for Sustained Development', see notes 38 and 40, p. 196.
10. Naqib, 'Prospects for Sustained Development', 52.
11. 'Property Violations Report' (July/August 1995) and Arab Studies Society, 'Land Research Committee Report' (March 1995).
12. Naqib, 'Prospects for Sustained Development', 144.

Part II

The Between-ness of the Palestinian Position

4

Between the Arms Race and Political Lobbyists: How Pax Americana Threatens Middle East Peace

Stephen Zunes

Peace between Israel and its Arab neighbors is a necessary but not a sufficient criterion for the economic development of the Middle East. Unfortunately, as the Peace Process stands, predictions of an economic boom in the Middle East resulting from the end of the decades-old conflict, much less the kind of economic growth that meets the basic needs of the people, is unlikely. First, as the Likud government becomes more confrontational, progress will continue to wane. Second, as long as basic economic needs are not met, true peace will be difficult to achieve, regardless of the government in power. As in many underdeveloped regions, the adoption of neoliberal economic policies in the Middle East is becoming an increasingly prevalent phenomenon. This is likely to increase investment and economic growth. However, because of the biased nature of funds flows such policies may actually set back those development efforts which would benefit the majority of the region's population and provide the basis for long-term economic and political stability.

Unfortunately, while there are some particular obstacles to sustainable economic development in the Middle East, a large part of Arab negotiators' problems relate to the fact that the Peace Process itself appears to be geared towards more of a Pax Americana than a real regional peace. Most observers believe true peace requires a comprehensive settlement to the Arab–Israeli conflict, a dramatic reduction in military expenditures, and support for democratization and human rights (see Glasser and Findley in this volume). US policy in the 1990s worked contrary to these goals – that is, with American economic and strategic interests in the region taking precedent – which means that a comprehensive peace which allows the region to form its own terms was impossible.

The Peace Process and the Fate of Palestine

American opposition to a comprehensive peace settlement goes back for at least a quarter century. When former Egyptian President Anwar Sadat made peace overtures toward Israel in 1971, the then US Secretary of State Henry Kissinger successfully pressured the Israelis to ignore it, ultimately precipitating the October 1973 War. Only after the war did the US support disengagement talks, and then only under American auspices. Subsequent peace plans brought forth by the Europeans, the United Nations (UN) or Arab states (such as the Fahd Plan) were also undermined by the US. The Camp David Accord, orchestrated by the Carter Administration, successfully derailed ongoing efforts to organize an all-parties conference, by working out a separate peace between Egypt and Israel, and not effectively including the PLO (or only via the efforts of people acting without formal authority, (see Findley, Chapter 1)) or the Soviet-supported Arab states. By including promises of strategic cooperation and more than $5 billion of military aid annually to the two countries, the Camp David Accords were more of a tripartite military pact than a true peace agreement. The Accords also placed Palestine between Israel and Jordan without the threat of aggression from the south, weakening the territories' strategic position (see Diwan and Walton in this volume). In addition, by neutralizing its biggest military rival, and in turn by weakening the internal Palestinian threat, Israel was able to invade Lebanon in 1982 and redouble its colonization and repression programs in occupied territories.

Continuing to reject calls for an international conference under UN auspices, the US set up the Madrid Conference in 1991, which was conducted largely within a bilateral format designed to keep Israelis and Palestinians separated by an American chaperon. The US went as far as excluding the PLO from the talks, allowing for Palestinian participation only on the grounds that they came as part of the Jordanian delegation, that they had no direct affiliation with the PLO, and that their representatives were not from the Palestinian diaspora (meaning many of the community's most powerful and wealthy members were excluded, not to mention Arab-American lobbyists) or even from the Palestinian capital of Jerusalem (meaning local Palestinian politicos). Progress was made on the Israeli–Palestinian track only when Israel and the PLO did an end-run around the restrictive US formula and met secretly in a third country, talks which resulted in the Oslo Accords.

In subsequent conferences organized to facilitate peace talks, the US, rather than pushing for compromises on Arab demands, actually took a harder line than did the Rabin government. To begin with, the Declarations of Principles, signed in September 1993, though limited in many respects regarding the Palestinians' right to self-determination, were far more generous to the Palestinians than a 'compromise' proposal offered by the US less than three months earlier. Palestinian officials described the US proposals as 'closer to the Israeli Likud position', referring to the Rabin government's right-wing predecessors. This position was later recognized and seized upon by the Netanyahu government and provided the backdrop for its increasingly strident positions.

There was a clear consensus in Israel that a Palestinian state in the West Bank and Gaza would be an inevitable outgrowth of the Protocol. All but a handful of the world's governments supported such a two-state solution. The US, however, was not one of those governments and it remained adamant from 1972 onwards in its opposition to Palestinian statehood. The Clinton Administration was the first in US history to see the West Bank and Gaza as disputed territories, insinuating that the Israelis and Palestinians had equal claim to the land, rather than the view of the UN and others in the international community which continued to recognize East Jerusalem and other lands gained during Israeli advances in 1967 as territory under foreign military occupation. This position placed the US overtly at odds with earlier UN resolutions on Palestine, and irritated the EU and other countries.

Most observers recognize that one of the major obstacles to Israeli–Palestinian peace is the expansion of illegal Israeli settlements in the occupied territories. Included here, too, is even a 1997 UN resolution against settlement expansion, which the US has also opposed. In a reversal of policy pursued by previous administrations, the Clinton Administration did not oppose the expansion of existing settlements and even vetoed a United Nations Security Council resolution condemning Israeli seizure of Palestinian lands in greater Jerusalem. The Clinton Administration also intimated that Arab East Jerusalem and environs, seized by Israel along with the rest of the West Bank in 1967, should remain exclusively part of Israel. This is counter to the position taken by every previous administration and reiterated in several UN Security Council resolutions.

While even Palestinians do not want to see Jerusalem redivided with barbed wire and sentry posts as it was 30 years ago, no Palestinian can accept an agreement which denies them equal rights to what is their capital city as well. Many nations see this as an affront to UN authority. Moreover, by insisting that issues regarding settlements not even be discussed until the very latest stages of negotiations, the US gave the

Israeli settlers more time to establish their occupation, thus justifying that they should not be displaced by further expansion of Palestinian control.

President Clinton even bypassed a US law which required the administration to deduct the costs of additional Jewish development in the occupied territories from the controversial $10 billion American loan guarantee to Israel signed in 1992: he has simply increased aid to Israel by the same amount subtracted from the loan.

At the time, the relative weakness of the more inclusive Labour Party-styled peace movement, as compared to its right-wing counterpart, was made clear by Netanyahu's election as prime minister and his survival of several scandals and ethics investigations. There was inadequate domestic pressure to force this Likud Israeli government to take the steps necessary to achieve peace: putting Israel in compliance with UN Security Council resolutions, including a total withdrawal of Israeli troops and settlers; and granting Palestinians control and real independence. Therefore, the only truly effective counter-pressure could be expected to come from the US, which provides the military, economic, and diplomatic support for Israeli occupation forces. Members of the Israeli negotiating team in Washington, DC privately asked the Clinton Administration to openly push the Israeli government to compromise further so as to give them sufficient political and public relations cover needed for more substantial concessions.[1] The Clinton Administration, however, refused to follow this tactic and in effect supported Likud's campaigns.

Meanwhile, the Clinton Administration continued to wage a vigorous campaign to rescind all the previous UN resolutions which were seen as critical of Israel, its occupation of the Palestinian territories, and its more recent positions on building new Jewish settlements in and around PA-controlled areas. The Clinton Administration labeled these resolutions as anachronistic, even though they addressed issues that are still relevant – human rights violations, illegal settlement policies, expulsions of dissidents, continuing development of nuclear weapons, and ongoing military occupation. And, the appointment of Martin Indyk as Under Secretary of State for Near Eastern Affairs all but assured that these policy initiatives would be pursued with continued vigor. As a result, it was inevitable that a Clinton Administration-directed peace process would not lead to a settlement meeting legitimate Palestinian demands for self-determination. Rather, the goal seemed to be the establishment of economic and political structures that would severely limit the PA *vis-à-vis* Israel and thus lead to virtual continuation of Israeli control. The economic implications are disheartening, and much of what was feared by Arabs attending the Madrid Conference (and other interested parties), about peace process initiatives making conditions worse, has come to pass. Historically the Gaza Strip was once a prosperous seaport and citrus-growing region, but under 27 years of Israeli military occupation it has deteriorated into a vast slum of unemployment or cheap labor, workers Israel now refuses to employ (see Sara Roy in this volume). Similarly, the West Bank, once the most economically advanced part of the Kingdom of Jordan, fell victim to systematic Israeli efforts to destroy the indigenous economy and make Arab entrepreneurs servile to Israeli contractors. As a result of these policies, the Palestinians of the West Bank and Gaza have grown dependent on employment in Israel for their economic survival. Moreover, after creating these labor market-related dependencies, Palestinians have seen Israeli governments shift toward forced separations of the economies by enforcing border closures and thereby severely restricting Arab workers from entering the Israeli marketplace, replacing them with thousands of guest-workers from Europe, Turkey, and the Far East. The PA has been left with an economic catastrophe and inadequate resources to handle it.

More problematically, it appeared likely that the final peace agreement would result in a patchwork of tiny densely populated Palestinian areas surrounded by heavily-armed Israeli occupation forces and Jewish settlers. With the Israelis maintaining control of the roads and communication centers, which also includes enforcement of border crossings between PA areas and neighboring Arab states, any real integrated commercial activity continued to be on a severely limited scale. Indeed, Israel appears determined to continue its control of, or effective veto power over, such important areas as 'water, energy, financial development, transport and communications, trade, industry, environment, labor, media and international aid', essentially all 'matters directly related to economic development'[2] (see Diwan and Walton on how this relates to Jordan's trade).

Most development schemes envision something resembling the *maquiladores* in Mexico: places where Israeli manufacturers can take advantage of a cheap labor force to assemble components for Israeli markets, offering little opportunity for fostering spin-off industries which could create a viable indigenous economy. Even this scenario has not gone very far, with Israel insisting that the PA 'harmonize its tax and customs regime with the high levels in force in Israel',[3] Palestinians find that their products are too expensive for much of their own population, as well as losing their comparative and competitive advantage in exports, manufacturing, and skilled crafts production. This customs union maintained by the Israeli authority further compromises the

Palestinians' ability to take advantage of cheaper labor and less regulation. Furthermore, with subsidies and protection for key Israeli manufacturing sectors, the problem of water supply for agricultural production, and setting a value-added tax on Palestinian goods that is just one percentage point below that of Israel, any competitive advantages are all but gone.

As outlined in various agreements since the Declaration of Principles, the PA was denied any real independence in economic decision making. This was particularly true with regard to setting policies relating to imports and trade finance. Besides Israel, Palestinians are only allowed to import from Egypt and Jordan and then only if the Israelis determine it can be justified by the needs of the market. These import restrictions take on additional significance in the face of Israel's continued confiscation of Palestinian agricultural property in order to expand illegal settlements. Israel also continued to control the majority of the water reserves in the occupied territories, making expansion of the Palestinian agricultural sector extremely difficult (see Rouyer, Chapter 8). Many military orders and other laws restricting Palestinian economic life were even strengthened by two successive regimes that supported a closed borders policy. In addition, the Cairo Agreement specifically exempts Israelis from financial reparations due for the destruction of property or for the illegal expropriation of resources and taxes. The Hebron Protocol also served to further limit PA security and Palestinian mobility.

Such scenarios denied the statehood and economic prosperity promised by Palestinian leader Yasser Arafat to his people and have led to widespread disillusionment. The result of this has been that radical Islamists and other extremists have gained further support (see Sara Roy). Under such a regime, it was predictable that the violence and militant response to new Israeli encroachments would come and, in turn, create further cycles of repression in the name of security. In addition, it would justify the imposition of greater restrictions on PA autonomy, in general, and on Palestinian labor mobility, in particular. Such cycles could hardly be conducive to economic growth.

Clearly, there can be no real peace unless the Palestinians are able to build their own state and develop their own autonomous economic institutions. The Netanyahu and Clinton Administrations rejected such a scenario, arguing that even a Palestinian mini-state on the West Bank and Gaza would be too much and that the Palestinians should be satisfied with limited local autonomy. In effect, the Israeli and US governments gambled that the Palestinians would continue to accept biased agreements which, deny them not only statehood, but also their long sought-after economic and political independence. That gamble has yet to pay off and, in fact, gave the Barak government fewer negotiating options than either the Rabin or Netanyahu administrations.

Israel and neighboring Arab States

The direction of the Peace Process elsewhere also showed some rather troubling signs which challenged the more optimistic scenarios of near-term peace and prosperity. For instance, Syria entered the peace negotiations in Madrid in 1991 on the understanding that UN Security Council resolutions 242 and 338 would be the basis for negotiations. Long considered the cornerstone of the Middle East Peace Process, these resolutions were based on the principle that Israel would withdraw from Arab lands seized in the 1967 war in return for security guarantees. However, Israel also insisted on full economic and diplomatic relations prior to a full withdrawal from the occupied territory, which would, at any rate, be more and more difficult to sell to Arab negotiators because of Israeli deployments and redeployments of armed 'police' forces into several towns and villages in PA-controlled areas. Israeli authorities endeavored to hold the trade card close at hand by not allowing Palestinians to export to or import from Arab countries that did not recognize Israel or had not lifted their trade embargoes. This effectively meant no exports to the oil-rich Gulf states.

While Israel's desire for such a comprehensively based peace regime was understandable, and certainly closer economic cooperation would be beneficial for the region as a whole, it went well beyond Syria's obligations as outlined in the Madrid formula. In effect, Israel had moved the goalposts. Despite the legal weakness of the Israeli position, the US pushed Syria to give in on a number of economic, political, and security issues, but was rebuffed in its efforts by Syria's President Hafez Assad.

There was an irony in this; for years, the US considered Syria to be too intransigent for its rejection of resolutions 242 and 338. More recently, the US has said that it considers Damascus too intransigent for its insistence on their strict implementation.

While Assad had expressed a willingness to eventually normalize relations, he insisted that it be done gradually and not as a precondition to Israel's obligation to withdraw. He was concerned that Israel and the US would take advantage of his gradual privatization of state enterprises by grabbing a large share of Syria's economy. The lifting of the trade ban with Israel, should peace be secured in the areas surrounding the Golan

Heights, could have provided Syria with some market access in Israel and the US, and may thus have served to defuse some Syrian tensions. But, in reality, it was the US's hypocritical positions that stung Assad, and likely his son too, the most.

However, there were other influential forces in Syria which, while desiring trade with Israel, made it contingent upon waiting until Syrian enterprises were strong enough to withstand expected competition. President Assad was also resentful of the heavy-handed tactics being used by US diplomats. For example, Syria remained on Washington's list of states sponsoring terrorism, precluding its access to a variety of American products and services, including certain critical technologies and export items. The US admits that it has no proof of direct ties by the Syrian government to terrorism since 1986, that Syria has pressed radical Palestinian groups to refrain from terrorism, and that Syria was instrumental in securing the release of American hostages held by Muslim extremists in Lebanon.[4] However, US officials claim that known terrorists are still being granted sanctuary in Syria and that this factor alone is sufficient reason for keeping Syria on its list of terrorist nations. No other nation is on this list solely on those grounds, although some of the US's closest allies are also known to harbor suspected terrorists. Indeed, the US has provided sanctuary for a number of right-wing Cubans wanted in several Latin American countries for terrorism and has allowed their organizations to operate openly within American borders. The Syrians felt they were kept on the list as a bargaining chip to acquiesce to Israeli and American desires to open the Syrian economy.[5] Such pressure served to increase suspicion of American and Israeli intentions and engendered resistance from key Syrian leaders to join the Peace Process.

Another rather revealing episode regarding US economic pressure in the peace process came with the signing of the Israeli–Jordanian peace agreement in the fall of 1994.[6] Sharp reductions in international aid in the previous years, increased aid competition (see Glasser), fallout from the Gulf War in terms of refugee and returnee influences and the continual decline of the Iraqi economy, have all combined to place the Jordanian economy in a state of crisis. With then-ailing King Hussein's domestic markets reeling (see Colton) and his budgets suffering from an enormous foreign debt, President Clinton offered him a lucrative, although short-term, bail-out package if he would sign an agreement recognizing Israel and lifting its trade embargo. During the meeting between Jordanian and Israeli leaders in Washington in July 1994, which laid the groundwork for the later peace agreement that was signed between the two countries, Clinton agreed to cancel $702 million of Jordan's debt to the US, representing nearly three-quarters of the Kingdom's outstanding loan balances with the US, the first $220 million to be canceled the following year and the remainder to be written-off over the next two fiscal years (with the expectation, of course, that relations would continue). In addition, the White House agreed to write members of the Paris Club – Western lenders who control the bulk of Jordan's unpaid debt – encouraging them to extend debt relief assistance to Jordan as well.[7]

While both sides publicly denied this was a quid pro quo agreement, Arab journalists accompanying King Hussein on the Washington trip reported that the Jordanian leader acknowledged that the Clinton Administration had made clear that a peace agreement under US terms was a prerequisite for debt relief and other favors.[8] In addition, prominent members of Congress – many of whom influence committees that approve foreign aid and loan forgiveness packages – were explicit in their insistence that the remaining debt relief be tied to a formal treaty with Israel regardless of a comprehensive peace settlement that would recognize full Palestinian rights, which had been Jordan's original condition for a peace agreement with Israel.

The US also offered Jordan new military equipment, increased foreign aid, and the encouragement of US investment. Moreover, Clinton officials promised to help end the Gulf States' effective boycott of Jordanian goods and labor. Part of the deal also involved possible US support for $50 million in water projects.[9] The US also agreed to lift the US-led blockade of the Gulf of Aqaba, ostensibly in place to enforce the embargo against Iraq, which had severely hurt Jordanian trade by forcing every ship entering the country's only port to be searched. (Lloyd's Register, a private British firm, took over the responsibility of observing the cargo as part of regular Jordanian customs inspections on land.)[10] In short, the US – after making a series of policy decisions which backed Jordan into a desperate economic corner – offered a bail-out package, but only if they cooperated with the US-led peace process. The Clinton Administration appeared to have effectively bought an Israeli–Jordanian settlement. And, by dragging out the debt forgiveness over three years, it ensured continued Jordanian cooperation with American designs in the region.

Similar pressures are being brought to bear against Lebanon. At the time, the US refused to offer any reconstruction aid to Lebanon, despite the fact that much of the war damage was caused by US-made armaments (and some was inflicted by the US directly). Until the summer of

1997, the Clinton Administration also continued to uphold a travel ban on Lebanon that forbade US citizens from visiting or conducting business, even though it was far safer than countries not on the list like Afghanistan and Algeria. Ironically, this situation forced the loss of Millions of US dollars to American firms, or forced them to share any contracts they received with foreign partners of subsidiaries, who were often Arab firms. The travel ban also barred potential investors and lenders from entering the country, and therefore served to further impede Lebanon's reconstruction efforts. The apparent goal of maintaining this pressure on Lebanon was to force the government to crack down on Hezballah guerrillas fighting against Israeli occupation forces in the southern part of the country, and to encourage the government to participate more freely in the peace process by making substantial concessions to Israel as part of a new agreement. This came in spite of the fact that UN Security Council Resolution 425 and ten subsequent resolutions require Israel to withdraw completely from south Lebanon.

Efforts at Regional Integration

With the asymmetry of political power between the Israelis and Palestinians now firmly established, with trade regimes in place that surely enhance Israel's economic power long into the next century, with Syria and Lebanon still facing full and partial occupation of their lands by Israeli forces, and with the Clinton Administration ruling out pressuring a Netanyahu-led Israel government to soften its position on Jerusalem, the settlements, and so on, one of the few tools which could have pushed the Israeli government to compromise was the threat of a renewed Arab economic boycott. As a result, the US greatly escalated its pressure against the Gulf states, in particular, for an end to their boycotts of Israel, and even of Israeli-taxed Palestinian products. In effect, the US wanted the Arab states to lift all trade sanctions against Israel before it would agree to pressure Israel to further recognize Palestinian needs for self-determination, to withdraw from Lebanon and Syria, or to come into compliance with UN resolutions and international law.

The Arabs see US opposition to a boycott against Israel as hypocritical because, in recent years, the US has successfully pushed for international sanctions against Arab states such as Libya and Iraq for violations of UN edicts and it has maintained a unilateral boycott of Cuba for 36 years. In statements about the future of the Middle East, US officials consistently avoided references to human rights, international law, self-determination, or disarmament, and instead emphasized the need to end commercial pressure against the Israeli occupation and integrate the region economically. Moreover, not only did the Israelis want an end to the embargo, but they also seemed to be establishing structures that many Arabs feared would lead to regional integration and economic domination. Indeed, Israel appeared to be linking projected economic development projects in Palestinian-administered areas to a regional development program of trade and economic cooperation, in order to force an end to the boycott and gain access to potentially lucrative investment funds and markets which had long been denied to them. In addition, Israeli desires for economic penetration of Syria and Lebanon with minimal restrictions were major goals for peace negotiators with these Arab neighbors. The US clearly backed Israel in this process.

Economic integration is a worthwhile goal, as is peace. The combination of Israeli technology, Palestinian industriousness and Arabian oil wealth could transform the region in many positive ways and better link it with global markets. However, as with the Peace Process itself, the emphasis on economic integration appears to be largely seen in terms of American interests. In many respects the situation is not unlike apartheid-era South Africa's efforts to promote economic integration with black southern African countries. These neighboring states resisted such efforts, on the grounds that they could not cooperate with the white-minority regime that was actively repressing their black brethren and also because of the fact that South Africa was so much more powerful economically than the rest of southern Africa combined, that their own economic independence, already undermined by colonial legacies and international lending institutions, would be compromised still further. The difference in the Middle East situation is that the world's largest economic power is repeatedly pushing for just such an integration.

As a result, while calls for greater economic cooperation between erstwhile enemies are in themselves reasonable, they are premature as long as Palestinians are denied their independence, and as long as the resource-poor Arab states are unable to enhance the competitiveness of vulnerable sectors of their economies. Furthermore, by using its considerable economic leverage to push for bilateral peace pacts that are kept separate from broader and more comprehensive agreements promoting regional economic development, supporting cooperative security agendas and arrangements, and facilitating enforcement of international laws and recognitions of their rights of self-determination, the US could create a backlash which could retard peace, stability and economic cooperation.

It is noteworthy that in 1991, efforts by the Arab Monetary Fund (AMF), based in Abu Dhabi, to establish a Middle East Development

Bank were effectively undermined by the US. The plan, which received favorable response from potential Arab, Japanese, and European investors, would have helped steer greater oil wealth back into the region, and would also have facilitated reinvestment of petro-dollars into business development and joint-venture projects enhancing labor and production markets (labor supply shocks being the most serious problem facing the northern Arab countries, see Colton, Chapter 6 in this volume). The oil-rich Gulf states agreed to contribute substantially more to regional development than previously through existing institutions as long as developed countries would share the burden. The AMF predicted that the bank would be self-sufficient within five years. The major obstacle was securing US support, which the George H. Bush Administration refused to offer, effectively halting the project. Subsequent efforts toward economic cooperation appeared to be geared primarily toward encouraging foreign investment and trade from industrialized nations rather than encouraging greater regional self-sufficiency.

On this issue, however, the American position is more pragmatic than it is pro-Israeli. The US would much prefer that petro-dollars be invested in the US than in the Middle East. As with Japanese investments, such infusions of cash are quite welcome, despite occasionally stimulating a mild nationalistic reaction in the US. Encouragement of such investments has other advantages: since many Gulf states have large amounts of capital invested in the West, there are fewer incentives to raise oil prices, since this could result in a drag on industrialized economies, which could lead them to lose more money than they could gain. For example, Kuwait now makes more money from interest on its international investments than it does from oil sales.[11] Therefore, on many international economic questions, the Gulf monarchies often find they have more in common with the industrialized North than they do with Arabs in the Levant.

A symbolic turning point was reached in the Damascus Declaration, signed by the Arab Gulf Cooperation Council (GCC) States – Bahrain, Kuwait, Oman, Qatar, Saudi Arabia, and the United Arab Emirates – plus Syria and Egypt, in 1991. In the document, the eight signatories committed themselves to national control over natural resources, which essentially codified the oil giants' determination not to share their wealth or entitlements with their Arab brethren in Palestine. Syria, in particular, once a defiantly nationalistic country, sorely misses Soviet aid support (see Wilson) and has now been forced by a sagging economy to look to the West and the Gulf for salvation. Egypt, also facing severe economic conditions, fears the loss of US aid. Thus, any pretense of pan-Arabism has effectively been put to rest as economic and strategic ties with the US have greatly increased throughout the region. This long-sought triumph for American policy makers – to divide the oil-rich monarchies and their allies from the potentially radical nationalists in the poorer Arab countries – has come to fruition, and has left, in many peoples' views, the poorer nations bereft of real influence. Indeed, the Arab League has largely been supplanted by the pro-Western GCC as the major policy-coordinating body in the Arab world.

Arms transfers and military spending

Military expenditures in Middle Eastern countries have steadily increased over the years, and have skyrocketed in the Gulf states since the Gulf War. The Arms Control and Disarmament Agency (ACDA) verifies that military expenditures for Middle Eastern countries come to nearly 55 percent of combined central government expenditures, and to more than 20 percent of gross national product. Force ratios – representing the number of people under arms per thousand – stand at around 14 percent for the Middle East, nearly twice that of industrialized countries and well over three times that of most underdeveloped countries.[12] But the world's arms trade is immensely profitable. And, according to ACDA, the Middle East's share of the international arms market rose from 36 percent to over 41 percent in the decade covered in the most recent study, a sizable majority of total transfers to poorer countries.[13] These figures do not include Turkey (which is included with European countries on such surveys), one of the world's major arms importers. It should also be noted that these increases came despite the international arms embargo against Iraq and Iran's ongoing economic crisis and international ostracism. This means the Arab Gulf countries and Israel are making massive arms purchases.

Ironically, then, it is unlikely that the Peace Process between Israel and its Arab neighbors will serve to reduce substantially the level of arms transfers, since such high military expenditures by Middle Eastern countries have little to do with actual security needs. In a survey for the Middle East Research and Information Project, Joe Stork argues that the ongoing Middle Eastern arms race continues for three reasons:

(1) that arms sales are an important component of building a political alliance, particularly with the military leadership of recipient countries;

(2) there is a strategic benefit coming from the inter-operability of having US-manufactured systems on the ground in the event of a direct US military intervention and;

(3) arms sales are a means of supporting military industries faced with declining demand in Western countries.[14]

One revealing episode was a 1993 off-the-record seminar with Assistant Secretary of State Richard Murphy, top Saudi Arabian officials, and the Vice-Chairman of Morgan Guaranty (the bank which organized the financing of Saudi Arabia's 1991 war effort), where it was acknowledged that arms transfers had little to do with US strategic requirements or objective security needs for the Kingdom.[15]

Despite occasional lip service to the contrary, President Clinton and his predecessors, have all opposed serious arms control in the Middle East because this would threaten corporate profits. While US officials insist that the Saudis alone are responsible for the sales, the Defense Department routinely defines the Kingdom's supposed security needs which lead directly to purchases of specific US weapons – a practice which can be traced as far back as the 1940s.[16] In May 1995 the State Department acknowledged that Saudi arms purchases have contributed to the country's budgetary problems and economic downturn and undermined its political stability. In addition, many senior observers believe debt financing for Saudi Arabia's arms purchases threatens the Kingdom's already fragile social pact of distributing oil rents to favored power constituents and political patrons.[17] The Saudis have also made it clear that they intend to place weapons procurement ahead of continuing subsidies to their citizens at current levels.[18] And yet, the massive arms transfers continue. Indeed, to ensure that the financially-strapped Kingdom keeps purchasing weapons, the US has provided billions of dollars' worth of credit and has further eased the terms of payment, despite warnings that it is threatening the economic viability of the regime.[19] According to Robert Vitalis:

> If the billions have not been useful to the Saudis, they were a gold mine for Congresspersons compelled to cast pro-Saudi votes, along with cabinet officials and party leaders worried about the economy of key states and electoral districts. To the extent that the regime faces politically destabilizing cutbacks in social spending, a proximate cause is the strong bipartisan push for arms exports to the Gulf as a means to bolster the sagging fortunes of key constituents and regions – the 'gun belt' – that represents the domestic face of internationalism.[20]

Another noteworthy factor, which is often overlooked, is that a number of Middle Eastern states became highly dependent on Saudi Arabia's aid and/or workers' remittances for financial assistance in the 1970s and 1980s. With the financial crisis being accelerated by unnecessary arms acquisitions, Saudi Arabia became less generous, leading to serious budget shortfalls throughout the Arab world. Much of the Saudi aid that remained was being used to finance arms purchases by Egypt and to subsidize Morocco's occupation of Western Sahara. Therefore, there are economic and political multipliers at work in the region that are directly tied to continuing support for purchasing arms from US manufacturers.

What is clear is that the implications of ongoing, indeed heightening, arms procurement is ominous on several levels. One of the most striking is that the food deficit in the Middle East is the fastest-growing in the world, and that water aquifers supporting agricultural development are falling at alarming rates.[21] As a result of these factors and because of high Arab population growth, food demand in the year 2000 is expected to be twice what is was in 1980. But in the face of these obviously serious problems, continued high military spending has effectively resulted in a fall in investments in agriculture and water development. While normalized relations would allow Israel's innovative agricultural techniques to be shared more widely, the push by neoliberal American and Israeli economists to dismantle subsidies to agriculture could lessen the potentially positive benefit that would be gained from reduced military sales.

While the lack of a peace dividend to the Arab world is increasingly apparent to some analysts, what is less appreciated is the impact of ongoing militarization on Israel. Many analysts predicted that American military and economic support for Israel in the 1990s would decline. This analysis was based on two factors: first of all, it was argued that Israel was no longer needed as a surrogate for US interests, because the Cold War's end simultaneously ended Israel's role as a counterweight to Soviet influences in the Middle East. In addition, the dramatic increase in military cooperation and arms transfers to the GCC states during and after the Gulf War demonstrated that Israel was not the only Middle Eastern country upon which the US (and its arms producers) could rely for maintaining its interests in the region. Indeed, the GCC states have proven themselves to be close allies although, as I have noted in other articles, the US–GCC alliance is based on a very fragile pact.[22]

However, it should be noted that Israel's role as a surrogate for US strategic interests has never been limited solely to concerns over Soviet influences in the region. As in many other parts of the developing world, the Cold War was more the excuse than the actual reason for

US concerns over instability and challenges to US economic and political hegemony in the international arena. Indeed, radical nationalism and, more recently, Islamic fundamentalism (as defined by Sara Roy) have been seen by American policy makers as at least as threatening to American interests in the region as was communism, and Israeli support in challenging such perceived threats to US-led hegemony has always been, and will continue to be, quite welcome. In addition, the potentially unstable Gulf monarchies, still suspicious of real US (and, indeed, UK) intentions, and in any event lacking the advantages Israel brings to its superpower patron – including well-trained armed forces, technological sophistication, an ability to mobilize their human and material resources, and substantial electoral influence – can never make themselves substitutes for Israel in US eyes. Given that continued support of Israel does not interfere with an unprecedented degree of cooperation with Egypt and the Gulf regimes, or with rapprochement with Syria, there are few risks involved with the US continuing such an alliance with Israel, even as the US cultivates closer strategic relationships with authoritarian Arab regimes.

A second factor involves the enormous costs to the American taxpayer for its ongoing economic and military support of Israel. Given the high level of aid to Israel, such aid would appear to be susceptible to major reductions by policy makers in a new administration eager to place priority on programs benefiting domestic US programs rather than a foreign country. What such arguments ignore, however, is that the large amounts of US aid to the Israeli government have never been particularly beneficial to Israel and have actually supported politically powerful sectors of the US industrial structure. It is striking that such a huge infusion of capital to such a small country has not led to more real economic growth. This is in large part because the economic aid that remained in Israel has gone primarily to finance non-productive sectors, such as settlement construction in the occupied territories, primarily built with Palestinian labor, and for military salaries. Instead, most of the economic aid in recent years and virtually all of the aid projected in the coming decade will likely be used to finance interest and loan repayments to American banks.

In addition, the $1.8 billion in annual military aid is in fact simply a credit line to American arms manufacturers, and actually ends up costing Israel two to three times that amount to train operators, to staff maintenance crews, to procure spare parts, and to support other related costs.[23] The overall impact is to increase Israeli economic and military dependency on the US and to drain Israel's increasingly fragile economy. Matti Peled, the late Israeli major general and Knesset member, reported that this $1.8 billion figure – which he claims was arrived at 'out of thin air',[24] and is far more than Israel needs to replenish arms support stocks – is unrelated to specific security requirements.[25] This observation thereby reinforces the impression that the Israeli military is little more than a US government subsidy for the American arms industry. This benefit to American defense contractors is multiplied by the fact that every major arms transfer to Israel creates a new demand by Arab states – most of which can pay hard currency through petro-dollars – for additional US weapons to challenge Israel. The resulting arms race is a bonanza for US arms manufacturers.

The prospects for peace will not reduce the close military relationship between Israel and the US because American military support for Israel was never and is not based on any actual concerns for Israeli security. Indeed, US aid to Israel has increased since the signing of the Oslo Accords and the peace treaty with Jordan, as Israel's strategic needs have lessened. Continuing US arms transfers to both Israel and the Gulf states serve important political functions for the recipient Middle Eastern states, despite the enormous costs and negative impact on their respective economies. For the Israelis, Arab militarism serves as an excuse for continued control over much of the occupied territories and for maintaining subsidies – in and of themselves labor subsidies – for its entrenched militarized industrial structure (for analysis of Israeli voter reaction within this context, see Shimson Bichler's contribution to this volume). For the autocratic Arab leaders, Israeli military power provides an excuse for their unwillingness to promote internal democratization programs, and affords them rhetoric allowing them to avoid making badly needed social and economic reforms (on aid competition, see Glasser). It is likely that both sides will continue to work on the assumption that these weapons will never actually have to be used. However, given the history of the region, this may be an overly-optimistic assumption.

Conclusion

As long as the Peace Process is advanced through what is essentially bribery and extortion, as long as the Palestinians do not have a greater say in their political and economic future, as long as the arms race continues, and as long as Israelis heavily influence US policy, there is little reason to expect real peace with its concomitant economic benefits and dividends. Only when the US government redirects its Middle East policy toward demilitarization, democratization, and a comprehensive settlement, recognizing the national rights of both Israeli Jews and Palestinian Arabs, can sustainable economic development take place and political stability be assured. Instead of US economic pressure and diplomatic clout being used as a bludgeon to make possible a Pax Americana, America's superpower leverage should be used to force all parties to recognize the right of self-determination.

The future of the economy of the Middle East may ultimately depend on economic choices made in the United States, for it is doubtful that American policy toward the Middle East will change until priorities at home are similarly redirected. There is unlikely to be any incentive to curb the arms race in the region, for example, until the US government implements a policy aimed at converting more weapons production facilities into industrial facilities that manufacture goods needed for domestic civilian consumption, and for export. At the same time, until US energy needs are met less through the import of Arab oil and more through energy conservation and the use of safe, renewable domestic sources, US strategic and energy priorities in the Middle East are unlikely to shift. And, until economic priorities at home are based less on corporate profits and more on meeting human needs, it is unrealistic to expect that any US economic agenda and political policy overseas will become more enlightened, no matter what party is in power. These structural flaws in the US economy and the crucial failures they create in American politics, present significant impediments to peace.

Notes

1.   Interview, November 1993.
2.   E. Murphy, 'Stacking the Deck: The Economics of the Israeli–PLO Accords', *Middle East Report* (August 1995), 194–5.
3.   *Financial Times*, 21 October 1993.
4.   *USIS Briefing*, Damascus, Syria (January 1992).
5.   Also see Zunes, 'Israeli–Syrian Peace: The Long Road Ahead', *Middle East Policy*, II (1993–94) and 'Disenchantment with the New World Order: US–Syrian Relations in the Post-Gulf War Era', *International Journal*, III (Spring 1995).
6.   Also see Zunes, 'The Israeli–Jordanian Peace Agreement: Peace or Pax Americana?', *Middle East Policy*, III (Spring 1995).
7.   P. V. Vivekand, 'Jordan to lobby Paris Club for debt relief during IMF talks', *Jordan Times*, 1 October 1994.
8.   *Jordan Times*, 29 July 1994.

9.   P. Kidron, 'Peace Treaty Agreement', *Middle East International*, 21 October 1994.
10.   *Jordan Times*, 15 October 1994.
11.   Briefing, National Council on US–Arab Relations, 30 December 1991.
12.   US Arms Control and Disarmament Agency, 'World Military Expenditures and Arms Transfers' (Washington, DC: US Arms Control and Disarmament Agency, 1994) 6–7 and 22–3.
13.   'World Military Expenditures and Arms Transfers', 8.
14.   J. Stork, 'The Middle East Arms Bazaar after the Gulf War', *Middle East Report* (November–December 1995).
15.   R. Vitalis, 'Gun Belt in the Beltway', *Middle East Report* (November–December 1995).
16.   'Saudis Go for Broke on US Arms', *Arms Sales Monitor* (July 1995).
17.   Vitalis, 'Gun Belt in the Beltway'.
18.   J. Gerth, 'Saudi Stability Hit by Heavy Spending Over the Decade', *New York Times*, 23 August 1993.
19.   S. Engleberg, 'US–Saudi Deals in the 1990s Shifting Away from Cash Toward Credit', *New York Times*, 23 August 1993.
20.   Vitalis, 'Gun Belt in the Beltway'.
21.   J. Shira-Starr, 'The Middle East Food Alarm', *Christian Science Monitor*, 26 October 1996.
22.   See Zunes, 'The United States and the Gulf Cooperation Council: A Fragile Alliance', *Middle East Policy*, 2 (Summer 1993).
23.   Interview with Matti Peled in Seattle, Washington (12 May 1992).
24.   Interview with Matti Peled (12 May 1992).
25.   See Zunes, 'The Roots of the US–Israeli Relationship', *New Political Science*, (Spring–Summer 1992).

5

Between Jordan and Israel: the Economics of Palestine's Uneasy Triangle

Ishaq Diwan and Michael Walton[1]

Will progress in the Middle East Peace Process spur regional integration? Peace would, theoretically, increase Israeli–Arab trade by removing the political motivations behind Arab economic sanctions against Israel. It could also reduce strategic motives for state intervention in economic affairs in Arab countries, which could lead to a generally more liberal economic order throughout the region. Many people in most camps believe this would be an unqualified good. Indeed, many observers go further by arguing that active policies promoting regional trade agreements between Israel and its more distant Gulf Arab neighbors are needed to facilitate the Peace Process. Others, especially on the leftist and nationalist sides of Arab politics, argue that a resolution of the Palestinian question should not include creation and promotion of trade structures facilitating Israeli commercial and economic domination of the Middle East.

In this chapter, we approach the issue of regional economic integration by focusing on the triangular economic relationships that have existed between the areas under the control of the Palestinian Authority (PA), Jordan, and Israel, and then by turning to the broader regional considerations, dimensions, and reasons that hold this relationship together. First, the linkages between the economies of the West Bank and Gaza Strip, Jordan, and Israel have been the most intensive of those crossing the Arab–Israeli divide. Second, the structures dominating the new regional order will have to accommodate the needs of all three economies – that is, Israel's desire for regional commercial insertion, the Palestinian's need for regional trade diversification as well as their need to develop broadly-based employment, and Jordan's drive to defend its interests and draw some benefits from the peace process.

The initial economic forces supporting the triangle

Strong but varied economic forces support the continuation of the Palestine–Jordan–Israel economic triangle, if only tensely. The key linkage in the triangle is the Palestinian economy's connections with Israel and Jordan through their labor, goods, and capital markets. Historically, of those Palestinians who did not relocate to Jordan after occupation in 1967, up to 35 percent worked in Israel. This was one of several factors that enabled trade in the West Bank and Gaza to be dominated by Israel.

On its other side, Jordan has traditionally served as a gateway for trade with the Gulf states. In addition, large quantities of Jordanian and Israeli currencies are in circulation in the West Bank and Gaza, where the dinar and the shekel are both legal tender. Because of these linkages, monetary, as well as supply, shocks that arise in any one of the three economies are invariably transmitted to the others (see Wright and Colton). As examples, the oil boom in the Gulf states induced a significant Palestinian labor migration, whose remittances provided Jordan with significant financial resources; Israeli inflation in the early 1980s led to a rise in demand for Jordanian dinar in the territories; in the 1990s Russian immigration to Israel reduced demand for Arab labor in Jerusalem, which further depressed the Palestinian labor market.

As a result, policies affecting relations between any two countries will inevitably affect the third. This situation is clear in the case of intra-triangle trade, where Israeli protectionist policies have reduced the flow of Jordanian exports to the West Bank and Gaza. A similar situation is evident on a broader basis because the Arab trade embargo on Israel also severely limited the ability of Palestinian producers to export to the Arab world. These indirect influences thus encouraged Palestine's greater economic integration with Israel. Even so, while the Israeli economy is much larger than the Palestinian's – in 1993 Israel's GDP was 15 times that of Jordan and 28 times that of the West Bank and Gaza – dependencies could be favorably affected by more liberal policies toward monetary and trade enhancement, the idea being that Israeli initiatives would be less effective if the PA would support freer markets, reduce tax rates below the levels prevailing in Israel (especially indirect taxes), and build more open trade structures.[2]

Our main objective is to investigate the basis for tensions affecting economic relations within the Palestinian–Jordanian–Israeli triangle, and thus delineate the elements of possible arrangements on trade, labor movement, and finance that could be stabilizing over the medium term. We will begin with a discussion of the particular interests of each

Table 5.1 Strategic objectives of the three sides of the triangle

Objective	Overall strategy	Trade	Labor	Capital
Israel	• Insertion into region via WBG and Jordan • Continue to pursue efficiency-improving economic reforms	• Access to regional market (including construction) • Transitional protection for labor-intensive industries	• Limit use of Palestinian construction labor • Minimize inflow of Palestinians into West Bank and Gaza	• Avoid outflows of Israeli capital • Keep official capital flowing in • Encourage foreign private capital
West Bank/Gaza (WBG)	• Increase economic autonomy • Balance economic relations towards the Arab World • Labor-demanding growth	• Maintain existing Israeli markets • Open to Arab countries • Open to ROW • Open rest of Israeli market • (Maybe) nurture infant industries • (Maybe) protect agriculture from Jordanian competition	• Slow phase out of labor from Israeli labor market • Manage inflow of returnees to West Bank and Gaza, in line with private capital (for jobs) and official capital (for services)	• Create conditions for private capital inflow; including open capital account • Increase official inflows • Expand banking services • Increase macroeconomic autonomy, including over currency
Jordan	• Reduce macro risks • Restructure the economy onto a new growth path	• Get wider market access to WBG • Open up in long term to ROW • As soon as politically acceptable get access to Israeli market • Transitional protection for inefficient industries	• Avoid disturbances to delicate internal labor situation • Avoid large deskilling through losses of skilled Palestinians	• Avoid shifts of portfolio or direct investment into WBG • Keep official capital flowing • Secure debt reduction • Resist withdrawals of Dinars from the WBG

of the three economies. We will then summarize the early bilateral economic agreements that have been reached to date between the parties, before we discuss feasible strategies with respect to labor, trade, and capital. Finally, we will turn to the broader issues presented by regional and international economic integration. In particular, we will ask what kind of market model can be best applied.

Perspectives on what is at stake in the Peace Process

Different motives existed in each of the Palestinian, Jordanian, and Israeli economies for rapprochement with the others. Jordan and the West Bank and Gaza all suffer from high unemployment, estimated at between 15 percent and 20 to 30 percent respectively in 1995, and 10 percent in Israel. In some areas, the unemployment problems are even worse. At a sectoral level, the problem is worse still among the youngest. As examples, 37.2 percent of first-time job seekers and 58 percent of labor market entrants under age 25 were unemployed in Jordan.[3] Similar figures existed in neighboring Egypt and Syria. The situation was likely worse in PA-controlled areas, especially Gaza.

Many economic observers feel the unemployment problem could have been eased, at least in the intermediate and medium terms, with the opening of new and regionally integrated market opportunities. This perspective recognized ways the PA and Israel shared strategic motives for greater integration with the Arab markets, but for different reasons. However, key considerations divided their positions. For example, the opening of additional trade routes could lead to employment losses in less efficient local sectors in Jordan and Israel, could reduce policy dominance/independence of economic institutions in each of the three economies, and could affect strategic balances with respect to long-standing political conflicts. Table 5.1 summarizes the strategic objectives of the triangle's players. Later, we analyze in more detail their positions regarding commodity, labor, and capital mobility.

The Palestinian perspective

The PA's central objective has been to increase its autonomy in economic decision making and policy planning concerning job creation and export growth. The PA sees trade diversification as the key factor to be addressed before unemployment-related problems can be tackled. Under Israeli occupation, the economy of the West Bank and Gaza evolved into one that was highly dependent on external employment structures, resulting from a combination of squeezes on domestic production, an opening up of Israeli labor markets, and an enormous expansion of demand for skilled labor in the Gulf states. Both sources of employment faltered from the mid-1980s, steadily declined in the late 1980s, before crashing in the 1990s. Following the Gulf War, Arab employment in Israel declined dramatically, from over 120 000 in 1992 (one-third of the labor force), to a low of 20 000 in 1993 (10 percent of the labor force), before recovering to some 50 000 in mid-1994.[4] These labor scenarios have become permanent aspects of the Palestinian employment structure. Moreover, there are few prospects to indicate another sharp rise in Gulf demand for Palestinian labor (see Wright). And, the fall in labor demand in Israel reflects tense security situations as well as the implementation of political agendas.

On another level, if the only motivations were market forces and real earnings differentials, there would be massive labor flows into Israel, where wages are two to three times higher. Labor flows from the territories, however, are likely to remain highly managed. In addition, while some Palestinians in the diaspora have maintained residence rights in the West Bank and Gaza and are, in principle, free to return under the terms of the September 1993 Declaration of Principles, the return of a large majority will be subject to future PA–Israeli negotiations. The Protocol dealt only with labor movements between Israel and the PA-controlled areas. This is one of several issues where the PA feels it does not have the 'decision' independence it needs in order to implement growth-oriented policies.

Furthermore, if peace is achieved, Palestinian workers could encounter stiffer competition in the region from Jordanian and Egyptian workers and they could also face substitution by new Jewish immigrants. In fact, this second factor has been somewhat hidden by the Israeli construction boom in settlement housing, the only sector within which Palestinian workers are still in high demand. Meanwhile, the Palestinian labor supply expanded rapidly throughout the 1990s, as has workforce growth in the Gulf states and North Africa, through a combination of exceptionally high population growth rates and the return of guest-workers who had migrated to the Gulf states.

It is worth noting again that the Israeli occupation substantially limited domestic production opportunities.[5] On the demand side, this occurred through Israeli restrictions on competitive exports. Restraints were also caused by the Arab boycott, which had the reciprocal effect of prohibiting Palestinian exports to neighboring Arab states. On the supply side, constraints were placed on the Palestinian economy through regulatory restrictions on investment and finance, through the underprovision of public goods, and through a declining natural resource base. Therefore, Palestinian dependence on outside labor markets was not merely the result of the expansion of Gulf markets, but was more so founded in biased regulations. The consequence of this legacy is that Palestinians felt from the beginning of the peace process that even with the huge aid packages pledged by donors, a transition without trade diversification and rapid expansion of the domestic labor market would lead to a deterioration of living standards and the destabilization of an already fragile Palestinian social-economic and political order.

Understandably, the Palestinians want solutions that take into account the interlocking interests of the whole triangle, but their position has contrasted with the short-term interests of each member. Even so, the PA may want to keep the flow of both commuter and unskilled return migrants gradual in order to avoid adverse labor market supply shocks; and yet it is likely to want skilled Palestinians back in growing sectors.[6] These considerations suggest a solution based on managed gradualism, including both a phase-out of Palestinian workers in Israel and a phase-in of skilled and then unskilled returnees from Jordan and elsewhere. The successful implementation of such a managed process, of course, is clearly subject to other shocks, such as those created by renewed violence on both sides.

The Jordanian perspective

For Jordan, the key economic objectives have been and remain defensive: to avert a sudden attack on the dinar, to retain Palestinian capital in the host economy, and to avoid the sudden exposure of inefficient industries to competition. However, these considerations fall within a context of significant potential structural change. Following a deep recession in the aftermath of the 1967 war, Jordan enjoyed unprecedented growth between 1973 and 1984 due to foreign assistance and substantial increases in workers' remittances. This ended, however, with the collapse of oil prices and, less directly, with the implementation of employment localization programs in the Gulf states. Aid levels also declined by 1991, real per capita income in Jordan had declined to about one-half of its levels in the early 1980s. The Gulf War complicated matters further, leading to the loss of the lucrative Iraqi market, which absorbed 30 percent or more of Jordan's exports in 1989. Relative to these situations, Jordan's traditional comparative advantages, namely providing skilled workers to the Gulf and receiving aid for its promise of maintaining a secure border with Israel, have largely faded.[7]

Even so, many of the ingredients for autonomous development existed. Most of the returnees from the Gulf to Jordan have marketable skills. Returnees' deposits into domestic savings were high (with additional savings abroad estimated at over 100 percent of GDP). The 1980s pattern of growth left Jordan with an expanded relatively efficient infrastructure. However, macroeconomic risks remained cause for deep concern. These risks included a high degree of past dependence on potentially fickle sources of foreign receipts, including trade with Iraq, potash sales, and private capital inflows, while falling workers' remittances had equalled approximately 17 percent of GDP. In addition, bilateral grants accounted for approximately 9 percent of GDP.

Moreover, there were two potential debt problems: an external public debt totaling 120 percent of GDP, and holdings of Jordanian dinars by West Bank residents totaling between 15 and 20 percent of GDP. Despite deep spending cuts, more fiscal adjustment was needed to service the country's debt, accommodate the recent returnees, and better integrate the Palestinian refugees into the economic and social fabric.[8] US and other debt forgiveness programs have helped alleviate these negative consequences. Even so, scheduled debt relief plans are linked to continuing support of the peace process.

Jordan has also been under significant international pressure to realize that its productive inefficiencies are mainly the result of protected and monopolistic industrial policies and extensive government involvement in most facets of the economy. A reformist strategy of gradually removing price controls and easing trade restrictions has been followed in the past few years, with some success – such as being granted entry into the World Trade Organization. However, there has been little real economic restructuring. As a result of its combination of unused capacity and limited competitiveness, Jordanian markets are seen as ones Palestinian producers could penetrate if allowed to do so. From this perspective, Jordan fears the introduction of Palestinian (or Israeli) competitors because they might have potentially devastating effects on local production and employment.

In addition, dinar holdings by Palestinians living in the territories are large, and the potential for a shifting of current deposits and future remittances away from Jordan's banking system could deepen the country's liquidity problems. And, over time, if Israel opens its markets to Palestinians alone, Jordan's firms (especially those which are Palestinian-owned) could begin to relocate to the West Bank and Gaza. Obviously, these underlying concerns force strategic choices concerning the balance between cooperation and competition with the rising Palestinian entity.

The Israeli perspective

For Israel, stable relations with the region's commercial sectors are crucial for its planned transformation from a state-dominated economy to one that can better appeal to domestic and foreign investors. A gradual liberal reform program aimed at enhancing growth was initiated in the late 1980s, but significant response has been elusive. Growth was fragile and dominated by immigration-related construction. Foreign investment stabilized at relatively low levels and there have been few new capital infusions into dynamic growth industries.[9] Starting in 1993, however, the economy picked up as expectations over the Peace Process gathered momentum. By 1995, unemployment had fallen below 10 percent, its lowest level in many years. As they looked past the year 2000, Israeli proponents of regional economic integration wanted more than gains from trade, foreseeing larger indirect gains from increased stability.

While regional economic insertion would enhance Israel's long-term goals, improving immediate trade relations with the West Bank and Gaza and opening its borders to Jordan involved short-term costs. Therefore, many Israelis feared that a more liberal commercial structure could cause a trade diversion away from Israeli producers and toward cheaper producers in PA-controlled areas and Jordan. The real effects would be small relative to the size of the overall Israeli economy, but resistance remained, especially in agriculture and several labor-intensive industries which have traditionally been shielded from foreign competition. Given the extent of public sector involvement in the economy, increased competition was expected to raise fiscal pressures unless privatization accelerated. In addition, these financial costs were accompanied by political costs, based on fears of wage losses to Palestinian workers.

The potential loss of policy effectiveness was also an important concern for Israel. If Palestinian and Israeli trade and fiscal regimes differed significantly, a border would be required to prevent the smuggling of goods from whichever country had lower customs rates and value-added taxes.[10] In the absence of a border, a more liberal Palestinian economic environment would reduce policy influence since Israelis would purchase in the Palestinian territories the goods that are more heavily taxed at home. On the monetary front, Israel stood to lose on two counts if the PA increased its policy independence. Israel would be concerned about losses associated with its currency in circulation in the autonomous areas, estimated at about $1 billion. And, if the foreign exchange and financial controls were freer under PA regulations, illegal leaks would become inevitable parts of the system, and reduce the effectiveness of

Israel's monetary and fiscal policies. These concerns would conceivably decline over time as the Israeli economy became increasingly liberal but, in 1995 and for now, they are immediate concerns, particularly at a time when Israel promises to pursue greater privatization and when its largest firms are reorganizing in the face of globalization.

Elements of the new economic order

With such a complex web of interests involved, what relations are likely to shape the Palestinian–Jordanian–Israeli triangle? The considerations above suggest that many market opportunities exist. However, in order for the parties to minimize transitional losses, preserve policy effectiveness and independence, and stabilize their strategic balances, market forces would also have to be restricted along geographical and sectoral lines in the short to medium terms. As a result, several areas of market integration would likely be carefully managed. In order to allow for cooperation in some areas, pressures would have to be contained elsewhere by enforcing market segmentation and minimizing leakages. This would require a tight balance between forces of competition and cooperation, as are already reflected in the economic agreements between the PA and Israel, the PA and Jordan, and Jordan and Israel.

A triangle of agreements

Economic agreements that were reached earlier in the Peace Process form the basis of the Palestinian–Jordanian–Israeli triangle. In December 1993, Jordan and Israel signed a Memorandum of Understanding concerning the reopening of Jordanian bank branches in the territories. A Palestinian–Jordanian economic agreement, which set the broad outlines of future economic cooperation, was signed in January 1995. A Palestinian–Israeli Protocol on Economic Relations (henceforth referred to as the Protocol) was signed in April 1994. Israel and Jordan also signed an Agreement on Trade and Economic Cooperation in 1995. However, these early agreements must be seen as being subject to continual change, at least until final status treaties are signed. For example, the Israeli–Jordanian banking agreement was superseded by the Palestinian–Israeli Protocol. Even in the Protocol, a mechanism for renegotiating was established in the form of a Joint Economic Committee. The Protocol also only covered a transitional period, and subjects many issues to renegotiation. The Palestinian–Jordanian agreement only officially set the stage for cooperation, but required follow-on negotiations for more specific arrangements, many of which are still being discussed. More fundamentally, most observers felt that these agreements were unlikely to stand the test of time because renewed sets of relationships and changes in power throughout the region (Israeli elections, the succession of new heads of state in Jordan and Syria, and parliamentary shifts in Lebanon) that would change the interests of all three parties would inevitably emerge.

In reality, what was being established under these agreed-upon principles are biased trade structures. For example, the economic agreement between the PLO and Israel was supposed to open the door for increased Palestinian exports and other trade between the Palestinian-controlled territories and Israel. This increased exchange would be managed within an essentially free market system, with common tariffs to be established (except on some specific imports for which the PA could set tariff rates independently) and with agreed-upon quantities. Still, a number of significant impediments to Palestinian producers were carried over from former Israeli edicts. For example, goods exempted from the customs union included oil, some foods, construction materials, automobiles, and some investment products. However, exemptions are valid only when these goods are not marketed in Israel.

In the banking sector, the Palestinians and Israelis agreed that a Palestinian Monetary Authority (PMA) would be responsible for the licensing, regulation and, supervision of banks operating in PA-controlled areas, and that it would be the area's lender of last resort. The new Israeli shekel would remain the 'circulating currency', meaning it must be accepted by the PA, and throughout the banking sector. The terms of foreign currencies convertibility were that the Israeli central bank has committed itself to exchanging shekels for foreign exchange, but only up to a maximum level. In addition, the bilateral agreement on estimated current account deficits between the PA and Israel insured that shekels circulating in the West Bank and Gaza could be withdrawn for reasons motivated by currency substitution agendas that could be set by the PA in the future. Both sides agreed to continue discussing the establishment of a Palestinian currency, but no timeframe was set. Meanwhile, the framework agreement between the PA and Jordan, signed in 1995, cleared the way for Jordanian bank entry into the territories and provides for the legal initiation of the Jordanian dinar as a circulating currency.

With respect to trade, the primary agreements between Jordan and the PA were about intentions and did not include substantive economic liberalization requirements. Both sides agreed to work on creating procedures aimed at increasing trade between the two countries. The agreement also called on Jordan to facilitate the transit of Palestinian goods to Arab markets, and for the establishment of new infrastructure including the construction of bridges, road networks, and storage and freight facilities. The trade agreement reached between Israel and Jordan was more substantive in that it officially 'normalized' commercial relations between the two countries and ended Jordan's boycott on Israeli trade. However, this agreed upon 'normalization' was left intentionally vague in order to ensure more negotiations. During the discussions leading to the agreement, the Israelis argued for a preferential trade relationship converging over time into the constitution of a free trade area. Jordan preferred instead to postpone talks about free trade, opting for a more limited formula whereby trade was to be normalized within the framework of the World Trade Organization, to which it had not acceded at the time. Jordan also managed to get preferential treatment for some selected goods (cement, furniture, foodstuffs, and pharmaceuticals). A transport agreement was also signed, and while intending to enable a freer transit of both goods and people, such movement remained constrained by a host of regulations and indirect costs.

The dynamics of integration under the existing structures

The agreements obviously reflect a complex mixture of factors. We will now try to evaluate the implications that these agreements have had and attempt to look forward toward what could be feasible and desirable scenarios in the next century. A key point here was that from each of these players' perspectives, effective administration of the labor market also means acquiring and managing finance. Effectively managing labor and capital movements, both in or out of the triangle's three economies, was critical to the degree to which macroeconomic stability can be maintained. The overriding issue, then, was one of balancing the creation of new employment opportunities with the defense of existing finance and production structures. In this section, we discuss possible ways of easing the tensions outlined above, which, if they were relatively easy to determine, were not easy to affect politically: capital inflows from outside, managing regional public investment projects, and the trickier issues of intra-triangle trade.

Capital inflows from the rest of the world

The Palestinian, Jordanian, and Israeli economies continue to face common interests in getting more money from the international donor community. But there is a complication: for all the West's enthusiasm for the Peace Process, it is probable that war is more conducive for official capital inflows than is peace. It was true that the West provided financing to get peace negotiations going as a means of averting a severe crisis. However, it is less clear as to whether or not they will renew their pledges mainly because initial expectations continue to fail. This situation makes it plausible that official financial contributions will continue to taper off. Or, capital inflows will continue to dry up if investments made in the 1990s do not meet their expected returns. Unfortunately, too many of these investments did not reach their expected destinations, or were lost to corruption. Above and beyond the donor community's prognosis of the economic and political efficiency of their donations, private entrepreneurs and financiers will certainly require more assurances of economic stability before they start investing significant amounts of capital. This is a strong argument for keeping the economics of peace running in tandem with the politics of peace. This also suggests that commitments for future assistance – multi-year aid packages for the Palestinian areas and debt reduction packages for Jordan – play a key role in advancing the process. That said, however, the international donor community will want to see better results than have been evident so far.

Regional projects

Of all forms of regional cooperation, investments in physical infrastructure and efforts aimed at harmonizing the region's trade services present the most promising routes to short-term growth because they strengthen areas common to each players' interests and they are directly manageable. This is especially obvious for infrastructure projects designed to foster inter-regional transportation and tourism. Another example is found in the building of power systems projects, where the least costly solutions from both design and maintenance perspectives require the participation of several countries. But a concerted regional effort will be most critical if the serious problems of environmental degradation and water scarcity are also to be addressed (see Rouyer). In fact, a number of projects are either under way or under consideration via the 'Multilateral Working Groups on Regional Economic Development'. These include plans for reconstruction and improvement of the coastal highway along the eastern ridge of the Mediterranean running mainly through Syria, Lebanon, Israel and Gaza, and upgrading the roads and rebuilding the bridges forming the three east–west corridors between the Israeli coast, the West Bank and Gaza, and Jordan. In the power sector, projects include the interconnection of power grids for Egypt, Jordan, the territories, Lebanon, and Syria.

The issue of trade relations lies at the heart of the uneasiness in the Palestine–Jordan–Israel economic triangle because expansionist and defensive considerations are involved. The Israeli market is attractive to both West Bank and Gazan and Jordanian entrepreneurs, since open access to a larger and geographically closer market could do much to reduce unemployment and raise incomes and living standards. For Israel, the expected gains are more macroeconomic and indirect, but no less important because they could eventually gain access to Gulf markets and/or lower their costs by securing energy deliveries. Jordan, of course, aims to profit on trade that moves across its borders and it hopes to secure market shares in Palestinian areas and to use them for gaining indirect access to Israeli markets. Still, the Arabs generally remain leery of transitional losses and economic domination.

From a Palestinian perspective, a change in the present trade structure is crucial for renewed growth. And while much can be gained with a more liberal environment, their very small industrial base means there is little in the Palestinian economy that is not vulnerable. Ideally, the PA-controlled territories should want to promote business development by combining the advantage of duty-free access to Israel, which could stimulate short-term growth, with increased discretion in long-term trade policies toward the rest of the world, and, in particular, the Arab world. Indeed, a key isolating factor has been the Arab's refusal to trade not only in Israeli products, but also in Palestinian products on which Israelis have assessed taxes. In an attempt at setting a new precedent, the economic agreement between the PA and Israel recognizes as Jordanian goods with only 30 percent of their value added in Jordan. A further relaxation of the embargo would allow Palestinian and Jordanian entrepreneurs to play an important role in disseminating Israeli goods and services.

Moreover, a key strategic concern for the Palestinians is to strengthen their independence in dealing with Israel. But two of the most thorny political issues which have yet to be negotiated, Jerusalem and Israeli settlements, make it impossible to contemplate the imposition of customs gates between Israel and the West Bank and Gaza, a precondition for trade policy independence. In the absence of a well-defined border, goods imported to the PA-controlled areas could easily leak into the Israeli market. This opportunity will be resisted in Israel for two reasons: the first is economic, namely the absence of trade relations based on reciprocity; the second is strategic, namely that Israel will not want to buy products from countries with which it has not signed peace treaties. As a result, the development of strong relations between the autonomous Palestinian areas and their neighboring Arab states is likely to remain contingent on concrete improvements in relations between the broader set of Arab states and Israel.

The contents of the Palestinian–Israel economic protocol clearly reflects this tension. On the one hand, it opened the door for Palestinian exports to Israel, providing an important source for future growth. On the other hand, it effectively subjugated the development of Palestinian–Arab trade relations to progress in the Peace Process. In addition, Jordan and Egypt's 'special treatment' in their access to the Palestinian market was nevertheless continued to be determined by the way in which the Israel–Palestinian agreement would be applied in the future, mainly because it contained the important provisions that quantities exported and imported must remain below some prescribed ceilings and that imports above these ceilings from other Arab countries be treated in accordance with Israeli regulations. This clearly implied that increased imports would not be allowed from countries that would not recognize official commercial relations with Israel. Thus, the main decisions about Palestinian–Arab trade could not be made by the PA: imports would depend on how liberal the Israelis would be in their interpretation of ceilings, and Palestinian exports would continue to be constrained by the Arab embargo, in its official or unofficial forms, until removed functionally as well as politically.

How was the Palestinian–Israeli Protocol supposed to affect Jordan? Amman continues to want to develop preferential relations with the West Bank and Gaza in order to expand its export base. The former territories are attractive because of their proximity, whether geographical or human, and to the market opportunities they provide, particularly in terms of industrial goods, foodstuffs, and services. The Protocol provided a favorable start and was expected to enable Jordan to export as much as US \$200 to \$300 million worth of goods annually to areas under Palestinian control. But, while this could be an important development, it would not be a substitute for direct access to the Israeli market. This was especially true since there has been continued decapitalization in Palestine throughout the last decade.

Under those circumstances, Jordan would find it difficult to play a pre-eminent regional role unless it is able to secure access to the Israeli market on equal terms with Palestinian producers in the West Bank and Gaza. There are several reasons for this, the first being that real openings to Israel would strengthen Jordan's competitiveness relative to the Palestinian territories and helped it retain factors of production at home. In contrast, Jordan would remain at a disadvantage if the autonomous

Palestinian areas were to retain a privileged relationship with Israel since the temptation would be to relocate factors of production to the West Bank and Gaza. Second, Jordan's initiation of preferential relations with Israel would facilitate relations with the Palestinian areas since those would not have to be restricted by the need to minimize leaks into Israel. Under those arrangements, Jordanian goods admitted into Palestinian-controlled territories under the agreed upon aggregate ceilings will find their way to the Israeli market. But the penetration of these goods into Israel remain constrained by their imperfect access to the autonomous areas. A liberal interpretation of import and export ceilings by Israel could be a way of establishing a similar degree of access that Palestinian producers have. For Jordan, however, such an indirect strategy of securing market access to Israel presents many risks, the main one being its vulnerability to a PA veto.

The alternative would be to establish free access to both the Israeli and Palestinian markets. But Jordan cannot secure a wide access to the Israeli market without reciprocating. However, opening up the Jordanian market to Israel on a preferential basis – for example, in the context of a functional free trade area – presents high short-term costs, both economic and political. For an economy as closed as Jordan's, sudden trade liberalization with a relatively competitive partner would be devastating for large segments of industry. Indeed, Jordan continued to be keen to maintain balance in its external relations, if for no other reason than wanting to avoid the political turmoils supply shocks have already caused (see Colton). If Israeli producers face no tariff, their advantage over far-away exporters will be enormous because their product's prices would bear neither the high transportation costs nor the 25 percent average tariff most Jordanian imported products carry. Given Jordan's substantial reliance on imports, approximately 80 percent of GDP, this would clearly represent an unacceptable strategic advantage for Israeli firms. In the future, two requirements are needed if a preferential trade agreement with Israel is to become a functional reality: (i) that Israel accept an asymmetric relationship in the short term, converging towards a relationship based on reciprocity in the long term; and (ii) that Jordan simultaneously extend liberalization efforts in order to raise exports to other markets, and thus keep the composition of its trade balanced over the long term.

In sum, a free trade area comprising Jordan, Israel, and the West Bank and Gaza may emerge in the long run if the Peace Process moves forward under the new leaderships that exist in the region. The driving force would be provided by the implicit competition between the Jordanian and Palestinian economies which would create incentives for both to bid for a preferential link with the Israeli market. For such a solution to emerge, however, a managed transition is required, supported by a continuation of the peace process, an Israeli willingness to bear some of the costs in exchange for strategic gains, an economic take-off in the Palestinian-controlled areas, and an active reformist agenda in Jordan.

Intra-triangle capital flows and currencies

The allocation of both long- and short-term capital will have powerful macroeconomic effects. The allocation of long-term capital between the Palestinian, Jordanian, and Israeli economies are driven by the relative economic stability of each as well as by the mercantile opportunities that flow from the various trade choices previously discussed. Patterns of regional public funding for industrial and social infrastructure, the relative levels of bureaucracy in the legal and business environments, and tax structures also affect the locational attractiveness of each of these economies for private investment. This tends to encourage intra-triangle competition and is likely to impose the need for some degree for policy coordination and infrastructure harmonization, especially between the (relatively) similar Jordanian and Palestinian economies.

A continual concern for both Jordanian and Israeli negotiators is the allocation of short-term capital, usually based on aid distributions. On this front, some degree of policy coordination is taking place and is likely to increase given the potential for highly destabilizing money flows. Jordan has a strong interest in protecting itself from capital relocation to the Palestinian-controlled areas. The Palestinians, in turn, have an interest in avoiding importing macroeconomic instability from Jordan. Avoidance of instability in the Jordanian economy can, to some extent, be caused by the greater independence resulting from a separate Palestinian currency. In practice, however, there are likely to be limits to the degree of insulation the Jordanians can receive or even want to receive. Consequently, the autonomous Palestinian territories have an interest in reducing macroeconomic risks in Jordan as a means for building internal stability.

The issue of currency is indeed of great concern to the three players in the triangle. Presently, the Palestinian-controlled areas enjoy a de facto unregulated currency system. The dinar, the shekel, and foreign currencies like the US dollar circulate side by side and can be exchanged freely through a well-developed network of money changers and now through an equally well-developed system of banks, most of which are Jordanian. As mentioned earlier, the PA has agreed to allow the dinar and shekel to be the primary currencies used in the territories. The agreement with Israel on the creation of a PMA, however, might suggest that, ultimately, the areas under PA control will have their own currency. The main questions from Jordanian and Israeli perspectives are when and how this transfer of monetary control should happen.[11]

There are several reasons why the Palestinian authorities want to introduce an indigenous currency. Besides its symbolic value, an independent currency is a source of seigniorage revenues, it ensures greater autonomy in the conduct of macroeconomic policy, and it can reduce monetary instability and the potentials for paying inflation taxes associated with the use of 'weak' currencies. But the Palestinians cannot act alone with respect to developing a domestic currency. Not much can be gained by policy independence given the extent of capital mobility and the competition provided by the Israeli and Jordanian currencies and banking systems. Moreover, the most precious commodity in macroeconomic management is credibility, something that is hard to earn, but that can be obtained by membership in a currency union or unions, or by establishing a track record of prudent macroeconomic, and especially fiscal management.

When viewed from another perspective, Palestinian ownership of dinar and shekels can be seen as a liability. Because a Palestinian currency is likely to be introduced sometime in the future, the substantial holdings of Israeli and Jordanian currencies by Palestinians can be considered external debts that will have to be repaid at some point in time. It is a key concern that this process proceed in an orderly fashion and that financing be made available. International assistance, especially to Jordan, may be necessary to reduce macroeconomic risks in the short term and to help finance the withdrawal of its currency in the medium term, with debt reduction as a major objective. In the short term, then, the Palestinian-controlled areas are likely to continue within the current structure of competing currencies. However, the effective management of such a system will require tight coordination between Israel and Jordan since it could easily generate variations in money demand in the Palestinian areas, which could affect the value of the dinar and shekel. Therefore, Israel and Jordan will likely continue to ask for compensating monetary balances in their banking systems so they can ensure that lapses in PA policies will not adversely affect the value of their own currencies on the open market.

However, the net effect of this on Israeli and Jordanian wealth remains unclear. Benefits would flow from possible increased seigniorage revenues, which may be large in the future given the expected flow of external assistance to the areas under Palestinian authority. The costs, however, will result from three developments. First, there will be a counter-balancing tendency for money demand to fall over time as the availability of financial services increases in PA-controlled areas. Second, the risk of financial instability will increase. The perceived threat of a sudden withdrawal of currency in circulation, even if it is unfounded, could form a self-fulfilling prophecy. This calls for an increase in foreign reserves, especially in Jordan. Third, the multiple currency system could reduce the scope for monetary policy independence, especially in the Palestinian-controlled territories and Jordan. Since currency shifts in the Palestinian areas will remain possible, at least between the dinar and the shekel, short-term interest rates will tend to be equalized in Israel and Jordan. In both countries, this will exert pressure for further openings to foreign financial markets and, in Jordan, for a lowering of financial repression to a level compatible with Israel.

The pressure is not as high, however, on Israel as it is on Jordan. This is because the Israeli–Palestinian Protocol does not allow for a quick withdrawal of shekels from PA-controlled territories, or at least not via official channels. This situation was achieved by placing an aggregate ceiling on the amounts of shekels that the PMA can convert at the Israeli central bank. The ceiling is provided by the estimated current account surplus between the autonomous territories and Israel. This also creates incentives for the Palestinians to find ways to ensure that Israeli capital flight does not transit via the West Bank. Potential capital flight from Jordanians to Palestine is also a major concern. Extending the Jordanian banking system into the territories substantially lessened the risk of destabilizing financial outflows and reduced monetary controls. Indeed, as long as Palestinians are placing their deposits into Jordanian bank branches, there are potential gains to be made.

For the Palestinians, finance is seen from a very different perspective. They feel the existence of a dynamic banking system is a prerequisite for any progress in investment and trade. Given the scarcity of ready-made options, a banking system was simply imported from Jordan, together with the dinar. But it is unclear whether this situation will remain an attractive option for Palestinians given the dinar's weakness, the level of financial repression in Jordan, and the fear of a loss of independence with regards to credit market policies. If the PA should decide to initiate an indigenous banking system, it would present a real threat to Jordan. One solution allowing the Jordanians to avoid this threat would be to pursue joint bank ventures. Another might be for Jordan to appeal to Israel to use its bank licensing veto power.

Thus, just as with the issue of currency, it is not clear that the Palestinians have the option of acting alone in the field of banking. The provisions making the PMA the formal lender of last resort recognize that this role is necessary in order for a banking system to operate efficiently. And yet, because the PMA is unable to issue dinars or shekels, the function of controlling market liquidity ultimately rests with the central banks of Jordan and Israel. For the PMA to be able to count on this, it would have to give up policy independence and enter into agreements on the size and use of reserves, especially now when the PMA's dollar reserves and its access to foreign lines of credit remain low. In sum, the PA is unlikely to promote an independent currency or banking system in the short or medium term because of the threats such a system would present. As the Palestinian financial sector grows, the parallel use of the Israeli and Jordanian currencies in these areas will place increasing pressures for closer monetary policy coordination between Israel, Jordan, and the PA.

Designing a new structure: will a European Union or a NAFTA model work?

Finding arrangements that can allow for free movement of goods, capital and labor is likely to remain an elusive goal in the Middle East for some time. Even beyond the severe policy changes seen since the demise of the Peres government, the Netenyahu government and the Barak government we see the many ways complications can arise, even within the Israel–Jordan–West Bank and Gaza triangle. This conclusion is only reinforced when considering a broader Middle East perspective. Certainly, the most widely cited models of regional integration, the European Union (EU) and North American Free Trade Agreement (NAFTA), are not applicable to the Middle East under the present circumstances.

In the case of the EU, economics were put at the service of politics because increased commercial interactions were sought in order to make it too costly for the European states to entertain the thought of war. Moreover, the goal of establishing a common market over time, with member states espousing similar laws, regulations, and a high degree of policy coordination, was not seen as being excessively costly from a budgetary standpoint because the main partners had roughly similar production structures and levels of income. Labor mobility was relaxed, but most of the Union's migratory movements took place after poorer countries, such as Spain and Portugal, joined the EU, and following the establishment of a subsidy system as a means of compensation for losses to be incurred by their entry into the Union.

In the Middle East, while the political motive for integration may be the same, policy coordination would, given the regional disparities, come at a much higher cost. A NAFTA model for Israeli–Arab rapprochement may be more suitable from an economic standpoint, but its political appeal remains more limited. The main reason for this is a reversal of goals in the sense that the repatriation of Palestinians is a given in the minds of the triangle's diplomats. In effect, the agreement between the United States and Mexico within NAFTA sought to increase trade flows in order to reduce migration pressures and encourage firm relocation on the basis of comparative advantages. Policy independence was preserved, with Mexico expected to retain standards below those enforced in the US on a range of manufacturing, labor, or environmental issues. The deal is expected to result, over time, in the relocation of many US labor-intensive factories to Mexico and it is anticipated that gains will result both from savings in production costs and, in the long run, from the dynamic effects related to the increased pressure on US firms to innovate and upgrade. The NAFTA agreement clearly presupposes political stability, since massive firm relocation may otherwise end up being detrimental to the national interests of both countries. While it is probable that a NAFTA model could be applied more readily in the Middle East than an EU (or a US-styled) model, it is equally clear that the political preconditions necessary for successful implementation do not exist.

A more critical problem with the NAFTA analogy, when considering its potential applications in the Middle East as a whole, is that in terms of market size and opportunities the region is home to much greater economic disparities even than are found between the US and Mexico. Unlike the EU or NAFTA, where the richer partner's masses are several times larger than that of the poorer partner, Israel's GDP is smaller than the combined mass of its Arab neighbors, but at the same time volume in the Israeli market outranks each neighbor. Thus Israel cannot be for the Arab world what the US is for Mexico, and at the same time it cannot expect its private sector to make the kinds of foreign direct investments that American companies are making in Mexico. At best, Israel can play a locomotive role for the West Bank and Gaza, and perhaps Jordan, but, as discussed previously, this is unattractive in the medium term given their strategic need to diversify economic relations in order to enhance their long-term bargaining position. This is all the more true given the two-track structure taken by the peace process with the more delicate issues of Jerusalem, the refugees, and the settlements relegated until the end.

Therefore, it is unlikely that these modern western models can be imported for use into the Israeli–Jordanian–Palestinian triangle. Moreover, regardless of the theoretical model that is chosen as a basis for future negotiations, three main factors will constrain the emergence of a freer regional market. First, countries with closed trade regimes and uncompetitive productive structures will oppose open trade until their reform agendas are well advanced. This is particularly the case in Egypt and Syria. Second, reformist forces will remain constrained by generalized instability, and will be encouraged by progress in the Peace Process. This is especially true for Israel and Jordan. And, third, Arab countries are unlikely to be willing to increase their exposure to trade with Israel unduly soon or until the Peace Process is well advanced and until there is further evidence that their trade relations with the rest of the world will expand to an extent sufficient to cover the costs of integrative structural change.

These considerations imply that the regional market is likely to remain fragmented in the short term, but that it will broaden over time if the Peace Process gains strength and domestic policies continue to converge toward coordination. The most promising strategy, then, seems to be one that moves on two tracks, with an opening up of multilateral trade with the rest of the world emerging as a crucial element in the development of regionalism. This two-track process also has its virtues: as regional links develop, regional instability will decline, and multilateral economic liberalization will become more attractive. This process may be helped by the fact that Egypt and Jordan have both acceded to the World Trade Organization and have committed themselves to long lists of trade policy reforms and standard compliance obligations aimed at economic liberalization. At the same time, as exports to the rest of the world rise and competitiveness improves, it will become less threatening to open up to Israel. In a way, the process may start with NAFTA-like agreements linking the region to global markets, leading over time to a regional EU-type arrangement at the speed at which regional disparities are reduced and regional convergence – both economic and political – becomes more advanced.

The process of gradual integration – both regional and international – could be greatly facilitated by the policies adopted in the Gulf states, the EU, and the US. All three of these powerful economic blocks can open their markets to Arab goods on a preferential basis. The EU Mediterranean Initiative proposed to establish a 'balanced triangular relation' between them, the Arab world, and Israel, with a long-term convergence toward symmetry as the implementation of economic reforms set in the peace process gather steam. The process of convergence can continue to be accelerated by internationally supported financing arrangements aimed at alleviating the costs of continued reform, including debt reduction, particularly for Jordan and Syria, and financing reconstruction, whether in the autonomous PA territories or in Lebanon and Iraq. This is especially true outside the Palestinian–Jordanian–Israeli triangle, where competitive forces are less important, and where Israel's economic power is too limited to serve as an effective locomotive for full regional growth.

Notes

1. Another version of this chapter was presented at the Cairo University Conference on Regional Cooperation in the Middle East (1993) and was later published in *The Beirut Review* in 1995. This version was updated for republication in this collection, with permission from the *Review*. The views expressed here reflect those of the authors and not those of the World Bank or its Board of Trustees.
2. J. D. Angrist, 'Wages and Employment in the West Bank and the Gaza Strip: 1981–1990', The Maurice Falk Institute for Economic Research in Israel, Discussion Paper No. 92.02 (Jerusalem, 1992).
3. The World Bank, 'Will Arab Workers Prosper or Be Left Out in the Twenty-First Century?', Regional Perspectives on World Development Report 1995 (Washington, DC: The World Bank, 1995) see chapter 1, 2–9.
4. See G. Abed (ed.), *The Palestinian Economy: Studies in Development Under Prolonged Occupation* (New York: Routledge, 1988); E. Kleinman, 'Economic Independence of the West Bank and Gaza Strip and Israel', Working Paper no. 220 (Bethlehem: Hebrew University, 1992); The World Bank, 'Developing the Occupied Territories: An Investment in Peace', (a six volume series) (Washington, DC: The World Bank, 1993); I. Diwan and M. Walton, 'Palestine: From Dependent to Autonomous Growth', *Finance and Development* (Fall 1994).
5. G. Abed, 'The Economic Viability of a Palestinian State', IPS Papers (Washington DC: Institute for Palestine Studies, 1990); see also the papers in G. Abed (ed.), *The Palestinian Economy*, and Kleinman, 'Economic Independence'.
6. A. A. Shokor, *The Labor Market in the East Bank and Gaza* (in Arabic) (Al-Najah University, 1987); along with Diwan and Walton, 'Palestine: From Dependent to Autonomous Growth'.
7. For a review of the effects of these policies prior to the Gulf War, see Wright's chapter 3 in this volume; and R. E. Wilson, 'Jordan's Trade: Past Performance and Future Prospects', *International Journal of Middle East Studies*, 20 (1988).
8. I. Diwan and L. Squire, 'Financial Flows in the Middle East', Working Paper no. 3 (Cairo: Economic Research Forum, 1994).

9. D. Razin and E. Sadka, *The Economy of Modern Israel: Malaise and Promise* (Chicago: The University of Chicago Press, 1993). After a recession in 1987–89, real GDP growth averaged 6 percent a year in 1990–93. But given that population has risen by about 10 percent between 1990–92, growth was relatively small on a per capita basis (about one percent a year). On the impact of increased Russian immigration, see K. Flug, N. Kasir, and G. Ofer, 'The Absorption of Soviet Immigrants into the Labor Market from 1990 Onward: Aspects of Occupational Substitution and Retention', Working Paper no 9213 (Jerusalem: Bank of Israel, November 1992).

10. A strategy of tax competition can be appealing to the PA. Now that a tax clearing agreement with Israel has been negotiated, the fiscal situation could improve substantially. The PA's fiscal advantage stems from the fact that it does not have to contend with the debt burden faced by Jordan, nor with the dense welfare functions played by the Israeli government. Instead, it will continue to benefit from large external assistance. Thus, a competitive policy of low fiscal burden is feasible in principle, once the fiscal situation is stabilized and the set-up costs of the new administration are brought under control.

11. To prepare for the introduction of a Palestinian currency, two intermediate steps are likely. In the very short term, the PA is likely to develop a Palestinian unit of account to serve as the basis for a tax schedule and public sector payments, and perhaps borrowing. An important issue for analysis is how this unit of account will be defined. In a second stage, the introduction of a relatively restricted version of an independent currency, as in a Currency Board, would help establish credibility and withdraw foreign currencies gradually. This could evolve into a full-fledged currency that brings greater discretion and discipline, and the associated demand for the currency, when it is well-established. There are other implications. In particular, use of multiple currencies creates risks of foreign exchange losses for the banking system.

6
Between 'Supply Shocked' Markets: the Case of Jordanian and Palestinian Returnees

Nora Ann Colton[1]

After the Gulf War hundreds of thousands of migrant guest-workers in the Arab Gulf states were forced to relocate (the case for most Palestinians living in Kuwait), or chose to move because conditions in the Gulf made jobs less profitable and more difficult to find. The bulk of these returnees were people of Palestinian origin who decided to relocate to Jordan, and, to a lesser extent, to the West Bank and Gaza. Most of these returnees had no choice as to where they should relocate: they held Jordanian passports because they or their parents had at some point been provided with citizenship after conflicts with Israel. As was true of earlier migrations, the return of labor following the Gulf War affected every sector of Jordan's economy, but this time it did so in ways that were not easily explained by traditional theories of 'migrant economies', 'returnee influence' and/or 'supply shocks'.

This chapter reviews literature in these areas and illustrates reasons for the Palestinians' unique labor and living positions in Jordan. It intermixes dialog providing historical contexts as well as presenting new research concerning returnee versus non-returnee attitudes toward occupational structures in Jordan. In combination, these discussions illustrate the magnitude of returnee-induced supply shocks – in food and water, housing, labor, and investments (see Wright on labor and finance) – that placed the Palestinians in-between markets, in the midst of political upheaval. By using Jordan as a case study, several theoretical paradigms concerning supply shocks are explored. New light is shed on how to study returnee migration and on the structure and behavior of Jordanian–Palestinian occupational markets. These insights are useful in understanding the response options of Palestinians residing in Jordan and the pros and cons of moving this labor.

The Palestinians of Jordan

To consider the implications of the Peace Process on Jordanian labor markets, one must understand how this market has behaved historically and understand the characteristics of the workers who would be affected by a comprehensive settlement.

When the peace Process Began, the United Nations Relief and Works Agency (UNRWA) accounted for 1 824 179 Palestinian refugees registered in Jordan. This represented 43 percent of the population, and included 227 719 people living in ten refugee camps located in Jordan.[2] Unlike other host countries in the region, Jordan had maintained a policy of integration since the 1950s, when the government devised a policy of granting Palestinians citizenship while simultaneously preserving their status as refugees (enabling them to receive UN assistance). This stance essentially granted Palestinians the right to seek employment and to acquire land and housing but, from the beginning, the granting of these rights was seen as a temporary measure until a final settlement could be reached between Israel and Palestine.

This dual policy worked well in its early stages, especially because of the UN's ability to positively impact the situation through its refugee relief and rehabilitation programs. UNRWA's vocational training schemes were a significant part of educational efforts that ended up making the Jordanian–Palestinians the most important manpower source for the developing Arab oil countries. Consequently, many Palestinians were able to use their education, coupled with their Jordanian passports, to gain residential and occupational mobility – unlike other refugee populations.[3] However, unable to cope with the employment consequences of this migration, Jordan encouraged labor migration for its indigenous population as well as for the Palestinians into the oil-rich Gulf states.

In contrast, the Gulf states wanted Palestinian workers but were not willing to provide them with citizenship. Consequently, when the Gulf crisis erupted and Palestinians joined the flood of returnees moving out of Iraq and Kuwait, they returned to Jordan. The Jordanian markets, from food to labor, were immediately subjected to supply-side shocks.

One of the most significant steps toward alleviating the dilemma faced by Jordan was the 1993 Declaration of Principles signed by the PLO and the Israelis. It recognized the 1967 war refugee's right to return (an estimated 800 000 Palestinians meet this criteria) and it allowed some groups to have temporary residency permits.[4] Unfortunately, because many returnees were people who had left the territories since 1984, the temporary nature of their residence permits made them more vulnerable than before. Technically, it meant they did not have the right to remain in Jordan if King Hussein decided to activate a relocation program.

The obvious question was: would the Palestinians want to return home and live within the structures defined by the peace process? Obviously Naquib's illustration of limited self-rule (Chapter 3) Diwan and Walton's analysis of the triangular economic dynamics that exist in the Levant (Chapter 5) do not paint an optimistic picture of development prospects upon return to PA-controlled areas. Still, there were indications that Palestinians would resettle in Palestine – throughout the diaspora, Palestinians had clung to their dream of one day having a state again.

Technically, return migration is defined as the return of people to their country or region of origin after spending a significant period abroad.[5] The important issues for this discussion relate to the reasons people return home. Unlike the forced movements out of Palestine and later Kuwait, many Palestinians, particularly those with Jordanian citizenship, found themselves facing with a new question: do I want to voluntarily change residence?

Reviewing resettlement literature is instructive. Cerase's work on migrants from Southern Italy led to classifications for people involved in return migration.[6] His first category was the 'return of failure', that is, those migrants who did not assimilate into the host society. Although the word failure is inappropriate for people who were forced to leave their homes involuntarily, the phenomenon of not assimilating into the host society was widespread among the Palestinians in Jordan. Records from the 1950s show that UNRWA attempted to resettle Palestinian refugees unsuccessfully. Many Palestinians refused to be resettled, asserting that they wanted to remain in camps until they could return home. UNRWA commentaries argued that this phenomenon would pass with time and that subsequent generations would be more likely to integrate into Jordanian society. However, large numbers of Palestinians never moved on. Staying in the camps was believed to be an important political statement, symbolizing that the occupation was temporary. Others moved to the Gulf where they were not allowed to assimilate. Consequently, the Declarations' signatories believed that Palestinian refugees would return to help create a Palestinian state.

The 'returns of conservatism' refers to migrants who have saved enough to achieve upward social mobility upon return through buying land, building a new house or opening an independent business. When Jordan initiated its policy on Palestinian refugees, King Abdullah justified giving Palestinians citizenship on the basis that 'they would return as masters and not as slaves'.[7] For many Palestinians, the level of savings acquired while working outside Palestine would be an important component in their decision to return. For many the opportunity to start a business, build a home or purchase land in the newly Palestinian-controlled areas would fuel their desire to return.

'Returns of innovation' refers to migrants who are assumed to have done well in the host society, but realize they are limited in what they can achieve as outsiders. Research on Palestinian labor market integration indicated that Palestinians in Jordan and Lebanon were seen to be extremely visible minorities, competitive in employment and wage markets. In the Gulf states, they were also seen as potential threats to the prevailing political structures. Related literature shows that such disenfranchised groups often end up as vulnerable participants in secondary labor markets, susceptible to insecurity via the indigenous elites. This situation made many Palestinians, even the most successful in their host countries, want to return to their homeland to work or retire. In addition, many saw returning to Palestine as a way of pursuing social and political opportunities.

Of these classifications, such as On-Jook's study of urban-to-rural return migration in Korea point out,[8] social and psychological reasons for returning often play a more prominent role than solely economic considerations. Certainly for Palestinians, a combination of socio-economic and political factors would motivate their decision to return to Palestine.

Ironically, there are parallels to be drawn between Israeli motives for relocating to Israel and Palestinian motives for relocating to Palestine – subjective reasons explain many Jewish migrants' decisions to move to Israel that from an economic view might appeared irrational. In the 1950s and 1960s, Israel saw much of its population emigrate a second time – to the US, Canada and France, among other western countries. Many of these people were labeled deserters after they remained abroad for extended periods. The extent of this out-migration was so large that the Israeli government began to provide incentives encouraging return migration. Even so, Toren's 1970 study of returnees from the US, Canada and France found that of the 199 persons interviewed, 39 percent returned for patriotic reasons, 30 percent because of family commitments, while only 17 percent for economic reasons.[9]

For Palestinians, too, the reasons for return are complex, but patriotism and family are likely to outweigh economic reasons. Yet, it was also clear that a flood of returnees to PA-controlled areas would be resisted by both Israel and the PA. Israel wanted to restrict the numbers who return to between 5000 and 10 000 people per year. The PA did not want to cope with more unemployment, feeling that it did not have the necessary resources to support the population.[10] It is estimated that the number of potential returnees from neighboring Arab countries is as high as 3 000 000, a figure that does not include Palestinians who have settled in the US and Europe.[11] Even if half of the estimated 800 000 eligible Palestinians who live in Jordan were to leave, supply shocks would certainly take place on both sides of the Jordan river.

The impact of supply shocks

Economic shocks are disturbances that dramatically shift a market's aggregate supply curve. They are often unusually quick changes in the money supply, labor availability, wage rates, pricing inputs, technology changes, productivity and so on. Supply shocks can be positive or negative, depending on the nature of the shock and its duration. For example, major declines in world oil supply following the 1973 OPEC embargo had a significantly positive effect on the Gulf Arab economies and their increased profits provided much-needed foreign exchange. The same market scenario, however, created a crisis in most of the industrialized world, which faced supply shocks that were both un-planned and expensive.

Indeed, much of the existing research on supply shocks is a by-pro-duct of the 1973–74 Arab oil embargo. The resulting world economic phenomena led many economists to study the effects of abrupt market changes. It also led many political analysts to study governmental pol-icy responses. There are two primary types of supply shocks. Adverse shocks arise when a sudden decline in supply leads to quick and sig-nificant price hikes which, in turn, force productivity and profits to fall in key industrial sectors. Positive shocks result from an easing of supply-side pressures caused by a quick lowering of input prices, presuming that profitability can be maintained and that too many producers are not forced out of the market. However, what is notable about this dialog is that, because it assumes one variable will shift in direct proportion to changes in the aggregate supply of another variable that might also shift the aggregate supply curve, it cannot reflect the dynamics caused by massive labor migration in conjunction with unplanned distributional and political conflicts, especially in the types of crises that arise in underdeveloped markets. This is certainly the case with Jordan, a coun-try that has had to balance an over-supply of labor, uphold a long-term commitment for supporting the Palestinian people, and meet pressures from the international aid community to reform its economic and political structures.

Historically, Jordan endeavored to produce a strong workforce more for purposes of labor exportation than as a means for enhancing local production. As part of its early development plan, Jordan developed a reliance on guest-worker exportation to the Gulf as (a) a safety valve for relieving the stress of local unemployment, and (b) as a source of financial liquidity due to remittance inflows, and also tax revenues generated as a result of increased exports and local purchases and investments made by these funds. As Wright points out (Chapter 7), the level of labor-finance dependency between Jordan and countries like Saudi Arabia had a significant impact on both sides of the Middle East's regional economic development equation. As early as 1975, Ismail Serageldin estimated that the Gulf region had a labor requirement of 9 728 000, but had less than half that number of workers available in local markets.[12] By the mid-1980s, even these figures increased substantially, with Kuwait alone needing approximately 1.5 million expatriate workers, roughly 67 percent of its population base. Jordanians and Palestinians, the most concentrated group, made up 35 percent of this workforce.[13]

The labor exchange between the oil-rich/labor-poor countries and oil-poor/labor-rich states began to decline as the price of oil fell in the mid-1980s. Consequently, even before the Gulf crisis, Jordanians and Palestinians were beginning to be sent home. In addition, there was an increase in Asian labor supply in the Gulf states which increased dramatically following the Gulf War. This placed downward pressure on wages and benefits that Jordanian and Palestinian workers could expect to receive. These economic phenomena, often coupled with extreme political pressure, made Palestinians even less welcomed guests in Gulf labor markets.

Even clearer incentives for return migration arose with Iraq's invasion of Kuwait and the resulting Gulf War. First the war instigated migration at a basic level. The PLO's blatant support of Saddam Hussein, during and even after the war, resulted in hard-lined diplomacy against Palestinians. For example, the embittered Kuwaitis, making few distinctions between those who did or did not support Iraq, began a sudden and sometimes brutal campaign to rid themselves of Palestinians. To complicate the problem, it was estimated that as many as 750 000 laborers from Asia, Egypt and Jordan passed through Jordan during the Gulf War period. Of this number, Jordan was forced to absorb approximately 300 000 people,[14] by some estimates 500 000. These figures, in relation to the population and overall labor force, constitute an increase in Jordan's population from 7.5 to 10 percent and a rise in the Kingdom's available workforce from 30 to 40 percent. Later reports showed that an estimated one-third of the returnees who had been employed abroad before the Gulf War remained unemployed two years later.[15]

The net effect was a major shift in Palestinian-Jordanian labor from the Gulf to Jordan. The alarming reality was that this migration caused more significant shocks than the figures revealed due to the returnees' demographic characteristics. For example, a large percentage of Jordan's workers were highly educated and trained for professional-class jobs. The returnees, by extension, were highly educated professionals with significant hands-on experience earned in the Gulf. A Ministry of Labor survey showed the returnee labor force had qualification traits consistent with a large number of educated and locally employed men.

In addition, one in five men and two-thirds of women had attended post-secondary level schools. The male–female ratio here has special significance in this discussion since it indicates that the returning labor supply was dominated by males. Because the Jordanian labor force already had a high male concentration (the workforce participation rate for males aged 25 to 60 is over 95 percent), the introduction of a returning labor supply dominated by men served to both crowd men into positions which they were overqualified to hold, and, more dramatically, to force women out of the workforce entirely (only 5 percent of women of working age were in the labor force).[16]

Consequently, this mass return was not only a shock to the household and labor supply but, due to the nature of Jordan's occupational structure, significant segments of the labor market were more affected than others. Moreover, studying the shock revealed that the Jordanian labor market had two important sectoral distinctions. The first was the education dynamic seen throughout the economy. The second was the competition among people seeking public sector instead of private sector employment.

On the issue of education, Jordan had a surplus of educated, skilled workers and a shortage of unskilled or semi-skilled workers. In fact, those who were considered newly, unemployed (non-returnees) in Jordan were predominantly young, educated, and often unwilling to take the many unskilled jobs that were being filled by expatriate labor (especially positions filled by Egyptians in the construction industry). This reality did not play out well for returnees who were also predominantly young and educated. Among this latter group, 43 percent were students, 49 percent had a secondary education or higher, and 30 percent had worked in professional positions when employed in one of the Gulf states. Regional birth rates in excess of 3 percent compounded this market imbalance.[17]

The fact that this mass return of labor is so concentrated in professional-class segments of the market has accentuated the income effects of the shock. The idea that returning migrants and, more specifically, refugee populations would be skilled and/or wealthy makes the Jordanian situation unique. This observation is not meant to discount the plight of the many people who remain impoverished and living in camps throughout Jordan, Lebanon, and Palestine, but it is a fact that the nature of remigration from the Gulf to Jordan contained this unusual dynamic. Thus, with such a skilled workforce becoming available, especially in a service-oriented economy, one might expect from reading supply shock theory that this abrupt increase would create a positive shock to which an economy would quickly adjust, and within which decreases in prices and increases in output would be seen. Unfortunately, this scenario has not occurred. In fact, Jordan's labor markets have been slow to adjust in the 1990s. Unemployment remains a major concern and output levels have dropped. There has also been a surge in imports as migrants shun domestically produced goods. This has fostered both inflation and the loss of foreign reserves. It has also been the cause of stagnating production and a declining new jobs base.

Table 6.1 illustrates the mixed economic results of this pattern of events (see also Diwan and Walton (Chapter 5)). On the one hand, unemployment rose significantly between 1990 and 1992, manufacturing wages fell precipitously by over 11 percent, and net exports also declined by roughly 45 percent. On the other hand, it appeared at first glance that Jordan achieved strong GDP growth. Unfortunately, when viewed on a sectoral basis, the growth did not represent nett business development, but was instead the result of a boom in housing construction pushed by the returnees' needs to secure permanent accommodations. This boom eventually became a drain on bank liquidity.

In the Jordanian case, two deviations from theory are obvious. The first is that most labor supply theories assume relatively free mobility

Table 6.1   The 1990–1991 labor supply shock[18]

	1990	1991	1992
Real GDP growth (%)	1.7	1.8	11.3
Real GDP growth/per capita (%)	−5.1	−9.0	6.8
GDP deflator (1985 = 100)	139.8	147.0	154.9
Index of manufacturing wages	125	115	111
Unemployment (%)	17	19	21

within and between markets and occupational segments. However, in Jordan wage rates tend to make rigid but rapid adjustments and market flexibility tends to be constrained by government intervention, sometimes in the form of work permit regulations, but certainly in the form of patronage employment. Thus, adjustments to changes in the labor force are slow and, in any event, are not allowed to move freely with supply and demand.

Second, the return of labor has been coupled with a return of capital in the form of returns of savings. This 'windfall income', coupled with a change in taste preferences that apparently took place while people were working in the Gulf, made buyers favor imported products in preference to domestically-produced goods. The return of capital or savings has also allowed some migrants to postpone entering the labor market. This fact was particularly pronounced among Palestinian returnees to Jordan, many of whom decided either to retire or were able to subsidize their standards of living costs by spending savings earned abroad. For the non-retirees, a main reason for not entering the labor market was the fact that wage rates for professionals were much less in Jordan than in Kuwait. The average returnee's salary in Jordan was approximately 30 percent of his/her average monthly pay in Kuwait. Many waited for opportunities to return to the Gulf rather than accept positions that did not pay well or that they perceived as being at a lower level.[19]

Third, skills and training transferability, coupled with overlapping market segmentation, arose as real problems. Many returnees had skills that were competitive rather than complementary to the local labor force and occupational structures. Others remained in peripheral sectors of their home economy. For example, many of the returning engineers had qualification specializations in the oil industry, which were not easily transferable to the labor market in Jordan.

Another key reason why Jordan's labor supply shocks did not yield positive results relates to the public sector employment structures that permeated the economy. Jordan was institutionally organized in a manner that did not allow market forces to work appropriately, i.e. a high percentage of its workforce was employed by the government or by aid-funded projects. Brand categorized Jordan as being a rentier state because (i) the state overly defined market structures and provided inordinately excessive control of the economy; (ii) the public sector was the largest employer and therefore the primary distributor of resources; and (iii) because it used foreign aid, grant, and remittance revenues and not production-based taxes to fund government interventions. The net effect was a structural rigidity induced by the public sector that, when coupled with its size, inhibited the market's ability to respond to dramatic changes in the composition and size of the labor force.[20]

Attitudes of returnees and non-returnees toward local employment

Attitudes toward occupational structures also played an important role in the employment process. In Jordan, attitudinal factors not only determine what positions people will and will not find acceptable, but also define the rigidity of competition between public and private sector employment. This section presents an analysis of a study focusing on Jordanian and Palestinian professionals' opinions concerning labor supply shocks. This group demonstrates many of the unique features of labor versus other inputs and the importance of the structure of the economy in determining market responsiveness.

The magnitude of the number of returnees to Jordan is worth repeating – 185 000 white-collar Jordanians and Palestinians worked in Kuwait alone.[21] At its height the Palestinian community in Kuwait was estimated to be more than 350 000, a number which declined to roughly 85 000 by the end of 1992.[22] Repatriation has been difficult for a variety of reasons. Many were resented by the local population because they were able to afford a higher standard of living as a result of their repatriated savings. In other cases Jordan was, or had become, an unfamiliar environment. For many 'returnees', their arrival in Jordan in 1990–91 was more of a forced relocation instead of a return home because, as children of 1948 Palestinian refugees who had lived in the Gulf for twenty or more years, Jordan was seen as a summer holiday spot and not as home. These variant perceptions of Jordan often rekindled West Bank versus East Bank hostilities that existed in earlier periods of the Arab–Israeli conflict. But regardless of personal discriminations, returnees were competitive in a job market already beleaguered by high unemployment and structural adjustment programs.

With these perceptions and sociological observations as background, an attitudinal survey, including extensive participant interviews, was distributed and collected in the summer of 1995. The survey focused exclusively on Jordanian and Jordanian-Palestinian (Jordanian citizens of Palestinian family origins) professionals who were either participating in the labor market or actively searching for work. It was hoped that the timing of the study, four years after the Gulf War, would set an appropriate framework for gathering information on the long- and short-term implications of the supply shock from the job-seeker's perspective.

The survey data confirmed that many of the negative effects of the labor shock to the economy were due to prevailing institutional and capital structures that tended to prevent resource mobilization. The majority of participants felt that their major concerns – persistent under- and unemployment – were consequences of the country's rigid institutional market structures, rather than an unwillingness to work.

The survey was conducted with the assistance of the Center for Strategic Studies at the University of Jordan in July 1995. Population samples included respondents from 766 households. Of this group, 396 were non-returnees and 370 returnees. The number of professionals who participated in the interview process in these households totaled 918, of whom 444 were returnees and 474 non-returnees. The term 'professional' was defined as anyone who was over the age of 19 with a minimum education of a secondary-school diploma. There was a preliminary screening process to determine if there were eligible members for the survey in each selected household. Since the project focused on professionals, interviewers asked preliminary questions in order to identify how many professionals there were in a household. A cluster-sampling technique was used for non-returnees while returnees were located from a distribution of houses in 'returnee neighborhoods'. The results of an initial analysis of the responses are presented in the following tables.

As can be seen from Table 6.2, the majority of returnees surveyed were between 20 and 29 years of age. 57 percent of returnees were male and 43 percent female, while 55.9 percent of non-returnees were male and 44.1 percent female. 46.1 percent of the returnees held a diploma after secondary school and 46.1 percent held a baccalaureate. For non-returnees, 51.1 percent held diplomas and 37.7 percent held baccalaureate degrees.

Before looking at responses to questions about career expectations, it is important to look further at the public sector's influence in the overall occupation structure. For example, in 1991 the labor force of Jordan was 920 000, with the public sector employing over half.[23] Although wages

Table 6.2 Age profile of returnees versus non-returnees in Jordanian labor markets

	Age Profile (years)			
	20–29	*30–39*	*40–49*	*over 50*
Returnees (%)	54.5	18.8	12	14.7
Non-returnees (%)	48.1	34.9	12.3	4.7

Table 6.3 Jordanian employment by sector

	Public (%)	Private/family (%)	Private/employees less than 20	Private/employees more than 20
Returnees	16	14.4	34.4	35.2
Non-returnees	50.4	9.6	21	19

in the public sector for skilled and educated workers were not high, the public sector provided a range of benefits and bonuses that were not necessarily determined by productivity. Consequently, many professionals were attracted to the public sector as they believed it offered job security which could not be obtained in the private sector. In the survey on the labor market in Jordan, more than 50 percent of the working non-returnees were government employees, while only 16 percent of the returnees were working in the public sector (see Table 6.3).

This situation was explained by the fact that the Jordanian government employed a large number of professionals in the 1980s, both as a means for using its foreign aid and remittance-generated revenues to expand public services, and as a means for providing political stability through patronage employment. Therefore, many of the professionals who remained in Jordan during this period were able to reap employment benefits from the state's labor policies. The public sector became the largest formal sector employer in Jordan. The survey reflected this – non-returnee respondents made up the bulk of the public sector employees. Furthermore, non-returnee public sector workers had been at their present positions for the longest period of time and were not planning to leave their positions in the immediate future. In contrast, 82 percent of private sector employees held their positions for less than five years. When age was controlled in length of tenure comparisons, 67 percent of private sector employees over 40 years were employed for less than five years, while only 27 percent of public sector employees over 40 years had similar employment terms.

Further responses by participants revealed that returnees generally felt they had fewer opportunities to work in the public sector. This perception is supported by other sources. For example, a World Bank poverty assessment report (volume II) shows that in 1991, when there were 128 000 unemployed people living in Jordan, a job search process by the Civil Service Commission for only 4200 jobs netted 67 444 applicants. In addition to the lack of employment opportunities for returnees in the public sector, they were also affected by that sector's size and influence on private sector employment. The effects were particularly notable for the way in which public sector wage rates provided downward pressure on private sector salaries. For example, among the engineers interviewed, the majority appeared to have similar wage levels regardless of whether they worked in the private or public sector. Around two-thirds (64 percent) of private sector engineers reported earning between 100 and 300 Jordanian dinars per month, compared to 58 percent of public sector employees. In reality, however, total compensation was actually higher in the public sector, because its agencies tended to pay more non-wage benefits and provide more job security than privately-owned firms.

Another important area in which the public sector affected the private was in terms of the former's growth potential. With nearly half of all employees in Jordan employed by the government, foreign aid and other sources of external financing for the country were needed to pay and sustain this workforce. Consequently, recirculation of these funds into capital investments or businesses that would have provided sustainable growth in productive sectors has been continually restrained. In addition, as government budget deficits have become increasingly strained, private investors and firms have assumed a large tax burden to pay the public sector debt. Needless to say, these crowdings-out have led to low levels of private sector investment in Jordan.

In spite of their private sector employment and equivalent education and age structures, returnees made less and were more often unemployed than non-returnees (see Table 6.4). One issue that became apparent during the interview process was that the status of public sector employment varied between returnee and non-returnee survey participants. Once an individual was employed in Jordan's public sector, there was very little job mobility. Moreover, these individuals did not see incentives to move into other sectors, even though they believed they were receiving less compensation than private sector counterparts – a perception that may not, in reality, have been true. When public sector employees were asked about their satisfaction with the level of compensation they received, 71 percent said they were

Table 6.4 Jordanian employment status

	Employed	Unemployed	Unemployed/worked
Returnees	55.9%	23.9%	20.1%
Non-returnees	65.6%	15.4%	19.1%

undercompensated considering their education, skills, and the duties they performed.

However, when asked if they would give up their jobs in order to work in the Gulf, if given the opportunity to do so, only 45 percent of public sector employees said they would. In contrast, of interviewees who worked in the private sector, especially returnees but also many non-returnees, 60 percent said they would accept an opportunity to work in the Gulf.

The private sector group was also more sensitive than the public sector group to the unemployment rate and more aware of the excess supply of professionals in Jordan. Almost all private sector employees, along with newly hired public sector employees, felt returnees had made employment more difficult to find. Again, it was clear that non-returnees saw returnees as competition. Those who had worked for more than five years in the public sector saw little correlation. Although the survey participants did not agree on many aspects of the job environment in Jordan, regardless of their background, approximately 60 percent of both groups felt the Jordanian economy was not faring well. This perception was important because it reflected overall expectations about the economy, which, in turn, affected their patterns of consumption and investment.

This negative impression of the economy carried over into views about the Peace Process as well. When asked whether or not respondents believed peace with Israel would be positive for Jordan, approximately 70 percent of the interviewees said no. For the majority of professionals interviewed, the Peace Process appeared to be another problem for a weak economy, rather than offering any solution.

What we see from responses to questions in this part of the survey is that returnee professionals felt they were confronted with a dual, public sector versus private sector labor market, characterized by a rigid wage scale and an inability to respond to supply or demand pressure. The public sector was hiring based on personal contacts rather than skills and was also a sector where job security weighed most heavily on a potential employee's decision to accept a position or transfer into the private sector. Among private sector employees, however, the decision-making process for pursuing, accepting and keeping positions was much more fluid. Education, experience and personal contacts were each seen as more significant factors when pursuing jobs, but private sector employees did not assume they would be allowed to stay in one position for very long. Rather, private sector employees tended to see their status as being dependent on the overall state of the economy, making them more sensitive to market fluctuations. This awareness, coupled with the perception that the Jordanian economy would continue to decline as a result of agreements written in the Peace Process, made public sector employment a more attractive option for job-seekers in Jordan, further skewing that sector's influence.

Still, it was clear in Jordan that small and usually family-owned businesses played an important role in Jordan's income structure. The appropriateness of policies for creating a positive investment climate was also questioned. Many felt that, if such an environment existed, returnees could potentially use the capital they held to create their own employment opportunities. It has also been argued that a primary reason for the government evolving into such a large employer was that there was little capital accumulation in the private sector. However, with the massive influx of returnee deposits that were made in the late 1980s and early 1990s, it would be logical to expect that this liquidity would be invested. This assumption was based on the opening of capital markets.

Responses of interviewees revealed that the majority worked in family businesses and that 60 percent of the others were employed by businesses with less than 20 workers. Only 16 percent of the private sector professionals interviewed worked in large-scale enterprises employing more than 20 workers. Only 15 percent had ever owned their own business and, of these 133 people, 51 had been forced to close their firms due to lack of capital, before the doors ever opened. The average cost of the businesses was 30 000 Jordanian dinars, which implied that they were small ventures. Of the businesses remaining open, they were highly concentrated, 55 percent selling imported goods. Almost all of these entrepreneurs felt a general inability in the private sector to attract investment and they felt that for professional returnees to be useful in Jordan there needed to be more complementary opportunities along with capital liquidity.

The occupational positions held by returnees did not significantly differ from those held by non-returnees (Table 6.5). Moreover, this occupational profile did not vary significantly when examined from a public versus private sector perspective. This confirmed to some degree the assertion that returnees and non-returnees had competitive and not complementary skills. Most notably, many of the employed informants were educators or engineers. What was also striking about these responses was that the occupational backgrounds of the informants did not point to any sub-sector in the economy that was absorbing the bulk of professionals' work. While Jordan was definitely a service economy with the majority of workers employed in this sector, it was

Table 6.5   Occupational profile of interviewees

Occupations	Returnees (%)	Non-returnees (%)
Accountant	7	6
Bank employee	3	2
Business persons	4	1
Computer technician	5	3
Doctor	2	3
Educator	23	27
Engineer	11	12
Fabric trader	1	1
Gold trader	1	2
Lawyer	1	1
Manager	4	
Office worker	2	3
Pharmacist assistant	1	2
Sales clerk	2	
Secretary	4	1
Other*	29	36

Note: *Other indicated occupations that usually have no more than one person reported in a given position. Examples of these occupations included health care workers, journalists, weavers, dentists, surveyors, financial analysts, masons, painters, and so on.

unfortunate that the services Jordanians and Palestinians offered in the labor market did not reflect any substantial comparative advantage. This reinforced the view that Jordan was a rentier economy dependent on imports bought with money from abroad.

What we also see in Jordan is that there was a group of returnees who were highly educated and skilled, but who did not fit into the present labor market, which was dominated by an unresponsive public sector and a capital-poor private sector. Therefore, without changes to this dual labor market, and without the generation of financial capital (nor the regulatory freedom to invest it) for entrepreneurial utilization, they remained peripheral to the labor force.

Political fallout

When the World Bank attempted to forecast the effects that large-scale returnee entrance would have on the Jordan labor market,[24] the report provided much food for thought, but, in the end, it was based on a number of limiting simplifications – such as the idea that returnee labor was homogeneous, that Palestinian and Jordanian workers would act as perfect substitutes, or that this labor market would behave as if it were less constrained or unconstrained by public sector employment influences – which made the report's conclusions less valuable than they could have been. Unfortunately, the Jordanian labor market has not proven to be very efficient while the structural rigidities caused by public sector dominance have been more severe. Moreover, we should anticipate that, if vacancies opened in the public sector, they would be filled by the backlog of applicants or an overload of first-time job-seekers.

However, even this scenario failed to come to fruition because of structural adjustment plans. As Jordan pursued an economic strategy of privatization and liberalization under guidance of the IMF and the World Bank, an exodus of Palestinians from public sector jobs might have provided the state with an ideal occasion to cut public sector employment without the same degree of political fallout normally associated with such actions. In either event, Palestinian returnees would not be first in line for filling public sector jobs and they have remained in weaker positions in the private sector. With unemployment in Jordan then ranging from 20 to 25 percent and a high cost of living with inflation at 6 percent, this situation no doubt fostered negative politics.

Conclusion

The attitudes displayed by respondents to this survey revealed that most Jordanians as well as Jordanian-Palestinians felt that the changes taking place in their society were from the top down and that they had had little or no say about the process, leading them to feel exceptionally frustrated.[25]

This survey shows that Jordan's segmented market for professionals was more complex than most due to its public–private competitive duality. Furthermore, Jordanian policies that placed constraints on the distribution of investment capital that would otherwise have been used to stimulate private sector employment remain problematic. The combination of issues reveals complicated impediments to solving Jordan's labor market paradoxes. If the labor supply-shock threat is to be dealt with, there probably needs to be an exodus of labor from the market. However, should this happen, shocks will occur in other areas, not to mention the turmoil a sudden influx could have in Palestine. Any real solution will force a massive restructuring of public sector employment, which would cause conflicts with the majority of Jordan's workers. Therefore, while theory may have initially led us to believe that a removal of the Palestinian labor surplus from the Jordan market might have fostered a state of full employment, when we take into consideration the segmented structure of this market with all its complexities, it appears that Jordan continues to have as much at stake in seeking a gradual return of Palestinians to the PA-controlled areas as does the PA, and as do the Israelis.

Notes

1. This research was assisted by an award from the American Center for Oriental Research and a CIES-J. William Fulbright Serial Grant. The author also wishes to thank the Center of Strategic Studies, University of Jordan for invaluable assistance in conducting the labor market survey in Jordan.
2. 'Facts and Figures About The Palestinians' (Washington, DC: Center for Policy Analysis on Palestine, 1992) 17.
3. A. Plascov, *The Palestinian Refugees in Jordan, 1948–1957* (London: Frank Cass, 1981) 44.
4. The World Bank, *Peace and the Jordanian Economy* (Washington, DC: World Bank, 1994) 38.
5. Russell King (ed.), *Return Migration and Regional Economic Problems* (London: Croom Helm, 1986), 4.
6. F. P. Cerase, 'Expectations and Reality: A Case Study of Return Migration From the United States to Southern Italy', *International Migration Review*, 8 (1974) 245–62.
7. A. Plascov, *The Palestinian Refugees in Jordan*, p. 46.
8. L. On-Jook, *Urban-to-Rural Return Migration in Korea* (Seoul: Seoul National University Press, 1980) 107.
9. N. Toren, 'Return Migration to Israel', *International Migration Review*, 12 (Spring 1978) 39–54.
10. The World Bank, 'Peace and the Jordanian Economy', 38; on PA motive see Diwan and Walton, Chapter 5 in this volume.
11. UNRWA, 'Palestine Refugees and UNRWA' (Vienna: Public Information Office UNRWA, 1993).
12. I. Serageldin et al., *Manpower and International Labor Migration in the Middle East and North Africa* (London: Oxford University Press, 1983) table 5–1, p. 46.
13. ESCWA, 'The Impact of the Gulf Crisis on The Economies of Western Asia' (Amman: ESCWA, 1992) 12.
14. ESCWA, 'The Return of Jordanian/Palestinian Nationals from Kuwait: Economic and Social Implications for Jordan' (Amman: ESCWA, 1991) 7.
15. The World Bank, *Poverty Assessment Report*, Vol. 1 (Washington, DC: World Bank, 1994) p. 47.
16. The World Bank, *Poverty Assessment Report*, Vol. II (Washington, DC: World Bank, 1994) p. 33; on women's participation rates see p. 12; for post-secondary figures see p. 2.

17. ESCWA, 'Return Migration: Profiles, Impact and Absorption in Home Countries' (New York: United Nations, 1993), for students figures see p. 53; for post-secondary see p. 24.
18. Sources used in this table include: Central Bank of Jordan, *Monthly Statistical Bulletin* (Amman: Central Bank of Jordan, March 1995); World Bank, *Poverty Assessment Report*, Vols I and II; C. A. Pissarides, 'Labor Markets in the Middle East and North Africa', MENA Discussion Paper Series, No. 5 (Cairo: World Bank, 1993).
19. S. Al-Qudsi, 'Microeconomic Analysis of Labor Markets in Jordan and Kuwait', *Proceedings: First Annual Conference on Development Economics* (Cairo, 1993) 2.
20. L. Brand, 'Economic and Political Liberalization in Jordan', in I. Harik and D. J. Sullivan (eds), *Privatization and Liberalization in the Middle East* (Bloomington, IN: Indiana University Press, 1992) pp. 167–88.
21. R. Klinov, 'Recent Trends in Migration for Work in the Middle East', Delivered at the Conference on 'The Economics of Labor Mobility in the Middle East', Institute for Social and Economic Policy in the Middle East, John F. Kennedy School of Government, Harvard University (7–8 February 1992) see Table 5.
22. G. Feiler, 'Palestinian Employment Prospects', *Middle East Journal* 47 (Autumn 1993) 640.
23. The World Bank, *Poverty Assessment Report*, 1, 1.
24. The World Bank, *Peace and the Jordanian Economy*, 39–40.
25. R. Al Abed, 'Calm Returns To South After Bread Riots', *The Star: Jordan's Political, Economic and Cultural Weekly*, 22–8 August 1996.

7
Between Israel and Saudi Arabia: Structural Dependencies in Labor and Finance

J. W. Wright, Jr.

> The individual human being cannot by himself obtain all the necessities of life. All human beings must cooperate to that end in their civilizations. What is obtained by the cooperation of a group of human beings satisfies the needs of a number many times greater than themselves.
>
> Ibn Khaldun[1]

The Peace Process has not led to expected outcomes, especially on the economic front.[2] Economic integration was to be a cornerstone of Middle East peace and it was widely expected that the benefits of this cooperation would lead to a warm peace that would serve the needs of many more people than were being served by a cold peace. But gaps in the process's design have impeded economic interactions,[3] partially because the incentives in the region's labor-remittance structures were not adequately considered. More specifically, one of the key factors overlooked in the Peace Process is the connection between remittance flows between Jordanian and Palestinian guest-workers and bank liquidity. On the one hand remittances funded much of Jordan's economic development in the late 1970s and early 1980s, on the other hand these remittances represented substantial losses of liquidity to Saudi Arabia and the other Gulf states. This chapter establishes a connection between lending risk in Saudi Arabia and Jordan and draws some conclusions about what this situation could mean for the future of the peace talks, especially if the relationship is not recognized by negotiators.

There are without doubt structural and attitudinal factors in the Middle East that make bank system development difficult.[4] In fact, the region's entire banking and trading patterns are skewed against economic cooperation integration. Intra-regional trade has always been low in the Middle East and North Africa (MENA) region, but it has dropped from around 11 percent to about 6 percent in the 1990s. Given the fact that trade within the Gulf Cooperation Council (GCC) has increased, then the negative impact of this declining Gulf–Levant trade is particularly significant.[5] Finance has been particularly hard-hit.

Historically, Saudi Arabian finance has revolved almost entirely around industrial projects that are not efficient producers, leaving loan portfolios without balance. Nor have people trusted the government-run banking system.[6] Jordan's banks have repeatedly found themselves in seriously illiquid positions (or falsely liquid positions), and without committed patrons, situations which have grown worse since the Gulf War.[7] The Palestinian banking system, which became almost non-existent as a result of the Israeli occupation, is now completely dependent on Jordan and Israel. Islamic banks in the region have often been unstable and have therefore failed in their role of establishing an alternative means for mobilizing Arab capital. Or, more the case in the Gulf states, Islamic banks have maintained narrow reinvestment interests focused almost entirely on import trade finance.[8] For the most part, then, these massive external capital flows have created more economic confusion than structural adjustment or market efficiency. This is a situation further complicated by massive aid distributions that flow to the region which skews North Arab bank portfolios.[9]

Labor flows and financial stability

Moreover, while Diwan and Walton, as well as Colton, look at labor-related issues in this collection, there have been few attempts here or elsewhere to analyze the effects of labor flows in the Middle East on financial stability. Labor and remittances between Jordan (and Palestine) and the Gulf states, particularly Saudi Arabia, have created significant economic dependencies that should not be overlooked by negotiators in the Arab–Israeli Peace Process. On the one hand, the formerly oil-rich states can no longer afford to support the region through aid packages. On the other, without worker remittances and the tax revenues they create, countries like Jordan cannot afford food price supports. In addition, the redirection of remittance flows from the

Gulf states away from the Levant and toward Asia has created havoc in the region's informal trade regimes.[10] This chapter investigates the roles of labor and finance in Jordan's (and Palestine's) and Saudi Arabia's political dialog. In the process, it illustrates the economic dependencies these countries have with each other, and it looks at the ways new banking structures may support regional trade. Finally, possible turning points for regional labor mobility are discussed.

Liquidity risk in Saudi Arabia

During the 1970s, Arab countries became divided into two development categories, the rentier states (or oil-rich) and the rentier-by-proxy states (or oil-poor labor supplying).[11] The oil-rich rentier states financed unprecedented amounts of capital investment but needed labor to implement their development plans.[12] The oil-poor rentier-by-proxy states needed financial resources, some of which could be provided by the remittances of guest-workers employed in the Gulf States. It was in the mid-to-late-1970s that Jordan and Saudi Arabia formed a particularly strong labor/remittances interdependence. Saudi Arabia issued more work visas to Jordanian and Jordanian-Palestinians than to any other national group in the 1970s and 1980s.[13] The banks in both countries hoped they would be among the beneficiaries of this economic tie. However, in actuality the relationship that developed between Saudi Arabia and Jordan forced banks to sustain a high default rate risk in their portfolios. This caused the private sectors in both countries to be over-reliant on Saudi agencies for cash flow, which also made risk and return profiles almost impossible to write.[14] What one finds, then, is that the economic structures in both countries made it difficult for banks to distribute capital effectively.

In order to understand this economic interdependency and its effect on regional banks, one must understand that businesses in each country have pursued strategies aimed at exploiting oil revenues collected by the Saudi government. (Other countries in the Gulf were also the targets of Jordan's labor export strategy. Kuwait is the primary example in Colton's and Glasser's chapters while Saudi Arabia is highlighted here). Unlike most developing economies in the last 25 years, Saudi Arabia has been able to finance infrastructure development. However, it lacked the level of human resources required to build its social and industrial projects in the 1970s and 1980s (a situation that changed significantly in the 1990s). This situation led the Kingdom to import labor, ultimately making it highly dependent on foreign workers. For example, during the early 1980s, 81 percent of personnel in the Saudi financial sector were foreign. Other estimates show that 70 percent of the total of participants in the Saudi labor force were foreign.[15]

Although characterized by extremes, this strategy worked while cash flows from oil revenues could sustain financing of industrial production. In the period 1975–85, the number of operational factories rose 154 percent and the number of industrial permits issued increased 330 percent. By 1987, 2016 factories had been constructed, with enough production capacity to meet at least 70 percent of the Kingdom's consumer market demand. The average annual rate of real output grew by 16.6 percent in the production sector, 14.1 percent in the service sector, and 4.8 percent in the oil sector. By 1990, the industrial complexes at Yanbu and Jubail were nearly complete and coming on-line with huge production capacity, enough in some cases to manufacture supplies equal to import demand.[16]

Government attempts undermined

However, there is a negative side to the Saudi development success story because the lucrative incentives that supported urban industrial growth also undermined government attempts to facilitate private sector productivity.[17] In fact, an inordinate number of private sector producers can only operate at a profitable level if they receive government aid. It should also be noted that foreign bank operations tend to drain liquidity from the Saudi economy.

In truth, Saudi banks may have been overly generous during the 1970s and 1980s in interpreting their moral responsibilities. For example, at the Saudi Arabian Agricultural Bank loans were not based on business plans or on written risk and return profiles; rather, funds were usually distributed according to a project's priority in the Kingdom's Five Year Development Plans. Aid, grant, and loan policies such as these made the private earnings process completely dependent on the government's revenue cycle. When government revenues and expenditures declined in the 1980s, the profits of most Saudi businesses also fell. The highest number of bank loan defaults happened in 1987, only months after oil revenues hit their low and a year after the government began delaying payments on grants and subsidies. (See Figures 7.1, 7.2 and 7.3 at the end of the chapter to see how closely Saudi revenues and expenditures were tracked by Jordanian remittances, pp. 104–5. It is important to note that

1987 was a pivotal year in the region's economic relations, as it marked the beginning of serious economic decline in both North and South, as well as the renewal of conflicts in Lebanon, Palestine, Syria, and Jordan.)

When declining oil prices forced the government to curb spending, many businesses could not distinguish between cash flow, government aid and operating profits.[18] And, as subsidy payments declined on agricultural and manufactured products, as well as on many imported goods, a staggering number of businesses found they were so dependent on government disbursements that they could not survive, and they began to default on loans. The problem became so serious in 1988 that the Real Estate Development Fund, for example, offered 20 percent discounts for the timely repayment of loans, with an additional 10 percent if lump sum repayments were made.[19] In addition, the government's crucial role in the acquisition-produced resources, being the country's largest consumer, introduced a real bias toward real-estate projects; when oil revenues declined the result was a proportional increase in state disbursements to real-estate-intensive industries from 64 to 84 percent.[20] 54 percent of consumption was achieved through direct government spending, and up to 75 percent of private sector spending was supported by government-financed assistance programs. In 1982, 56 countries had joint-venture projects in Saudi Arabia; 41 of these were contracts with the government. The service sector accounted for 66 percent of the country's gross domestic product, 38 percent of which came from services provided to the government. Furthermore, in 1985, 80 percent of industrial labor in the Saudi Arabian economy was foreign.

Fifth Development Plan

These factors notwithstanding, the Fifth Development Plan encouraged banks to issue more medium- and long-term financing to the private sector in general and to small firms in particular.[21] In addition, semi-government financing agencies were expected to issue an additional SR 36.9 billion between 1990 and 1995 to real-estate- or equipment-intensive businesses. Over half of these loans were to be made through the Real Estate Development Fund, whose cumulative loan portfolio in 1990 was SR 92 billion. Planned investments in private sector development in the fifth plan are SR 144 billion, approximately 37 percent of the total planned investments. While planned spending fell short in funding these goals, the consequence remains the same because the private sector and their financiers still depend on state funds for liquidity. These policies produce asset values that are more closely linked to aid and government funding than to corporate efficiency. This situation became worse during the period since the Gulf War, when the Saudi government was forced to borrow money in order to support its security obligations. By 1990, Saudi Arabia was left searching for ways to finance the upgrading of its oil and gas facilities.[22]

The net effect of these factors was that banks could not write adequate risk and return profiles for prospective borrowers and they could not collect funds. This placed them in situations where portfolio risk was impossible to determine. Indeed, how can lending institutions create risk and return profiles if cash flows from subsidies are meant to keep inefficient businesses from failing? How can they distribute capital venture funds if businesses cannot prove the generation of non-government-linked profits? Likewise, without the threat of foreclosure, Saudi's banks become responsible for assuming most, if not all, of the Kingdom's private sector risk. This would not cause a problem if the government guaranteed support throughout the life of the loan, but widely fluctuating oil markets make these guarantees impossible.

It is also worth mentioning that the assertions Bradley Glasser makes about economic crisis forming the basis for liberalization also apply in the Saudi case.[23] Waste in the Saudi financial system was obvious throughout the 1970s and 1980s. Huge liquidity losses were either not recognized (although western advisors had long seen the danger inherent in the Saudi system) or were simply seen as an unavoidable cost of rapid economic growth. In addition, budgetary deficits were largely ignored or seen as politically necessary but temporary features of the system. However, following the 1987–88 bank crisis, both budgetary process and financial regulations were significantly reformed. To a large extent, the banking system was liberalized in ways that allowed it to better support the private sector. At the same time, the government faced many of its budgetary dilemmas and restructured numerous industrial subsidy programs, which, also, had the effect of forcing the economy to rely increasingly on the private sector for generating growth. Thus, while Glasser makes the point that oil revenues have allowed the Gulf states to avoid political liberalization, these regimes have also only pursued economic liberalization in reaction to financial sector crisis.

It is worth noting that the Israeli banking system also faced similar declines in the late 1980s, leading to the reorganization of several banks. While the Intifada hurt Palestinians much more than the Israeli economy, the loss of Palestinian deposits and remittance-generated investments was still significant. In any event, it was impending crisis that forced Israeli banks to implement reforms and privatize.[24]

Liquidity risk in Jordan

Another clearly defined objective of the Saudis' Fourth and Fifth development plans, and also expressed to a lesser extent in the Sixth plan (which actually focused more on localization of jobs training), was the displacement of expatriate workers.[25] Because the largest population of Saudi imported labor came from Jordan and Palestine, this change in policy intensified the level of business risk in Jordan and, by extension, in the occupied territories. Although Jordan is not an oil-exporting country, economic expansion and contraction has tended to follow oil price hikes and declines. Like a number of labor-exporting countries in the region, Jordan must attribute much of its prosperity in the 1970s and 1980s to the remittances gained by emigrant workers. Through this strategy Jordan became the region's premier 'rentier-by-proxy' state – that is, a state whose liquidity is indirectly dependent on the exploitation of natural resources; in this case they were dependent on employment generated through the sale of Saudi Arabia's oil. The labor/remittance dynamic between the two kingdoms cannot be overstated in a discussion of Jordanian bank risk or in discussions of regional trade development.

In fact, Jordan has, since the 1950s, turned labor exportation into its most profitable strategic resource, placing the highest premium on the placement of skilled (managerial) labor into the Gulf states. Labor exportation is an especially significant part of Jordan's economic development plans. It is a means for obtaining workers' remittances, financial assistance, and for facilitating the export of Jordanian products and services. More specifically, Jordan viewed labor exportation as part of a broader marketing strategy to expand export earnings, increase national liquidity, raise the level of employment, and decrease the country's persistent balance of payments deficits.[26] Jordanian workers abroad showed a high propensity for sending money to home-country banks, making remittances the dominant source of reported export earnings. In the 1970s, remittances doubled the value of Jordanian exports and, in the 1980s, remittances exceeded export revenues and became the primary income source of one million people. In addition, remittances produced one-third of Jordan's foreign exchange in the early 1980s. By 1989, migrant workers accounted for almost 57 percent of the country's exports.

70 percent of Jordan's commercial activities in the 1980s were funded through income from workers employed abroad.[27] Twenty percent of tuition payments were paid through remittances, a crucial point since Jordanian and Palestinian guest-workers living in Saudi Arabia mainly filled professional positions, a dynamic which Colton discussed before.[28]

Sharing oil revenues

In effect, Jordan's rentier-by-proxy strategy became so entrenched that its financial stability was critically dependent upon Saudi Arabia's (or the Gulf states') willingness to share oil revenues via the employment of Jordanian and Palestinian nationals.[29] Over the last 20 years trends in Jordan's consumption, the money supply, and industrial output mirrored the level of oil revenues received by the Gulf states.

Therefore, just as the oil-price declines adversely affected economic activity in the Gulf states, as Jankowski puts it, Jordan's 'economic boom of the 1970s had in the 1980s given way to declining national revenues, governmental retrenchment, and growing unemployment'.[30] Construction expenditures and the consumption of imported goods followed nearly the same patterns as oil revenues. In addition, an inverse relationship between remittances from the Gulf and domestic employment is evident. In the period 1979–1981, when oil prices were relatively high, unemployment in Jordan was less than 4 percent. Following the oil price collapses in 1982 and 1983, unemployment rose to 5.4 percent in 1984 and to 8.0 percent in 1986.[31] Estimates suggest that it was between 3 and 4 times that high following the Gulf War.

In fact, this inverse labor exchange dynamic did not continue as the condition of oil markets improved. Rather, as oil revenues rose in the late 1980s, and when theoretically unemployment in Jordan should have fallen as people returned to the Gulf, unemployment rose to 8.3 percent in 1987, 8.9 percent in 1988, and 15 percent in 1989.[32] What had begun to happen as early as 1987 was the implementation of the Saudi's Fourth plan's goals for repatriating guest-workers to Jordan. In response, the number of Jordanians returning from the Gulf increased and annual remittances continued to decline.

Overall money supply

There was a direct tie between the amount of Gulf labor importation, the level of remittance income, and overall money supply in Jordan (and presumably the West Bank and Gaza). Moreover, these figures on the economic impact of Jordan's changing political relationships with Saudi Arabia combine to make two things clear. First, the oil-revenue risks inherent in the Saudi Arabian system are also inherent in the Jordanian system. Secondly, the possibility of continued abrogation in the Jordanian–Gulf states' political relationship magnifies Jordan's level of economic and financial risk. In addition, the situation in the late 1980s reveals a fundamental change in Jordan's economic structure between 1987 and 1989 as an effect of Saudi's employment of more native labor and Asian workers instead of rehiring Arab workers after the period 1987–89.[33]

The future of the Jordanian banking structure's liquidity in 1990 was in serious jeopardy if remittances continued to decline (or, unless aid distributions could shore up deposits, which is what happened in 1996–97, but this too should be seen as a temporary market scenario). Alongside this dynamic stood the older confusion between measuring profit-generated cash flow seen in Saudi Arabia, except that in Jordan this valuation problem was based on emigrant-financed remittances. In essence, Jordan's private sector had become so biased toward foreign sources of cash flow, and toward foreign government purchasing agents as a source of sales, that asset values were too often determined by a firm's ability to gain aid, contracts, or financing from clients or agents in the Gulf states.[34] Jordanian banks, therefore, found themselves in the unfortunate position of having to assume not only the risks taken by their own clients, the risks intrinsic to their own economy, but also a new level of labor risk based on political dynamics over which they had no control. In fact, the level of employment for Jordanian and Palestinian workers in the Gulf and the state of Jordan's economy both continued to decline in the 1990s.

However, during the Gulf War another dynamic was added to Jordan's financial dependency on Saudi Arabia and the Gulf states. This was that liquidity unexpectedly rose after the war, as did the overall level of consumption and production, at the point when alien employment in the Gulf fell dramatically and when underemployment in Jordan reached its highest level. At this point it was even more difficult to determine what part of Jordan's liquidity was earned and what part was contributable to transferred savings from the Gulf by returnees (which also hurt Saudi Arabia's liquidity).

Jordan's structural dichotomy between sectoral growth and the number of returnees after the Gulf War was dramatic (Figure 7.4). The bulk of returnees came in 1990 following the Iraqi invasion of Kuwait, but the flow of Jordanians and Palestinians out of Saudi Arabia and the other Gulf states has continued since the end of the war. Because of this situation one might expect to see a declining national economy because as the number of returnees rose by approximately 26 percent in 1991 it could also be expected that revenues from remittances and their related purchases would subside. However, consumption in almost all sectors of the economy grew substantially, money supply in 1991 grew nearly 16 percent, bank deposits grew approximately 51 percent, and insurance premium receipts rose 30 percent. In 1992 the level of money supply continued to increase, leveling off by the year's end.[35]

Effects of structural adjustments

The between-the-lines effects of these structural adjustments are critical to understand. Many economists presumed that this situation meant that the Jordanian economy had more liquidity than before and, therefore, the level of financial risk in the Kingdom had decreased. (Neither the IMF nor the Central Bank of Jordan changed the way they calculated and reported returns of savings until their 1993–94 reports.) This was not the case. The real questions were: What did these increases in remittances reflect in the economic potential (or dependency) of the Jordanian economy? How could revenues rise during a period when increasing numbers of Jordanian laborers were forced to return from jobs they had held in the Gulf? And, did this increase in money supply really increase national liquidity?

The answers to these questions are not simple. In fact, the situation was more grim than it appeared from the numbers shown. The growth in bank deposits was not at all related to remittances. Instead it was the transfer of savings from the Gulf back to Jordan. The increase in consumption was not representative of economic growth but rather it was the use of savings liquidations required to support returnees' life styles, who, for the most part, were either underemployed or unemployed. In addition, the increase in money supply did not represent more liquidity in the country. It is true that the transfer of deposits from the Gulf to Jordan added money to the system. But, to which financial system and for how long?

First, consider that the rate of increase in money supply had begun to level off in 1992 even though additional people were returning from the Gulf. This leveling effect was caused by the relative increase in subsistence spending as compared to declining remittance revenues and the continued inability of returnees to find full, meaningful, or professional employment in Jordan. This spending, again, did not indicate growth but was unproductive savings losses. The more serious implication comes when the placement, redistribution, and reinvestment of deposits are considered. For example, most returnees' deposits were used by the Central Bank of Jordan, which means they were used to finance government- or ministry-approved projects and subsidies. Such transactions did not raise the level of liquidity available for use in the private sector. Instead, a rapid decline in available capital was experienced by local banks and there was a general decline in the amount of deposits that was available for local lending. There was a upward trend toward the end of 1991, but this was reversed in 1992 and by 1993 the level of deposits in local banks fell to JD 166 million, a 32.26 percent decrease. The situation looked even worse when the amount of Central Bank deposits in local banks was omitted. In this case, the level of deposits peaked in 1989 at JD 172.5 million, and fell to JD 169.6 million in 1990, to 149.9 million in 1991, and to 110.0 million in 1992. Therefore, in a period of less than three years, private sector deposits in local indigenous banks fell by 36.23 percent, and 44 percent in November 1992.

Indicators reveal problems

The graphical presentation of trends in this area is not possible because in 1993 the way in which these transfers were recorded was changed.[36] However, other indicators reveal continuing problems. Between 1990 and 1994 the level of currency circulation increased only from JD 1006 million to 1093, or only about 8.7 percent, during a time when the dinar was also becoming the circulating currency in PA-controlled areas. Private sector demand deposits declined in 1992 by over JD 100 million and by 1994 were still declining, by as much as JD 7.7 million in January alone. The Central Bank of Jordan's current account deposits rose from JD 5.2 million in 1990, to 12.4 million in 1992, but dropped to 2.7 million in 1993. What was clear was that available liquidity had not and probably could not return to prior levels. In addition, there were inter-bank investment activities that negatively affected the liquidity situation. For example, Jordanian bank investments in other local banks decreased from JD 227.2 million in 1990, to JD 166.4 million in 1991, to JD 137.8 million in 1992, a 39.35 percent decline. However, over that same two-year period Jordanian bank investment in foreign banks rose 2.24 times its normal level, moving from JD 628 million in 1990, to JD 1.254 billion in

1991, and 1.407 billion in 1992. Investments by licensed banks in foreign currencies rose from JD 357.7 million in 1990, to JD 459.8 million in 1992, to JD 488.5 million in 1992, to JD 504.5 in 1993. Therefore, less money was held or reinvested in dinars. This indicates further that even less of the available capital in Jordan was being reinvested into the indigenous private sector. By extension this meant that the level of business risk was increased due to lack of finance. And, it heightened the capital flight anxieties that Diwan and Walters discuss.

The messages were clear for Jordan, and should have been clear for others interested in the Peace Process's economic implications. Despite their positive effects, remittances were not a reliable source of cash flow in the 1990s. Failing political and economic relations with Saudi Arabia and the other Gulf states made Jordan's businesses less stable. Finally, financial groups had no intention of injecting money into the local economy. This situation in effect placed the future of the Jordanian economy more heavily than ever on the ability to renew its labor-remittance contract with Saudi Arabia and the other Gulf states' businesses.

Real declines in regional wages

It is worth noting that Jordan was obviously not the only country that faced problems caused by weakening labor relations. Indeed, each of the Levantine states needed to export labor in order to survive. Their increased inability to make this connection led to real declines in regional wages over the last ten years in Egypt, Jordan and Syria. Egyptian real manufacturing wages fell from 181 percent of the 1970 levels in 1985 to 114 percent in 1992; and Jordanian wages fell from 157 percent of 1970 levels in 1985 to 111 percent in 1992. Syrian manufacturing wages had actually fallen to 92 percent of their 1970 levels by 1992. Much of these wage declines can be attributed to sectoral growth in the Northern Arab labor markets. As examples, 78 percent of first-time job-seekers in Syria and 76.6 percent in Egypt remain persistently unemployed and unable to earn sustainable incomes from the formal sector.[37] Overall unemployment in Gaza is estimated to exceed 60 percent, possibly being as high as 74 percent.

It would be unfair to not recognize Israel's contribution to the region's unemployment-conflict dynamic. In response to both domestic and international political pressure – domestic pressure based on security issues surfacing in the Israeli electorate's mind due to the Intifada, and internationally on increased pressure from American and European Jews that Israel should accept more Soviet block immigrants – Israel significantly reduced its dependence on Palestinian labor during the late 1980s and the early 1990s (see Bichler, Chapter 12 and Roy, Chapter 11). In the decade between 1987 and 1997 Israel's contribution to Gazan employment fell from 80 000 to less than 7000. In 1995 and 1997 an estimated 2000 additional jobs were eliminated, and most of the remaining workers who travel to Israel have had their wages significantly reduced by persistent border closures. Average per capita GNP in Gaza fell below US$500 by the year 2000, because of these employment trends.

This situation followed a period when Israel had absorbed much Arab labor. According to Fadle Naqib:

> between 1972 and 1990 the (Palestinian) labor force increased by around 64 percent, while domestic employment increased only 28 percent. The difference was mainly absorbed by the Israeli market, in which employment of Palestinians from the West Bank increased 86 percent, and from the Gaza Strip by 128 percent, in the same period.[38]

One can see how Gazans, in particular, were frustrated that the most dramatic declines in Israeli employment have occurred since the Peace Process began. The potential for conflict in the region has grown due to the rise in unemployment but neither the Gulf nor Israel is acting in ways that will mitigate this situation.

Private sector finance risks

This showed that at least two structural problems existed in Jordan that made the risk of private sector finance extremely high, inhibiting both employment and investment growth. The first of these was that the banking problems that were present in the Arab rentier states were compounded in the 'rentier-by-proxy' states, which puts lending officers in exceedingly difficult positions. In order for financiers to fill finance gaps through equity finance, they must write risk and return profiles on a capital-venture model. And, in still too many cases Jordanian firms cannot distinguish cash flow from profits or from remittances, or from the reduction of savings deposits transferred from Gulf banks. This places Jordanian banks in a much riskier competitive situation when pursuing the distribution and reinvestment of new capital.

This situation creates one in which the politics of finance and trade become an ultimate source of conflict in the Arab–Israeli Peace Process. And if the stakes are high in Jordan, they are worse in Gaza!

Would the labor-remittance contract ever be renewed?

Probably not, but for reasons that have little to do with political malfeasance. The fact is that the Gulf states face very different problems today from what they did in the 1970s, when the first labor-remittance contract was established. Indeed, the Gulf states' population has grown at incredibly high rates, meaning that they are now looking to create new employment opportunities on their own.

More specifically, with population growth rates in the Gulf countries averaging over 4 percent, labor supply scenarios have significantly changed. In fact, the Middle East maintains the highest labor force growth rate of any region in the world. Based on International Labor Organization figures, the annual growth rates of working-aged populations were as follows in selected Arab countries between 1975 and 1990: Bahrain 4.61 percent, Egypt 2.58 percent, Iraq 3.57 percent, Jordan 3.33 percent, Oman 4.51 percent, Saudi Arabia 5.17 percent, and Syria at 3.52 percent. A trend worth noting is that the highest working-aged population growth rates are not in the countries that traditionally supply labor markets – Egypt, Jordan, and Syria. Rather, the three fastest growing workforce countries between 1975 and 1990 were Saudi Arabia, Bahrain, and Oman, respectively. Projections for the current period show that growth rates may be slowing somewhat in the Gulf states, but this is a relative conclusion simply because each of these countries still maintains labor force growth rates above 3 percent.[39]

The obvious implication is that the oil-rich nations are finding it necessary to localize their labor forces. For example, Saudi Arabia included notice of its ten-year schedule for 'Saudi-ization' as early as 1985 in its Fourth Five Year Development Plan. The Fifth and Sixth development plans continued these policies, although the Sixth plan in particular recognizes the benefit of managed, gradual repatriation plans (especially since so much has already taken place). At the other extreme, the United Arab Emirates attempted to implement a 30-day amnesty program aimed at localization, put into effect in September 1996. In both cases, these programs made economic sense in terms of raising citizen employment and – at least theoretically – community-level production. Gulf localization programs also served to dam the outward flow of remittances and lower the overall costs of import subsidies, social services provision, and visa processing.

Service sectors entry place

In addition, the service sectors are where the Gulf's projected labor force entry will most likely take place. This sector now comprises significant proportions of the Gulf economies – Bahrain 68.2 percent, Kuwait 74 percent, Qatar 65.4 percent, Saudi Arabia 66.9 percent – which have traditionally relied on university-level labor from Egypt, Jordan, and Palestine. However, statistics for higher education in the Gulf states show that enrollment figures in Bahrain exceed 18 percent, Kuwait 16 percent, Qatar 18 percent, and Saudi Arabia 20 percent. This pool of young and educated people in the Gulf will further facilitate the Gulf states' localization processes. Moreover, they are a pool of people caught within the region's conflicting labor agendas; the young in Jordan and Palestine fall into a category within which the Gulf states no longer need them, Israel no longer wants them, and wherein there is little hope that massive local employment will develop soon. A World Bank report, aptly titled 'Will Arab Workers Prosper or be Left Out?' (pp. 27–8) summarized the situation as follows:

> The main reason that reforms have not yet deepened in the region is that most governments have not yet been able to articulate a vision that is realistic and convincing. ... A key challenge is how to salvage parts of the old industrial base, and how to retain those workers whose skills have become outmoded. The Peace Process, if successful, will reduce the strategic uncertainty that has infected the region. ... [However,] with low or shallow investment, skilled workers will have to accept low productivity jobs, leading to harsh social distortions. Reforms thus pose a major political challenge, especially where public sectors are large and unemployment among the educated is of long duration. The difficult dilemma, however, is that lack of reform is likely to perpetuate low productivity and lead over time to rising poverty.
>
> [Thus...] both optimistic and pessimistic expectations may seem relevant. The projections for the World Development Report for 1995 illustrates well the fragility of the region's future. In the 'high case' scenario growth is fast and domestic inequalities fall. By 2010 the labor productivity and wages of unskilled workers are 60 percent

higher than current levels, those of skilled workers 40 percent. But in the 'low case' scenario the incomes of unskilled workers remain stagnant at best, and those of skilled workers rise only slowly, and inequities rise sharply. The main difference between the two outcomes is in the dynamics of transition. Bad outcomes are likely to perpetuate themselves with social instability and fleeing capital. Good policies could unleash opposite forces, bringing in capital and making success easier. There is a thin line between rising with a virtuous circle and falling with a vicious one. Good economic policies, strategies, and execution can make a big difference. But time is running out. The full force of the Uruguay round agreements will be felt in the next ten years. This is perhaps all the time left for governments in the region to build competitiveness.

Ten years is not a lot of time, especially if labor and financial markets in the region become increasingly disjointed instead of integrated. These widening divisions raised the level of investment risk for financial institutions. One had to wonder if continued moves by the Likud regime to disenfranchise the now PA-controlled territories, along with the reported corruption within the Palestinian administration, have not made achieving only the lower case scenario improbable. In any case, these situations leave the new Sharon government fewer options and poor negotiating partners, as it clearly did to Barak.

Peace process unlikely to help

Moreover, it seems likely that little help in the Peace Process can come from an opening-up of Gulf labor markets. This is due more to pragmatics than malice. The fact is that the Saudi banking structure has recovered fairly well from the trauma it experienced in the late 1980s. One reason for its recovery was a partial redirection of funds that were being lost via remittances made by guest-workers. And, with the Sixth Development plan clearly calling for the increasing retention of the system's funds for reinvestment in a private sector which can employ a burgeoning new generation of workers, the Kingdom is unlikely to release these funds as easily as it has in the past, and it is unlikely to force its banking system to assume the risks these losses imply.

Unfortunately, whether for pragmatic or other reasons, a refusal by the Gulf states to re-employ labor from the Levant continues to drive a cycle of decline in areas like Jordan and Palestine. With fewer remittances there is more risk in the financial system that constrains business development. This leads to fewer employment opportunities and more spending of returnee savings. This causes less financial sector liquidity and higher levels of banking and investment risk. And the cycle continues downward. The bottom line is that the dependencies that supported Jordanians and Palestinians in the past have been irrevocably altered since the Gulf War, meaning they and other ruling bodies in similar situations – Lebanon, Syria, and possibly Egypt and Yemen – must liberalize their economic policies in ways that attenuate government intervention and augment internal private-sector-employment generation programs. The realization that an outside savior is unlikely to buy Jordan out of its difficulties will be hard medicine for many in Jordanian ministries (and for PA ministries as well) to swallow. The alternative is to face decline into abject poverty, a more bitter pill. As Ibn Khaldun put it, an unkind ruler brings economic and social deterioration as

> a result of heavy taxation, expropriation, and social and political unrest...and financial pressures reduce the public demand for goods and services in the urban economy, [which will eventually lead to]...the emergence of diseases and epidemics accompanied by famine'. [However: A kind and benevolent] ruler serves as an incentive to the subjects and gives them energy [and]...civilization will be abundant.[40]

Postscript

If there is a positive side to Jordan's situation, it is that their economic crisis in the 1990s has forced them to reassess their policies and pursue economic liberalization. They seem to have seen that the best way to replace lost remittance flows is to create employment and enhance productivity through economic liberalization and new foreign investment.

The fortunate net result for Jordan is significant opportunities for attracting foreign direct investment have developed, especially in comparison to its neighbors. For example, while the gross dollar value is lower, Jordan's receipts of foreign investment as a percentage of gross domestic product far outperforms that of Egypt. According to the IMF's Global Development Finance report, for non-FDI capital flows as a percentage of GDP, in 1997 Egypt received 0.86 percent while Jordan

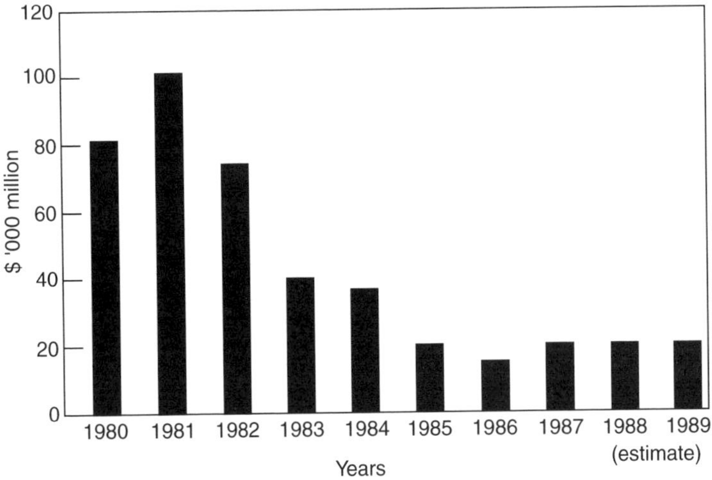

Figure 7.1   Saudi Arabia oil revenues, 1980 to 1989

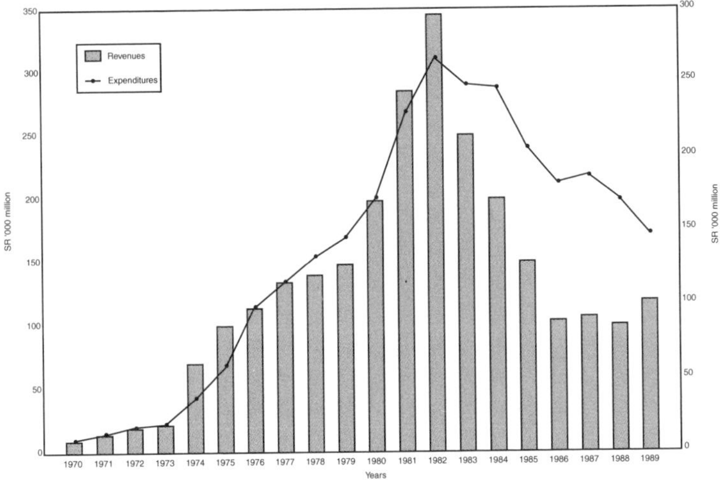

Figure 7.2   Saudi Arabia revenues and expenditures, 1980 to 1989

received 5.67 percent. Also by comparison, Egypt has lower M2 reserves than Jordan, Lebanon, Morocco or Tunisia. Also, according to a 1998 report, Jordan leads Egypt in gaining in technology transfer.[41]

Jordan's increase in foreign direct investment will also likely lead to other gains in global integration. For example, the percentage of exports

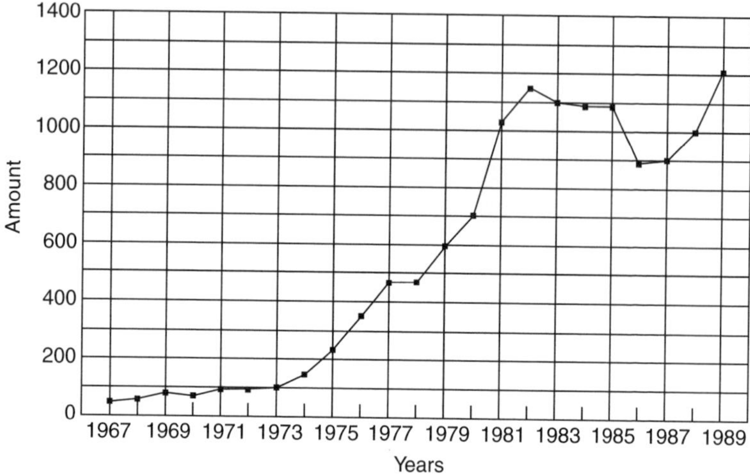

Figure 7.3 Jordanian remittances, 1964 to 1989

in sales of US majority-owned foreign affiliates increased from 20 percent in 1966 to 40 percent in 1993. Jordan's participation in this doubling of trade has been nominal, but this is likely to change. First, Jordan is making strides toward liberalization. They have also acceded to the World Trade Organization and increased their abilities to meet international standards. Second, because of this, Jordan has signed a free trade agreement with the United States, the first such agreement in the region. Given that US companies are growing at a significantly fast pace in the region, this raises the likelihood that Jordanian companies will share in this growth.

Jordan's work on trade liberalization is not complete. Unfortunately, according to studies on the 'speed of total trade integration', Jordan is not at the top of the list. The leaders are UAE with a growth rate of 10.2, Algeria 6.9, and Tunisia 6.9. These figures are confirmed by the 'Economic Freedom Index' (Egypt ranks even lower).

However, a World Bank report shows there is progress in trade integration. This is all to say that trade liberalization is the key to replacing remittance losses. To this end, Jordan is beginning to focus on trade policy reform and it is paying off. Jordan is becoming a regional success story and its national commitments to provide overall liberalization (political as well as economic) and policy stability, meeting core standards, and providing efficient trade services, seem to be paying off. Foreign investment is indeed taking place at a pace far above that of its neighbors. But is this enough? On one hand, the fact that Jordan has

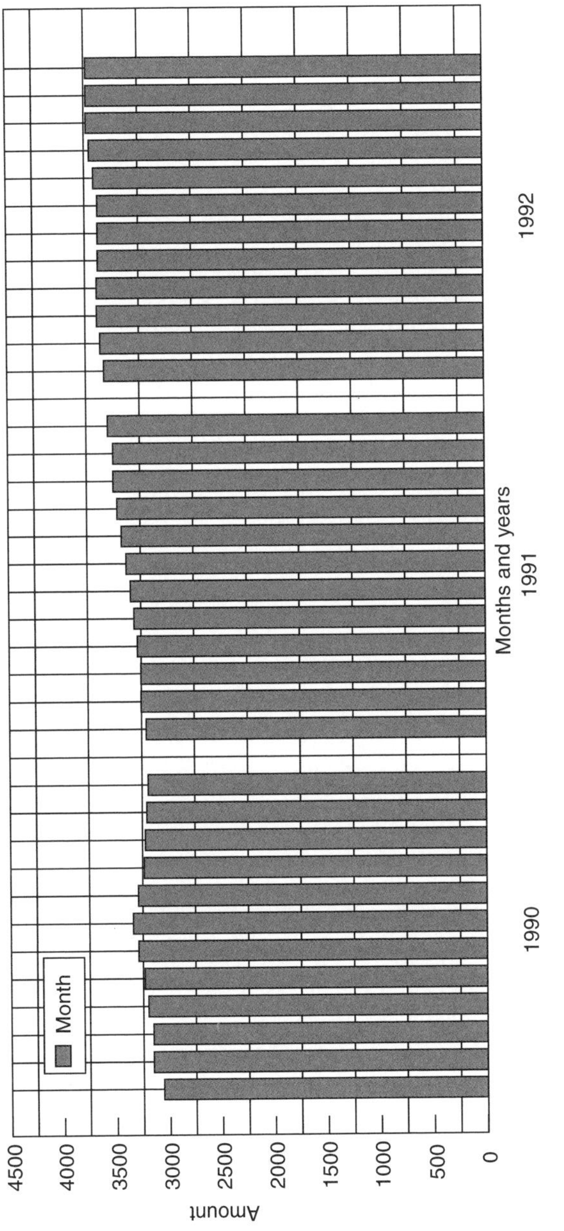

Figure 7.4 Jordanian remittances, 1990, 1991, 1992

historically not made real commitments to trade liberalization has put it into the 'late reformers' category, whose members have lost significant opportunities for economic growth. On the other hand, Jordan's moves in the last few years indicate that by a factor of at least 5 to 1, possibly 10 to 1, Jordan's economy could achieve higher trade-related growth if it pursues a consistent track toward trade liberalization and implementing core standards and harmonized business services. Given Jordan's historical presence as a supplier of services and as a supplier of human resources in the service sectors, the idea that they could become a real service economy is feasible.

Now, there are two final questions. The Middle East and North Africa region (MENA) has notoriously low rates of intra-regional trade. Of this, trade among the peace process states is worst. Can Jordan's moves toward trade liberalization be used to break this cycle? And, if so, will they assist Palestine to participate in the growth that will be generated from increased regional trade? If the answer to either, and preferably both, of these questions is yes, it will strengthen the peace process. If the answer is no, then current flaws in the structure will remain.

Notes

1. Ibn Khaldun's *Muqaddima* (2:271–72) translated and quoted by D. Weiss, 'Ibn Khaldun on Economic Transformation', *International Journal of Middle East Studies*, 27 (1995) 30.
2. See L. Andori, 'Redefining Oslo: Negotiating the Hebron Protocol', *Journal of Palestine Studies*, XXVI (Spring 1997) 17–30; E. Said, 'The Real Meaning of the Hebron Agreement', *Journal of Palestine Studies*, XXVI (Spring 1997) 31–6; M. Ellis, 'The Future of Israel/Palestine: Embracing the Broken Middle', *Journal of Palestine Studies*, XXVI (Spring 1997) 56–66; and H. Ashrawi, 'Guarded Optimism on the Peace Process: An Interview with Hanan Ashrawi', *Journal of Palestine Studies*, XXVI (Summer 1997), 81–9. On Ellis, his articles in the end identified a 'broken middle' that based on 'the broken dreams of Jews and Palestinians could provide as meaningful a meeting ground', but he also shows that an alternative position has been taken by negotiators. Andori, Said, and Ellis raise different points, but agree that the Hebron Protocol constricts rather than liberalizing the Palestinian position. Ashrawi claims some optimism, but comments throughout her interview expressed more stoicism than enthusiasm for the future of the Peace Process or for economic and political developments in the West Bank and Gaza.
3. H. Awartani and E. Klienmen, 'Economic Interactions Among Participants in the Middle East Peace Process', *Middle East Journal*, 51 (Spring 1997), 214–29.
4. Much of this chapter is based on my occasional paper, 'Islamic Banking in Practice: Problems in Jordan and Saudi Arabia', The University of Durham The Center for Middle Eastern and Islamic Studies Occasional Papers Series, No. 48 (May 1995). C. Vaughn and I asserted at the 1992 BRISMES conference

that 'remittances' were being misreported and should be listed as 'returns of savings'.

5. Awatani and Klienman give discussion of trade potential between these areas.

6. B. al Hajjar, J. Presley, and J. W. Wright, Jr., 'Structural and Attitudinal Impediments to the Effective Capital Distribution in the Saudi Arabia's Islamicizing Economy: Implications for Financial Sector Training', *Economic Growth and Human Resource Development in Islamic Perspective* (Herndon, VA: International Institute for Islamic Thought, 1993).

7. On economic stability in Jordan see my editorial, 'Is Jordan's Economic Recovery Real?' *Arab-American Business and Consumer Magazine*, 12 (1993) 8–9; and M. Abujaber and C. Vaughn (with J. W. Wright, Jr.), 'Jordan's Rentier-by-Proxy Economic Agenda: Recent Changes, Observations, and Opportunities', Proceedings of the 1992 British Society for Middle Eastern Studies Conference (St. Andrews, Scotland: St. Andrews University, 1992) 629–35. On patronage behavior in Jordan, see C. Erol and R. El-Bdour, 'Conventional and Islamic Banks: Patronage Behavior of Jordanian Customers', *The International Journal of Bank Marketing*, 8 (1990) 25–35.

8. See Introduction and Nicholas D. Ray, 'Asset Allocation Strategies for Islamic Financial Institutions,' in J. W. Wright, Jr. (ed.), *Muslim Attitudes Toward Islamic Finance*, Bloomington In: International Journal of Islamic and Arabic Studies, (1996).

9. B. L. Glasser, 'External Capital and Political Liberalizations: A Typography of Middle Eastern Development in the 1980s and 1990s', *Journal of International Affairs*, 49 (1995) 45–73. For a journalistic perspective on aid competition see A. D. Marcus, 'Israeli, Jordanian, Palestinian Banks vie to Service Aid Coming to the West Bank', *Wall Street Journal*, 2 February 1994.

10. A. Eichman, 'The Hawala System: A Model of the Informal Channel for Remittances in the Middle East and South Asia', in F. M. Hana (ed.), *Middle East Banking and Finance: Collection of Essays* (New York: Arab Bankers Association of America, Inc., 1995) pp. 27–65.

11. I use the term 'rentier-by-proxy' extensively, but it was applied by T. R. Stauffer, *The Journal of Energy and Development*, 11 (1985) 69–93. The term rentier finds its basis in Ricardo's work on depletable resources and by extension the term 'rentier-by-proxy' refers to resource exploitation via secondary transactions, such remittances gained from exported workers. I am not sure the term 'rent' is appropriately used with reference to seeking aid, but others, including authors herein, refer to exogenous aid directly as rents, which I do not object to, but do not prefer.

12. On capital investment see M. Ballool, 'Social Change and Business Policy in an Era of New Prospect: Strategic Investment Planning From 1970 to 1985', pp. 33–52; and A. Albatel's article 'Private Sector Finance: Problems Faced by the Fourth and the Fifth Five Year Plans', pp. 53–70, both in J. W. Wright, Jr. (ed.), *Business Development in Saudi Arabia* (London: Macmillan Press, Ltd., 1996). On labor needs, see also in that collection, H. Khashoggi and C. Vaughn, 'Labor Constraint on Saudi Business Development', pp. 97–104; and M. Schmidt and A. Garawi, 'The Saudi Managerial Environment', 87–96.

13. The possible exception is Yemen, but there are few official records on Yemani migrant to Saudi in the 1970s. Saudi Arabia's labor-import strategy

also affects other economies like India, Pakistan, the Philippines, Egypt, etc., but the largest number of official immigrants came via Jordan. See various ESCWA reports cited herein, as well as three dissertations cited below. Others debate this: Serengeldin claims the most labor came from Egypt. It is more feasible that the greatest number of guest-workers in Saudi Arabia came via Jordan, although many were actually Palestinian. This is certainly true in the other Gulf states, like Kuwait. Certainly, Jordanians and Palestinians were a majority at professional levels of employment.

14. J. W. Wright, Jr. 'Accounting in Saudi Arabia: Imperative Questions for the 1990s', Proceedings of the 1992 British Society for Middle Eastern Studies Conference (St Andrews, Scotland: St Andrews University, 1992) 636–43.

15. S. A. Tawi, 'The Impact of Expatriate Workers on the Economy in Saudi Arabia: Compatible General Equilibrium Results', PhD dissertation Oklahoma State University (1984) 24. This situation was even more noticeable in other Gulf Arab countries. Even today, some estimates put 88 percent of Dubai's population as foreign. However, it is true that most Palestinian and Jordanian labor were replaced.

16. These statistics come from various Saudi government reports, but are also discussed in secondary sources used here, namely J. Presley, and T. Westaway, *A Guide to the Saudi Arabian Economy* (London: Macmillan Press, 1989) pp. 9–48; B. al Hajjar and J. Presley, 'Managerial Inefficiency in Small, Manufacturing Businesses in Saudi Arabia: A Constraint to Development', Proceedings of the British Society of Middle Eastern Studies Conference (London: University of London, 1991) personal copy, and in the chapters in *Business and Economic Development in Saudi Arabia*.

17. On urban growth in Saudi see 'Cultural Continuity and Saudi Urban Planning: National, Regional, and Municipal', in *Business and Economic Development in Saudi Arabia*. On private sector dependencies see al-Hajjar, Presley, and Wright, cited above; and J. W. Wright, Jr. 'More Than Petroleum: A Diversified Economy', in A. Al-Sweel and J. W. Wright, Jr., *Saudi Arabia: Tradition and Transition* (Westland, MI: Hayden-McNiel, 1993) pp. 27–66.

18. al-Hajjar and Presley, 'Managerial Inefficiency'; Wright, Brismes; and Presley and Westaway, 48.

19. J. A. Shaw and D. E. Long, *Saudi Arabian Modernization: the Impact of Change on Stability* (New York: Praeger Publishing, 1989) p. 35.

20. On 'government assistance financing' see M. F. Y. Kurashi, 'The Social Responsibility of the Multinational Corporations Operating in Saudi Arabia', as summarized by C. B. Joy in A. H. Dahlan (ed.), *Politics, Administration and Development in Saudi Arabia* (Brentwood, MD: Amana Corporation, 1990) pp. 259–77. For population estimates see Shaw and Long, 38; and Presley and Westaway, 100–1 and 138. Saudi labor population figures vary widely. Shaw and Long estimate that 80 percent of the labor is imported, Presley and Westaway claim 70 percent, while some agency statistics put estimates as low as 40 percent.

21. A definite progression is made in the goals stated in the Kingdom's Five Year Development Plans. The First Plan focuses on the construction of human support services such as health care facilities, roads and schools. The Second and Third Plans concentrate on infrastructure development, with the Third

Plan outlining plans for industrial cities at Yanbu and Jubail. The Fourth Plan calls for the completion of the majority of government-sponsored infrastructure projects and places more attention on human resource development. Human resource development is the primary focus of the Fifth Plan, and is even further emphasized in the Sixth Plan. This progression from expenditures on construction to expenditures on intangible items such as training and small business development would normally indicate a move toward support for private sector businesses, especially as the economy becomes increasing service-based. But, while the progression is made in the Plans, it has not happened at the practical level. Small firms are still not participating in financial incentive programs for business development. See Presley, Westaway, and Wright.

22. A. Al-Mazeedi and Ruby Yaksick, 'The Oil Trust: An Energy Financing Mechanism: Linking Arab Banks and Oil Companies', in F. M. Hana (ed.), *Middle East Banking and Finance: Collection of Essays* (New York: The Arab Bankers Association of America, Inc., 1995), pp. 22–36. For a more general discussion of measures taken to correct budget deficits in the Kingdom see R. Looney, 'Saudi Arabian Budgetary Dilemmas', *Middle East Studies*, 26 (January 1990) 76–87.

23. In addition to chapter 6 herein, see also B. Glasser, 'Exogenous Capital and Political Liberalizations: A Typography of Middle Eastern Development in the 1980s and 1990s', *Journal of International Affairs*, 49 (Summer 1995) 45–73.

24. P. Levine, 'The Intifada and its Impact on the Banking System in the State of Israel', *The American Economist*, 37 (Spring 1993) 68–71; R. Melnick, 'Financial Services, Cointegration, and Demand for Money in Israel', *Journal of Money, Credit, and Banking*, 27 (1995) 140–53. Israeli economic restructuring is outlined in articles by S. Bichler and J. Nitzen, including 'Bringing Capital Accumulation Back in: The Weapondollar, Petrodollar Coalition – Military Contractors, Oil Companies, and Middle East Energy Conflicts', *Review of International Political Economy*, 2 (1995) 446–515; 'Putting the State in its Place: US Foreign Policy and Differential Capital Accumulation in Middle East Energy Conflicts', *Review of International Political Economy*, 28 (1996), and especially in 'From War Profits to Peace Dividends: The New Israeli Political Economy', forthcoming.

25. The Fourth Plan targets lowered the number of non-national employees by 600 000 between 1985 and 1990, and the Fifth Plan calls for the replacement of 220 400 foreign workers. The actual number displaced was about three-quaters of the target.

26. Examples include The Economic Adjustment Program of 1989–1993, the Encouragement of Investment Law No. 53, the Post Office Fund Act, the Development Bonds Plan. The Central Bank also encourages the opening of foreign accounts to facilitate the remittances process.

27. This is discussed in A. J. Munzer, 'A Rate of Return Analysis of the Education of Jordanian Workers', PhD dissertation, University of Wales (1980). For a more recent study leading into the Gulf War period see ESCWA, 'The Impact of The Gulf Crisis On The Jordanian Economy' (Amman: ESCWA, 1990), which surveys prewar conditions in its member countries: Bahrain, Egypt, Iraq, Jordan, Kuwait, Lebanon, Oman, Palestine, Qatar, Saudi Arabia, Syria,

United Arab Emirates, and Yemen. Also see M. S. Amerah, 'Major Employment Issues in Some Arab Countries' (Amman: Economic Research Centre for the Royal Scientific Society, 1990); and N.Choucri, 'Migration in the Middle East: Old Economics or New Politics?', *Journal of Arab Affairs*, 7 (1988) 10–18.

28. H. A. Yahya, 'Human Capital Migration From Labor-Rich Arab States to Oil-Rich Arab States and the Consequences for the Jordanian Economy', PhD dissertation, Oklahoma State University, 1980, 34; supporting statistics come from N. Abdalla, 'The Impact of The Gulf Crisis' (Amman: ESCWA, 1991) 10–14; and Hussein, 28. For additional support see A. Y. Abu-Ayyash, 'Absorption of Returnees in Small Industrial Enterprises: The Case of the Development and Employment Fund' (Amman: ESCWA, 1991), specifically pp. 13–14; also see Vaugh and Abujaber 629–35; and Amerah, 26–31.

29. There is some debate over the success of labor export plans. Choucri describes the danger of investing remittances into 'squanderables' in 'Migration in the Middle East: Old Economics or New Politics?', cited above. Before him, I. Serageldin stated: 'There is strong evidence that the marginal propensity of a migrant worker in the Arab world to remit is inversely related to occupational level' in *Manpower and International Labor Migration in the Middle East and North Africa* (London: Oxford University Press, 1983) p. 91. His study tends to draw conclusions based on Egyptian experience. The inverse relationship he finds may not be applicable to Jordan. I tend to agree with R. H. Adam's argument that the positive or negative effects of remittances must be measured relative to domestic employment and investment alternatives. See 'The Economic Uses and Impact of International Remittances in Rural Egypt', *Economic Development and Cultural Change*, 39 (1991). The reader should also see Adam's *The Effects of International Remittances on Poverty, Inequality, and Rural Development in Egypt* (Washington, DC: International Food Policy Research Institute, 1991). His position is more moderate, but still discusses poor reinvestment. I argue further that the remittance strategy began to fail in 1987.

30. J. Jankowski, 'Review: *Troubles on the East Bank: Challenges to the Domestic Stability*', by R. B. Sutloff, *Middle East Studies Association Bulletin*, 21 (1987) 219.

31. Amerah, 13.

32. 1987–1988 figures were taken from Amerah, 13, and were verified and extended to 1989 from data provided by Abdalla 8–9.

33. Serageldin, Socknat, Birks, Li, and Sinclair discuss the influence of Asian labor in the Gulf in the 1975–1985 period, speculating that Arab workers would be replaced in the future. M. Ali, M. Amerah, and I. Ibrahim discusses this in 'The Unemployment Problem in Jordan: Characteristics and Prospects' (Amman: Royal Scientific Society, 1987) as does I. Ibrahim in 'Status and Prospects of the Jordanian Labour Market' (Amman: Royal Scientific Society, 1989). Choucri shows this has been the case since the Gulf War and his claim continues to be justified.

34. It is true that purchases of goods consumed by families receiving remittances would become parts of a firm's cash flow like any other sale. However, several studies cited in this chapter discuss the fact that people reinvest remittance money into real estate or into the operations of family run

businesses. I agree with the argument that families in labor exporting countries pursue income portfolio strategies. This assertion is certainly supported by, albeit briefly and indirectly, Abujaber and Vaughn, Amerah and Ibrahim, Cantori (in his articles on corporate conservatism), and Serageldin. Also see K. Aziz Choudhry, 'The Price of Wealth: Business and State in Remittance and Oil Economies', *International Organization*, 43 (1989) 123–43, who indirectly implies this is the case while talking about the real costs of remittances on liquidity. M. Schmidt discusses the extent to which the notion of family-unit businesses transfers with families who emigrate to the US in 'The Family-Run Business: A Remnant of the Old Country for Today's Arab American', *Arab-American Business and Consumer Magazine*, 12 (December 1993) 11–12. The implications are much more severe, however, in an economy where between 60 percent and 80 percent of private sector profits come from sales to the government.

35. The money supply and deposit figures come from various Central Bank of Jordan, Monthly Statistical Reports, especially December 1992. The percent increases in insurance premiums collected reflects an index created from the annual reports of the leading Jordanian insurance firms.

36. Several factors make it difficult to continue this analysis in 1993. Among these are a reclassification of reporting categories for some economic indicators. Remittances, for example, are not presented for 1993. This is probably in response to the International Monetary Fund's recognition that what had been counted as remittances should have been reported as transfers of capital. In 1993 the Central Bank of Jordan does not list deposits in licensed banks and they do not list deposits in financial companies at all. These omissions make trend analysis difficult. However, the 'currency in circulation' accounts are consistent and are found in the Central Bank of Jordan's October 1994 *Monthly Statistical Bulletin* on p. 10; 'Private Sector Demand Deposits' are on p. 13; 'Current Account Status' is on p. 16.

37. The statistics in this report come from the Regional Perspectives on World Development Report 1995, 'Will Arab Workers Prosper or Be Left Out in the Twenty-First Century?' (Washington, DC: World Bank, 1995).

38. Fadle Naqib, 'Prospects for Sustained Development of the Palestinian Economy: Strategies and Policies for Reconstruction and Development' (New York: UNCTAD, 1995) 33.

39. All the statistics in this section come from World Bank, 'Will Arab Workers Prosper?' The longer quote later in this section comes from pp. 27–8.

40. Ibn Khaldun, see D. Weiss, 'Ibn Khaldun on Economic Transformation', 33.

41. For figures in the postscript see Mustapha Nabli and Annette De Kline, "Benefiting Globalization." Address to the Mediterranean Development Forum, Marakech, Morocco, September 3–5, 1998; and Nabli and De Kline, "Managing Global Integration in the Middle East and North Africa," Bernard Hoekinan and Hanaa Kheir-El-Din, eds, *Trade Policy Development in the Middle East and North Africa*, (Washington: World Bank Institute, 2000), pp. 7–50.

8

Between Desert Countries: the Political Economy of Water Under the Israeli Occupation of the Palestinian Territories and Beyond

Alwyn R. Rouyer

The Taba Interim Agreement, signed by Israelis and Palestinians in September 1995, represented a major milestone in the Middle East Peace Process. Whether this agreement, also known as Oslo II, was a step toward a Palestinian state remains to be seen. In the meantime, it brought at least a partial cessation to 28 years of Israeli occupation, along with further recognition of Palestinian Authority (PA) control over parts of the West Bank and the Gaza Strip. Moreover, under Israeli occupation, the Palestinians suffered from many forms of discriminatory policies, that they hoped would end with Taba.

One of the most blatant forms of discrimination faced by Palestinians was inequitable access to water, for agricultural and industrial purposes and basic human consumption. According to various estimates, Israelis consume around three to four times more water per capita than Palestinians. For settlers in the territories, favorable access has been even greater: they enjoy green lawns and swimming pools in their protected enclaves, while Palestinian villages and towns suffer from tap water shortages and intermittent service losses that can last for weeks, even during the dry summer months. The Taba Interim Agreement did not immediately alleviate these inequities, but it was considered to be a foundation upon which final status dialog and cooperation concerning water resources could be built. Under this agreement, Israel recognized Palestinian water rights for the first time, promised to release additional water for Palestinian consumption, and agreed to establish the rudiments of a cooperative framework for developing new water supplies. Still, difficult issues, including defining water rights, remained. This chapter examines the economic and political impact of Israel's water policies during the occupation and the changes brought about by the water accords of the Oslo II agreement.

The occupation and water allocation

Within weeks of Israel's conquest of the West Bank and Gaza Strip, water resources in the territories were put under military control. Military Order No. 92 of 15 August 1967 vested all powers dealing with water, as defined under Jordanian law, in the hands of an Israeli officer appointed by the Area Commander. Other orders and regulations followed which integrated the territories' water resources into the Israeli system. Arab water resources were thus strictly regulated by the Israeli Water Commission until the PA was established. Palestinians were involved in the decision-making process affecting water utilization, which rested entirely with the Civil Administration (Israeli Military Authority) and the Israeli Water Commission (IWC). As a result, a highly discriminatory administrative structure that penalized Arab consumers was formed. Their agricultural water consumption was frozen at 1967 levels, and domestic consumption was only allowed to grow gradually and at a pace far below that of Palestinian population growth. Palestinians were prevented from drilling new wells or replacing existing ones. In contrast, during this period Israeli authorities dug wells for the needs of growing settler populations. Particularly onerous were the greater differential prices paid for water by Palestinians and Israeli settlers.

Water infrastructure under occupation

The Israeli Water Law of 1959 vests ownership of all water resources with the state and formalized its central water system. The law gives the state the power to allocate water through licensing, rationing, and rate regulation. Israel's water distribution system is a highly-complex centralized structure that is managed by the Minister of Agriculture. The main administrative units are Mekorot, Tahal, and the Water Commission. Mekorot, sometimes called the Israel Water Company, is responsible for developing and supplying irrigation projects. Its most ambitious project to date has been the National Water Carrier system, which consists of a series of pipelines and canals that convey over 1100 million cubic meters per year (mcm/y) from the country's water-rich north to coastal cities and the Negev. The company supplies about 65 percent of the water consumed in Israel. Tahal, also called the Water Planning Company, is responsible for the long-range planning and design of new water development projects. The Israeli Water Commission is responsible for the overall planning and supervision of all matters related to water in Israel. The Water Commissioner, appointed by the Israeli Cabinet, has ultimate authority over issuing permits, setting tariffs, and allocating water access to all 'categories' of consumers.

A state-controlled water system had not existed in Palestine before the occupation. Under pre-occupation Jordanian law, water was considered to be a privately-owned resource. With the issuance of Military Order No. 291 (Order 291) in 1968, all previous water settlements became invalid. Many observers claim the result of Order 291 shifted the legal status of West Bank water resources and thus violated Palestinian rights under international law.[1] Objecting to this interpretation, Israel argued that Order 291 merely authorized a military commander in 'Judea and Samara' (ancient Hebrew names right-wing Israelis call the territories), to enforce pre-existing laws regarding land and natural resources. They contended that orders relating to the exercise of public water ownership applied only to 'previously non-utilized water' were appropriate.[2] Whichever interpretation one espouses, under occupation Palestinians lost control over the development and distribution of water resources.

Through the Israeli Civil Administration (ICA or Civil Administration) and under Israeli Water Commission (IWC) directives, water was supplied to Palestinians by local municipal companies, village councils, and by Mekorot. For example, the Jerusalem Water Undertaking in the Ramallah District supplied the cities of Ramallah and El-Bireh, and local Palestinian villages, as well as several Israeli settlements. The majority (67 percent) of this water came from Mekorot, with the rest coming from local wells. Mekorot sold water to the ICA, which in turn sold it to Palestinian companies, at a 50 percent profit. While the water itself went directly from Mekorot to the Palestinian utilities, extra costs were assessed for overheads, and then were passed on to Arab consumers. A Palestinian municipal water company director charged: 'the money the Civil Administration is generating from Palestinian institutions is being used to subsidize the settlements and army activities in the West Bank. Thus, in a way the Palestinian population is subsidizing the Israeli settlement of Palestine.'[3] This practice is an example of the discriminatory water policies under Israeli occupation.

Differentials in water consumption

Water consumption figures for Israel and the West Bank and Gaza bring into sharp focus the prejudicial nature of Israeli water policies. At the time Taba was signed, Israeli per capita water consumption was three to four times greater than that of the Palestinians.[4] While Palestinians constituted 31 percent of the area's population, they consumed only 10 percent of the water. Combined water usage for Israel and the territories was estimated to be 2100–2200 mcm/y; 100 to 300 hundred mcm/y more than could be safely extracted from available sources. However, year-to-year rationing depends on rainfall. Between 1986 and 1991, generally considered to have been dry years, Israel cut agricultural water consumption by as much as 30 percent. Later, after the dry winter of 1993–94, agricultural rations of potable water were reduced by 10 percent. Data from Tahal show lower consumption figures, of about 1900 mcm/y, but this is disputed by many experts on the hydrology of the Middle East. These disputed consumption figures reflect the difficulty in getting and sharing accurate data between Israelis and Palestinians.[5]

While over-exploitation and the lack of water sources remain major concerns, especially in Gaza, the crucial problem is not scarcity but distribution inequity. Israeli policies restricted Palestinian water consumption to around 110–125 mcm per annum. As mentioned above, water for agriculture was frozen during 28 years of occupation at roughly the levels of utilization prevalent in 1967, or about 90–100 mcm/y. The balance went to domestic use, with only a fraction going to industry. While domestic consumption was allowed to grow gradually, the territories' population has nearly tripled. As a result, Palestinian water allocation has not risen at a rate sufficient to support the community.[6] The water gap between Israelis and Palestinians can best be grasped by examining per capita consumption figures, as shown in Table 8.1.

While the numbers vary depending on their source, close approximations are possible. Whereas Israeli usage was about 280 liters per person per day (l/pd), Palestinian consumption is only 70–90 l/pd. However, actual water delivery to Palestinian consumers in the towns and cities is

Table 8.1   Water consumption: Israel and the Palestinian Territories circa 1990

	Total consumption (mcm)	Total consumption (m^3/p/y)	Domestic consumption (m^3/o/y)	Domestic consumption (l/pd)
Israel	1900	400	100	280
West Bank	120	125	31	76
Gaza	97	130	35	100
West Bank settlers	(45–160)	(350–1600)	110	300

Sources: See note 35.

a much lower 40–60 l/pd because leakage rates from the deteriorating infrastructure were estimated to have reached about 50 percent in the West Bank. As a result, during the summer dry season, water was supplied only irregularly, a situation that was even worse in the refugee camps. Estimates revealed that drinking water consumption in Palestinian villages was about one-third of that in the towns. Over half of the villages, housing about 37 percent of the population, did not have a piped drinking water supply and had to rely on roof-top cisterns or hand-carried sources from wells. Among refugees, about 40 percent of camp residents in the Gaza Strip had no internal plumbing. These stark inequities clearly stand out.[7]

In contrast, Israel's water consumption level depended heavily on how much water it shared with the Palestinians. Israel consumes 80 to 90 percent of the water from the central hill region's mountain aquifers, although only 5 percent of the re-charge area of the aquifer falls outside the green line. Roughly 25 to 30 percent of Israel's total water resources, and 50 percent of its drinking water, came from the West Bank. Many experts charge that Israel was over-pumping shared aquifers beyond what was considered safe yields. While these accusations are strenuously denied by officials at Tahal and Mekorot, a 1990 Israeli State Comptroller Report documents serious over-pumping in the mountain and coastal aquifers of upwards to 100 mcm annually throughout the 1980s.[8] The growth of Israeli settlements in the territories seriously aggravated the water problem. While data on settler water consumption is closely guarded, safe estimates were that settlers accounted for 30 to 50 percent of the water consumed in the West Bank. In 1994, settlers numbering around 130 000 consumed 60–100 mcm, while 1 200 000 Palestinians consumed 100–140 mcm.[9]

Restrictions on water utilization

The most burdensome water policy during the occupation was the prohibition on drilling. Military No. Order 158 of October 1967 states that, 'No person is allowed to establish or own or administer a water installation (any construction that is used to extract either surface or subterranean water resources or processing plant) without a new official permit.' The regulation applies to new wells, irrigation systems, and to the repair of wells drilled before 1967. Israeli authorities maintained strict metering of wells in the territories and imposed quotas on irrigation wells, fining those who exceeded limits. These regulations, in fact, were consistent with Israeli laws concerning drilling new wells and repairing old ones. However, permits for Palestinians had to be approved by both the ICA and the IWC, and were often delayed by red tape. Palestinians charged that these restrictions on drilling are gross violations of their property rights and that, since Jordanian laws in effect before 1967 were not recognized, this made the occupation 'belligerent' and thus breached international legal principles. Under Jordanian administration drilling permits were automatically issued for replacing wells and no meters were used on private wells.[10]

In contrast to the Jordanian system, ICA drilling licenses were very hard for Palestinians to obtain. Permits were not issued for new irrigation wells and, while there was no prohibition on new domestic-use wells, obtaining the licenses involved a long and complex bureaucratic process. In the 27 years between 1967 and the establishment of PA in Gaza-Jericho in the spring of 1994, Israeli authorities issued only 20 new drilling permits for domestic use and three for irrigation in the West Bank, according to figures supplied by the ICA. In addition, 15 permits were approved for repairing and replacing wells. But this number did not come close to meeting the need or the large number of requests for permits. Taher Nasserddin, the highest-ranking Palestinian in the West Bank water department, estimated in 1994 that an additional 26 wells were required for domestic purposes alone and many more than this if agricultural needs were also to be met.[11]

In response to these assertions, Israeli officials claimed that the regulations and restrictions on water use in the occupied territories were also applied in Israel. In Israel, wells could not be drilled or repaired without direct authorization of the Water Commissioner. All wells were metered and agricultural consumers had to adhere to quotas set by ICA. They also pointed out that in 1966 Jordan promulgated a 'Law of Natural Resources' requiring the installation of metering devices. Regarding the issuing of drilling permits Israeli water officials asserted that new permits were always issued when it became necessary to replace existing dried-up wells for domestic use. Licenses for new irrigation wells have been denied, they explain, because much of the mountain aquifer was already fully utilized. They also claimed that the high cost of sinking the bore hole was another reason why so few wells had been drilled for domestic purposes. One Israeli government briefing paper reported that in the first ten years of the occupation the ICA received 60 applications to drill new wells in the West Bank for domestic purposes and approved 20. However, none were dug because of the estimated cost of US $250 000 per bore.[12] Israel further contended that policies implemented during the occupation were not discriminatory, but were aimed at ensuring reliable water sources for both Jews and Arabs. But Israeli officials also emphatically stated they would never allow Palestinian farm water consumption to grow to levels where production could endanger their agricultural economy. This public Israeli position is often made by Meir Ben-Meir, a former Israeli Water Commissioner: 'Israel will not divert fresh water to cotton away from a Palestinian child to drink; but nor will Israel give-up irrigating orchards in Israel so that new orchards in the West Bank may be irrigated.'[13]

But Israel's water policies in the territories were never as benign or even-handed as these comments imply, even without consideration of the special privileges given to settlers, and particularly before the drought years of the late 1980s and early 1990s. Allocations to Palestinians remained virtually static after 1967 while those of Israelis, especially settlers, were made on the basis of need and supply.[14] Palestinians and Israelis also had highly unequal access to financial resources for water projects. Israeli projects were financed by the Israeli government, mainly through the Mekorot water company. By way of contrast, the Civil Administration made only minor contributions to water projects in the territories. Furthermore, because there were no banks in the territories until 1994, Palestinians found it difficult to obtain private loans to support the drilling of bores and the construction of other water installations. Consequently, what limited investment was made in water infrastructure generally came from NGO donors such as American Near East Refugee Aid (ANERA). Projects were also made more costly by the occupation practice of requiring Mekorot or private Israeli companies to do the construction.[15]

Other Israeli occupation policies put severe limitations on Palestinian water use and agricultural development. In the West Bank, Palestinians were not allowed to use water for farming after 4.00 p.m., despite the fact that in arid regions evening is the traditional and sensible time to irrigate.[16] Military Order No. 1015 of 1982 prohibited the planting of fruit trees, except on private plots, without a permit from the military authorities in order to promote maximum run-off to preserve water resources. Trees already planted were required to be registered within 90 days – after this period all unlicensed trees could be uprooted by ICA inspectors at the owner's expense. Subsequent military orders added to the list of trees and vegetable plants for which permits were required. Palestinians were not allowed to drill wells for any purpose in the western basin while, at the same time, Mekorot put 30 new wells in this basin, on both sides of the green line. Israeli water authorities justified this discrepancy by explaining that from a hydrological engineering perspective the best place to tap the mountain aquifer was over the foot hills and lower slopes of the plateau closer to the Mediterranean Sea, the major proportion of which is within Israel.[17]

And yet this explanation did not account for the very deep wells dug by Israel for settler use at the highest elevations of the eastern mountain plateau. Not only were few new wells approved for Palestinian use, but occupation regulations required that even newly-authorized ones could reach only a shallow depth. Bores range from 60 to 150 meters in the West Bank and 15–80 meters in the Gaza Strip. In contrast, wells dug by Mekorot in the West Bank for settler consumption are much deeper (400 to 600 meters) and equipped with considerably more powerful pumps. Deep wells yielded greater flow and better-quality water. Mekorot wells in the West Bank yielded, on average, 750 000 cm/y, as compared to 13 000 cm/y for Palestinian wells.[18] In addition, stiff penalties were imposed for the over-pumping of Arab wells, but until recently no such similar restrictions were placed on over-pumping Mekorot-owned wells. Even within the green line Israeli authorities maintained only minimal restrictions on the discharge of Mekorot wells. The 1990 report of the State Comptroller of Israel charged that Mekorot overutilized the western aquifer for over 25 years. In the West Bank, the State Comptroller found Israeli settlements to have exceeded their quotas set by the Water Commissioner by over 35 percent in the 1980s.[19]

The discrepancy in depth and quality between Israeli and Palestinian wells, along with excessive over-pumping by Israeli wells, produced serious consequences for Palestinian wells. Many Mekorot wells dug for settler use were near Arab towns and villages and there was a strong indication that they often lowered the water table, contributing to the drying-up or deterioration of the more shallow, nearby Arab wells and springs. The Palestinian Hydrology Group reported that 26 wells had dried up completely in the Jordan Valley by 1993.[20] One widely publicized case was that of al-Ouja Spring, one of the largest in the West Bank, which ran dry in the spring of 1979 during a drought, but also shortly after three deep wells were dug in the vicinity for nearby settlements. Over 3000 dunums of fruit and vegetable crops were lost (a dunum equals approximately one-quarter of an acre or 1000 square meters). Israeli hydrologists contended that the problem was not from the Mekorot wells, which tapped a deeper and different aquifer, but rather as a result of the drought. Drinking water was provided for the Arab inhabitants from the Israeli wells, but it was not allowed to be used for irrigation. While the flow of the spring partially returned, Palestinian hydrologists maintain the continued irregularity in discharge is due to the nearby Israeli wells. Whichever assertion was correct, the fact remains that Arab fields were allowed to dry up and farmers forced to seek work elsewhere while adjacent fields farmed by settlers bloomed.[21]

Al-Ouja was only one among numerous instances of shortages and deterioration of water quality in the West Bank under occupation. Deep wells dug for the settlement of Ariel and for settlements in the vicinity of Nablus significantly reduced the quantity and quality of community wells in nearby Palestinian villages. While some of these villages were connected to the Mekorot grid, most were not. In the West Bank, in 1994, only 15 percent of Palestinian villages obtained water from Mekorot. The cities of Bethlehem and Hebron also suffered from severe water shortages, especially in the summer months. In the summers of both 1993 and 1995, while settlements of the nearby Etzion Bloc received plentiful water daily, Bethlehem and the surrounding refugee camps and villages were supplied with water only two days a week. It was not unusual for the water pipes in the city of Hebron to run totally dry, requiring potable water to be trucked in at four times the normal price, while the nearby settlement of Kiryat Arba continued to receive enough water for flowering gardens and swimming pools. According to a study by the Palestinian Hydrology Group, the over-pumping of deep Israeli wells in the West Bank also resulted in a sharp increase in the salinity levels of Palestinian wells. In the Jordan Valley during the period between 1982 and 1991, salt content rose by 130 percent and chlorine concentrations by 50 percent in Palestinian wells. Other parts of the West Bank also experienced a marked deterioration in water quality during the occupation.[22]

Gaza under occupation

While Israeli water policies applied equally to the Gaza Strip before autonomy, they were never as strictly enforced as in the West Bank. Israel never considered Gaza to be part of their water system and thus it was not thought to be vital to Israeli water security. Furthermore, given the large number of wells (nearly 2000 in 1992), Israeli authorities found it much harder to enforce water restrictions in this area. Under Egyptian rule before 1967, the lack of regulation had resulted in chronic over-pumping and serious depletion of the water supply. Because Egyptian law considered water a private resource to which individuals could claim ownership, no permits were required to drill or operate wells. After 1967 in Gaza, as in the West Bank, the Israeli authorities imposed water quotas on Palestinian farmers and placed meters on all wells, including those dug before the occupation. Arabs were refused permits to dig new agricultural wells. As justification, Israeli authorities based this policy on the fact that water supply was already seriously harmed and continued overuse would lead to permanent damage. Yet as the Israel State Comptroller's report documents, over-pumping continued into the 1980s, most significantly by deep wells in the settlements. In addition, the quality of the groundwater continued to deteriorate due to the lower water tables, which allowed seawater to infiltrate. There was also increased seepage of agricultural chemicals and sewage into the aquifers. The sewage situation was worst in the refugee camps in Gaza, few of which had even partial sewage systems.[23]

Other actions taken by Israel contributed to Gaza's serious water problems. The most important surface water source for the Strip was the Wadi Gaza, which has its catchment areas in the West Bank and Israel and provides, by some estimates, 20 mcm to 30 mcm of water per year. (In Arabic a *wadi* is a water course which may have winter run-off, like an *arroyos* in the Southwest US). Israel impounds all this water before it ever reaches Gaza's boundary.[24] In addition, a significant amount of groundwater that would otherwise be available to the Gaza Strip was intercepted by Israel according to hydrologists' and development agencies' reports. These specialists contended that in the 1980s Mekorot dug between three and five deep wells close to Gaza's border so that water could be pumped from Gazan reserves. Other nearby wells, they charged, intercepted groundwater of the coastal aquifer inside Israel, perhaps up to 60 mcm/y, that would normally flow to Gaza.[25] Ironically, this was the same reason some Israelis gave for restricting Palestinian water utilization in the West Bank. ICA authorities adamantly denied these accusations, stating not only that they are not true, but also that the low transmissivity of the coastal aquifer made the latter assertion impossible. Unfortunately, because ICA's and IWC's water records and transmissivity data are not available for public examination, it is impossible to make an independent verification of the allegations or disclaimers.[26]

The price of water

Under occupation Palestinians were not only discriminated against in per capita water consumption, but also paid more for the limited water they received. Evidence indicated that not only did Israelis inside the green line pay a lower price for water than did Palestinians, but so did Israeli settlers in the territories, because their costs were (and still are) subsidized by the World Zionist Organization. Based on this evidence one must assume Israeli water pricing policy in the territories was aimed at discouraging Palestinian water consumption while encouraging that of settlers.[27]

More specifically, the Israel Water Law of 1959 vested the power to set water prices with the Minister of Agriculture following consultation with the IWC and after authorization by the joint committee of the Economic and Fiscal committees of the Knesset. The law provided for the establishment of the Water Rates Adjustment Fund, to be coordinated by the Water Commissioner. The purpose of this fund was to reduce the variation in water rates across the country by taxing consumption in low-cost regions and subsidizing consumption in high-cost regions.[28] As a result of these measures, the price of water was essentially the same no matter where you lived in Israel. The clear beneficiary of this bureaucratic arrangement has been Israeli agriculture. Each agricultural enterprise was assigned a water quota by the IWC but the price was highly subsidized, with prices for agriculture use set on a progressive scale. In 1994, for the first 50 percent of the quota, the price was 13 cents/m^3, between 50 and 80 percent of the quota, the price jumped to 17 cents/m^3, and for the last 20 percent it rose to 21 cents/m^3. If the agricultural consumer used more than 100 percent of the quota the price increased considerably, to about 70 cents/m^3, providing a strong incentive to stay within the assigned allocation. In periods of drought the IWC had the responsibility to reduce agricultural allocations in order to maintain the water balance. For example, after the relatively dry winter of 1993–94 agricultural allocations were reduced 10 percent.[29]

Water charges for the domestic sector in Israel were much higher than for the agricultural sector. After a price rise approved by the Knesset Finance Committee in April 1994, households paid, on a bimonthly basis, about 65 cents/m^3 for the first 8 m^3 rising to $1.40/$m^3$ after 15 m^3. Industrial users paid about 24 cents/m^3. The difference in the price of water between sectors reflected the power of the agriculture lobby in Israeli politics. It also presented a barrier to Israeli concessions in the final status water negotiations with the Palestinians. By one estimate Israel subsidized the agricultural sector on both sides of the green line by nearly $200 million per year.[30] It was difficult to believe that the core conglomerates and others with vested interests in maintaining this subsidy system would suffer the costs of restructuring lightly or without making a significant appeal to the electorate (see Bichler Chapter 12).

Officially, Israel does not support price discrimination: 'most certainly not on the basis of the religion or nationality of users'.[31] However, interviews with Palestinian water utilities officials revealed a very different story. In the territories, unlike in Israel, the price varied according to local municipality practices, the area's topography and hydrological conditions, the physical circumstances of the distribution network, and the ratio of locally produced water to water purchased from Mekorot. Arab towns and villages without an alternative to purchasing water from Mekorot paid a higher rate than Israeli consumers – Mekorot sold the water to ICA for nearly twice the price it charged local Israeli utilities.[32] ICA, in turn, sold the water to Palestinian utilities at an additional 50 percent mark-up.

In the spring of 1994 the price of water sold to the Palestinian utilities was about 65 cents/m^3, essentially the same price paid by Israeli domestic consumers for their first bimonthly 8 m^3. When the utilities added charges for overheads (up to 60 percent in some municipalities) and other fees, the cost for Mekorot water came to three times the price for which it was sold to ICA. For example, the price paid for Mekorot water by the Jerusalem Undertaking's, Ramallah District came to about \$1.30/m^3, while locally produced water typically cost 40 to 50 percent less. Thus, the overall price per m^3 of water delivered to Palestinian consumers was heavily dependent on the ratio of Mekorot water to locally produced water. In this case, the consumers' price came to about \$1.05/m^3. In real practice, Mekorot delivered the water directly to the Palestinian utilities and the sale by Mekorot to ICA is merely a paper transfer involving minimal clerical expense for the occupation authorities, but it adds significantly to the cost of water paid by Palestinian consumers. Unfortunately, this system of price discrimination was not addressed in the Taba Interim Agreement. But, if, in fact, a profit is being made from these 'sales', it violates the international law of occupation. Palestinian water specialists asserted that the money generated through this practice was subsidizing settlements and army activities in the West Bank, but no evidence supporting this charge has been documented.[33]

As with the consumption of water, the greatest inequity in the price of water came in relation to the settlers. Because settler costs were heavily subsidized by the World Zionist Organization, they paid a significantly lower price for water than either Palestinians or Israelis within the green line. According to figures compiled by the Israel State Comptroller for 1986, settlers paid one-third what Palestinians paid for domestic consumption of water, while the cost for agricultural consumption was one-fifth the Palestinian cost.[34] Ironically, a number of West Bank Jewish settlements had their water delivered by Palestinian utilities. For

Table 8.2   Comparative water prices

	Israel	West Bank/Palestinians	West Bank settlers
Domestic price	0.65*	1.00	0.33
Agricultural price	0.16**	1.00	0.16**

Notes: The prices are transformed to US dollars from Israeli shekels.
*price of first 8m^3 on a bimonthly basis.
**average cost per m^3 on total annual quota.
Sources: See note 35.

instance, the Jerusalem Water Undertaking, Ramallah District supplies four settlements in its region. The settlers were charged a price only slightly less than that paid by Palestinian consumers (approximately 92 cents/m^3). However, an interesting part of this administrative system was that money never changed hands. The utility's charge for this water was deducted directly from its payment to the Civil Administration for Mekorot water. It was thus impossible for either the Palestinian managers of the utility or other interested parties to ascertain exactly what the settlers themselves paid for the water. One estimate put the price of domestic water for West Bank settlers in the spring of 1994 at 33 cents/ m^3, which would have been about the same ratio to Palestinian cost as that given by the Israel comptroller for 1986 (see Table 8.2).[35]

The foregoing analysis leads one to believe that Israel's water policy in the territories has been motivated more by political rather than by environmental or economic concerns, as Israeli officials contend. Israeli restrictions on Palestinian well drilling, agricultural development, and consumption and access to drinking water have been justified in terms of the long-term protection of water resources and economic necessity. But these policies were not applied even-handedly. The prices charged even for drinking water were grossly unequal. During drought conditions Palestinian population centers often received water only one day a week while the water flowed continuously to the settlements next door. Environmental protection and economic growth concerns could not explain this kind of gross inequity in Israeli water policies in the Arab territories it occupied militarily, and over which it continues to exercise ultimate control.

The Taba Interim Agreement and the road ahead

Given the discriminatory nature of water policies during the occupation, the extent of the Israeli concessions in the 1995 Taba Interim

Negotiations were not widely expected to succeed. While the water dispute had been addressed in Oslo I, only statements on cooperation were made and nothing specific was decided. The Cairo Accord, which established the Gaza-Jericho autonomy area, gave the PA 'limited' control over water resources. Under that Accord, the PA gained management rights over water resources in autonomous areas, including the control over existing wells and the right to drill new ones. Israel retained control over wells in settlement blocs and military installations, but agreed to restrict water consumption to present levels and to provide the PA with information on monthly consumption and on the number of wells drilled in these blocs. Both sides agreed that exchanging data was necessary in order to prevent the further deterioration of the aquifers. These arrangements, however, failed to address the primary Palestinian demands. From the outset of the negotiations, the Palestinians had charged that they wanted equitable access to water. Their basic position was that their water rights must first be recognized by the Israelis before more advanced negotiations on sharing could take place. They felt these rights included the ability to resume drilling in PA-controlled areas, the cessation of Israeli drilling in these territories, and access to Israeli water-tables data.[36] Once these rights were provided, the Palestinians said they would be willing to discuss a jointly managed and equitable utilization formula. As one Palestinian negotiator at both the bilateral and multilateral talks told me, 'what we ask for is a water charter for the region that is accepted by all riparian users in the region. If a peace agreement is to last, water resources must be shared in an equitable fashion.'[37]

Israeli negotiators refused to address new drilling in the territories and they were adamant that access to the three mountain aquifers was non-negotiable.[38] Israel based its negotiating position on the international law principle of prior use. Throughout the negotiations the Israelis asserted that they had a legitimate right to the water because of their long-term development interests in these sources, dating back, they claimed, to springs sunk by Jewish farmers during the British Mandate. Since 1948 the Israeli government has invested over $30 billion in water resources development. Thus, Israelis felt the principle of international customary law, which, for example, protects Egypt's claim to Nile River water, also applied to their claims. They stated that the Helsinki Rules of 1966, which delineate the rights to riparian areas of water courses, and the more recent supplement passed in Seoul in 1986, specifically concerning groundwater, should be used in determining resource allocations. The Palestinians counter-charged that Israel had overextended its rights by preventing, by the use of military force, access to water resources. Israeli negotiators responded that Israel's allocations had not changed significantly since the 1950s, aside from the additional amounts going to West Bank settlements. These additional utilizations, Israel pointed out, came from the eastern basin mountain aquifer, not previously used by Arabs in the region. Rather than negotiate water volume division, the Israelis proposed a cooperative management approach for developing new sources of water.[39]

However, after some time the rhetorical exercises quieted and positions softened. The water accords of the Taba Interim Agreement represented a major shift from previous Israeli negotiating positions. First, while a permanent agreement on the issue was deferred until the final status talks, these accords represented a significant step toward accommodation. Most far-reaching was Israel's formal recognition of Palestinian water rights in the West Bank. While the meaning of these rights was to be negotiated in permanent status talks, and while the Palestinian claim to an allocation of Jordan River water was not mentioned in the agreement, the formal acceptance of Palestinian rights was more than most observers expected.[40] Second, the parties agreed to cooperate on the management of water resources and sewage systems 'while respecting each side's powers and responsibilities'.

Cooperation encompasses not only the management and development of water resources but also the exchange of relevant data. In order to accomplish this goal, they agreed to establish a Joint Water Committee (JWC) for the interim period to oversee and coordinate all 'issues of mutual interest in the sphere of water and sewage'. Responsibilities given to the JWC include: the licensing for drilling of new wells; the increasing of water extraction from any water source; the developing and updating of annual extraction quotas; the coordination of the management of existing systems; adjusting the levels of extraction in the event of drought or other natural conditions affecting water supply; and planning the construction of new water and sewage systems. Each side was to have equal representation in the JWC and veto power since all decisions are to be reached by consensus. In order to enforce these decisions, Joint Supervision and Enforcement Teams (JSET) would be created to inspect and monitor the utilization of water resources in the West Bank. The third and final principal agreement on water recognized the need to develop additional water sources for Arab–Israeli joint use.

Implementation of the agreement called for transferring the power and responsibilities over water and sewage in the territories to the PA, but ICA would retain responsibility for systems supplying Israeli settlements. Furthermore, Israel agreed to the immediate availability of an additional 28.6 mcm/y of water for domestic use by Palestinians in the West Bank and Gaza during the interim period. From its own water system Israel committed to supply the Palestinians 9.5 mcm/y, including 5 mcm/y for Gaza. The remainder was to be developed by the PA from the eastern aquifer. Both sides agreed that the total future need of the Palestinians in the West Bank would come to between 70 and 80 mcm/y for both domestic and agricultural use. This supply would be developed by the Palestinians from the eastern aquifer, slated for their exclusive use, and other West Bank sources to be negotiated in the final status treaty. In order to assist the implementation of these provisions Israel agreed to make available all the relevant water data collected by Tahal and other government agencies. Regarding water purchases by one side from the other, the purchaser would have to pay the real cost of the production of the resource. The means for development of new water resources was not addressed in the agreement, but Israel promised to present desalination proposals at the final status talks. The JWC was charged with setting one price that reflects the real costs of source development.[41]

Perhaps the most controversial provision of the water accords in the Taba Agreement was the joint Israeli–Palestinian–American Committee on water production and development. While the specific role of this committee was not made clear in the agreement, other than to facilitate projects agreed to by the JWC, it appeared to be a means to generate both American mediation on hard-to-resolve questions and to generate US funding. Because of their mutual distrust Peres and Arafat decided to establish a trilateral committee. In an interview with the *Jerusalem Post*, Avraham Katz-Oz suggested that because Israel recognized that the PA would be suspicious of any Israeli action regarding water management, they thought it best to involve the US. According to Katz-Oz, the Americans would be asked to set water prices and perhaps to take part in JSET inspections. Both sides clearly looked to Washington to contribute significantly to funding the large projects necessary to produce additional water and help to enlist further support from the EU and Japan.

While praised by outsiders, the Taba water accords had their critics. For instance, Palestinian critics, while they welcomed the recognition of water rights, charged that the agreement did not go far enough, providing the territories with far less water and addressing only current needs.[42] Israeli critics, equally sharp, called the reallocation 'a give away of our water to the Arabs', in the words of Dan Zaslavsky, who became Israeli water commissioner in 1992. Another former water commissioner, Meir Ben-Meir, criticized the joint management provisions, suggesting that the Palestinians could not be trusted with the safeguarding of water resources. 'Mutual management', he argued, 'is not mutual responsibility; someone has to be boss.' Other Israeli critics feared that American involvement could lead to the US dictating the terms of a permanent status water agreement which may be highly disadvantageous to Israel.[43]

Conclusions: what to expect

The result was a shift from a tight structure of Israeli control to a flawed structure that could not be controlled. The lifting of Israeli military authority in the Gaza-Jericho autonomy area following the Cairo Accord in May 1994 led to the uncontrolled drilling of private wells, by one estimate over 200, to meet pent-up demand.[44] This was sure to create conflict in the newly autonomous Palestinian areas of the West Bank. For one thing, under the terms of the Taba Agreement the JWC had to give approval for any new drilling in the territories. Given the importance of these water resources to both parties it was unlikely that any new drilling would be allowed by the JWC that was not previously allowed, making it inevitable that abuses could not be controlled.[45]

Moreover, inequalities remained between Israelis and Palestinians in water consumption and particularly in the price paid for that water. While each side, according to the negotiations, was eventually supposed to pay the same price for water, Israelis continue to pay a much lower rate. Mekorot water supplied to settlers continues to be heavily subsidized by outside sources while the additional amounts of water Israel is supplying to the PA under the terms of the Taba Accord's is sold at the real cost of the water. Israel has refused to subsidize the water going to the Palestinians. According to one Mekorot official, 'if they want subsidized water, let them ask the United States'.[46] While this problem is being discussed between the agriculture ministers of Israel and the PA, it is the type of question that must be resolved before a permanent status agreement can be achieved.

Israeli authorities at least acknowledged the highly unequal nature of water utilization during the occupation and accepted the idea that steps must be taken toward bringing water consumption into balance. Yosef Ben-Dor, Israeli Foreign Ministry official and coordinator of the Israeli delegation to the multilateral water working group, commented to me that 'for us, it is obvious that if the Palestinians do not have enough water, we shall not have peace'.[47]

In its acceptance of Taba provisions, the PA also appeared to realize that it would not achieve full control over the mountain aquifers and that a peaceful outcome of this dispute must involve a mutually managed and shared natural water resource supply system.

Five years later, the same questions remain: What further steps toward equity are the Israelis willing to take? What limitations will the Palestinians be willing to accept in the permanent status talks? For a sustainable agreement to be reached, Israel must definitively accept the fact that Palestinians have a right to an equitable share of the region's water supply, and they should outline a program of action aimed at achieving this goal. The PA must accept the fact that Israel depends on West Bank water and has a legal and historical right to a proportional share of that water. Moreover, a sustainable agreement will only be achieved when both parties are willing to go beyond legal and historical debates over often-minute divisions of the already scarce water supply. The final agreement must include a program for full cooperation and mutual management through an expansion of the JWC's role. Instead of arguing over 'rightful' national allotments, negotiators should recognize the individual minimum requirements needed by the people residing in the entire region. Only then, when both sides recognize that water security (and indeed peace itself) depends more on human well-being than on political (or religious) priorities, will permanent peace be achieved.

Notes

1. See S. Lonergan and D. Brooks, *The Economic, Ecological and Geopolitical Dimensions of Water in Israel* (Victoria, BC: University of Victoria, Centre for Sustainable Regional Development, 1992) p. 72; J. Dillman, 'Water Rights in the Occupied Territories', *Journal of Palestinian Studies* (Autumn 1989) 52; R. Shehadeh, *Occupier's Law: Israel and the West Bank* (Washington, DC: Institute for Palestine Studies, rev. ed 1988), p. 153; and United Nations, 'Water Resources in the Occupied Palestinian Territory' (New York: UN: A/AC.183, 1992) 39.
2. UN, 'Letter dated 10 October 1984 from the Permanent Representative of Israel to the United Nations addressed to the Secretary-General' (New York: UN, A/C.2/39/7, 1984), 7–8.
3. Interview with Abdel-Karim Asa'd, Director of the Jerusalem Water Undertaking, Ramallah District (March 1994). An interview with Danny Adar, chief water official in the Civil Administration in the West Bank, was requested but refused.

4. T. Naff, testimony before the House Committee on Foreign Affairs, 26 June 1990, published in 'The Middle East in the 1990s: Middle East Water Issues' (Washington, DC: House Committee on Foreign Affairs, 1990) 153; Tahal Consulting Engineers, 'Israel Water Sector Study' (Tel-Aviv and Washington, DC: Report submitted to the World Bank, 1990) 13–17; 'The World Bank, Developing the Occupied Territories: An Investment in Peace', Vol. 5: 'Infrastructure' (Washington, DC: World Bank, 1993) 55.

5. See Tahal Consulting Engineers, 'Israel Water Sector Study', 13; and Ben-Gurion University of the Negev and Tahal Consulting Engineers, 'Israel Water Study for the World Bank' (Washington, DC: World Bank, 1994), pp. 3–7. This view was communicated in an interview with Jehoshua Schwarz, senior water engineer at Tahal, Israel's water planning company (April 1994). The higher consumption figures are cited by T. Naff, 'The Jordan Basin: Political, Economic and International Issues', paper presented at the World Bank International Workshop on Comprehensive Water Resource Management Policies (Washington, DC, 1991), 10; and J. Kolars, 'Water Resources of the Middle East', *Canadian Journal of Development Studies* (Special Issue, 1992) 113–14. Some Palestinian geologists give a figure for Israel of upwards to 2500 mcm/y. See A.-R. Tamimi, 'Water: A Factor for Conflict or Peace in the Middle East', Israeli–Palestinian Peace Research Project Working Papers, (Jerusalem: Winter, 1991/92) 12–13.

6. Again Israeli and Palestinian scholars disagree. According to M. Benvenisti, West Bank agricultural water consumption was frozen at 20 percent above 1967 levels. See 'West Bank Data Project: A Survey of Israel's Policies' (Washington, DC: American Enterprise Institute, 1984) 14. In contrast, S. Elmusa claims Palestinian agriculural water use fell after 1967. See, 'Dividing the Common Palestinian–Israeli Waters: An International Law Approach', *Journal of Palestine Studies* 22 (Spring 1993) 64.

7. Comments on irregular supply were made in interviews with Abdel-Karim Asa'd (March 1994). Also see the World Bank, 'Developing the Occupied Territories', 52. On 'access usage' see Palestinian Hydrology Group (February 1994); The Center for Engineering and Planning, 'Land and Water Resources in the Occupied Palestinian Territories' (Ramallah: ESCWA, 1992) 27; and 'Water Resources in the Occupied Palestinian Territory', 63.

8. The 'denials' mentioned here come from interviews with Jehoshua Schwarz (April 1994) and Shmuel Kantor, a senior consultant at Mekorot (May 1994). On 'over-pumping', see 'Report on the Management of Water Resources in Israel' (Jerusalem: State Comptroller of Israel, 1990). See also S. Gabbay, 'Focus: The Impending Water Crisis', *Israel Environment Bulletin*, 14 (Spring 1991) 3–11.

9. Again, estimates differ greatly. N. Beschorner cites F. Zach, Israeli Deputy Coordinator for the Territories in 1990, saying per capita settler consumption was 354 cubic meters. See 'Water and Instability in the Middle East', No. 273, *Adelphi Paper* (Winter, 1992–93) 13. Alternatively, A. Mosely Lesch gives a 1990 figure of 1600 cm/p/y. See 'Water Policy in the Context of Palestinian Self-Government', address to 'The First Israeli–Palestinian International Academic Conference on Water' (Zurich, 1992) 5. In an interview with Abdel-Karim Asa'd (March 1994), I was quoted 450–600 cm/p/y, which seems to be a realistic figure.

10. Interview with Raja Shehadeh, Palestinian legal scholar (March 1994). Also see Shehadeh, *Occupier Law*, pp. 153–4; and J. el-Hindi, 'Note: The West Bank Aquifer and Conventions Regarding Laws of Belligerent Occupation', *Michigan Journal of International Law*, 11 (Summer 1990) 105–8.
11. Interview, March 1994.
12. Israeli Foreign Ministry 1982, 3. Also, interview with Moshe Yisraeli Israeli adviser to the Water Commissioner, Gideon Tsur (April 1994); and 'Letter from the Permanent Representative of Israel to the United Nations addressed to the Secretary-General', 8 and 17.
13. Interview, February 1994.
14. T. Naff, 'The Jordan Basin', 5.
15. Interview with Shedadeh Dajani, General Manager of the Arab Development Society in Jericho, March 1994. Also see 'Developing the Occupied Territories', 48.
16. Testimony by T. Naff to the House Committee on Foreign Affairs (June 26, 1990) *The Middle East in the 1990s*, p. 187.
17. Interview with Schwarz, April 7, 1994. Also see H. Shuval, 'Approaches to Finding an Equitable Solution to Water Resources Problems Shared by Israeli and Palestinians over the Use of the Mountain Aquifer', in G. Baskin (ed), *Water: Conflict and Cooperation* (Jerusalem: Israel/Palestine Center for Research and Information, 1993), p. 42.
18. H. Awartani, 'Artesian Wells in Palestine' (Jerusalem: Palestinian Hydrology Group, 1992) in Arabic; and S. Lonergan and D. Brooks, *Dimensions of Water in Israel*, p. 73.
19. State Comptroller of Israel, *Report on the Management of Water Resources in Israel* (in Hebrew).
20. Interview with Ayman El-Rabi, Associate Director of the Palestinian Hydrology Group, October 1993.
21. On 'drinking water' see W. Claiborne, 'West Bank Dry Well is a Sign of Distrust', *Washington Post*, October 4, 1979. I also interviewed Martin Sherman, of Tel-Aviv University and Senior Advisor to former Minister of Agriculture Rafael Eitan (December 1993), on this issue, and took an inspection trip with Muhamad Sbeih, from ANERA (March 1994). Also see, J. Stork, 'Water and Israel's Occupation Strategy', *Middle East Report*, 13 (July–August 1983) 22.
22. These comments are based on two interviews and an inspection tour, one with Sami Daoud of the Palestinian Hydrology Group Nablus field office (February 1994), and another with Thawki Issa, Associate Director of Land and Water Establishment, a Palestinian legal defense organization (October 1993). Also see J. Peres, 'In parched West Bank, valuable water ignites latest fight', *Chicago Tribune*, August 13, 1995, 4; D. Makovsky and J. Immanuel, 'TV report prompts cabinet to discuss water supply in areas', *Jerusalem Post*, August 20, 1995, 1; and H. Awartani, 'Artesian Wells in Palestine', p. 7.
23. For 1990 see, State Comptroller of Israel, 'Report on the Management of Water Resources in Israel'. On refugee camps see S. Roy, *The Gaza Strip: The Political Economy of De-Development* (Washington, DC: Institute for Palestine Studies, 1995) pp. 164–5.
24. I. Shawwa, 'Water Situation in the Gaza Strip', address to 'The First Israeli–Palestinian International Academic Conference on Water' (Zurich, 1992), 4; and S. Elmusa, 'Dividing the Common Palestinian–Israeli Waters', 63.

25. Interview with Jonathan Kuttab, Palestinian lawyer (January 1994); Roy, *The Gaza Strip*, p. 165.
26. 'Transmissivity' refers to water volume transmitted horizontally through an aquifer. Sandstone aquifers such as that of the coastal aquifers have relatively low transmissivity while the properties of limestone aquifers, like a mountain aquifer, are often highly transmissive. As a result, the range of interference in sandstone aquifers is only one to two kilometers while it is much greater in limestone ones. Interview with Jehoshua Schwarz, April 1994.
27. State Comptroller of Israel, 'Report on the Management of Water Resources in Israel', 12. Also see M. Benevenisti and S. Khayat, 'The West Bank and Gaza Atlas' (Jerusalem: The West Bank Data Project, 1988) 26.
28. Tahal Consulting Engineers, 'Israel Water Sector Study', (Tel-Aviv and Washington, DC: Report submitted to the World Bank, 1990) 52.
29. Comments on 'assigned allocations' come from interviews with G. Fishelson, Professor of Economics at Tel-Aviv University (January 1994), and S. Leshem (March 1994). Also see, 'Water prices rise sharply', *Jerusalem Post*, December 13, 1993. The figures given in the text have been converted from shekels (NIS) to dollars for convenience of the reader. I discussed 'draught' polices with Moshe Yisraeli (April 1994).
30. First see, 'Household water prices to rise by 7–10%', *Jerusalem Post*, April 27, 1994; On the economics of water in Israel and the water disputes with its neighbors, see D. Wishart, 'An Economic Approach to Understanding Jordan Valley Water Disputes', *Middle East Review*, 21 (Summer, 1989) 45–53; and H. Zarour and J. Isaac, 'The Water Crisis in the Occupied Territories', Paper presented to the VII World Congress on Water, Rabat, Morocco, 1991, 12.
31. UN, 'Letter from the Permanent Representative of Israel to the United Nations addressed to the Secretary-General', 18. This denial was reiterated to this author by an official representative of Mekorot; Interview with S. Kantor (May 1994).
32. These and the following descriptions are based on interviews with: Abdel-Rahaman Tamimi, November 1993; Abdel-Karim Asa'd, March 1994; and Taher Nasserddin, March 1994. Also see 'Developing the Occupied Territories', 57–9.
33. Interview with Raja Shehadeh (March 1994). Also see, J. el-Hindi, 'The West Bank Aquifer and Conventions Regarding Laws of Belligerent Occupation', 1405–19. Comments on 'subsidized settlements' came from an interview with Abdel-Karim Asa'd, March 1994.
34. State Comptroller of Israel, 'Report on the Management of Water Resources in Israel', 12.
35. Interview with Abdel-Karim Asa'd, March 1994. The 'price' estimate was made by Abdel-Rahaman Tamimi, General Director of the Palestinian Hydrology Group, in an interview with the author (May 1994). Requests for information on the price paid for water by West Bank settlers were made to officials of Mekorot, Tahal and the Civil Administration in the spring of 1994, but all my requests were refused.

    The figures in Table 8.2 come from the international agency sources cited in notes 4 and 5, along with Israeli comptroller of Currency Reports cited above. These figures were discussed in interviews with G. Fishelson, A.-K.

As'ad, S. Leshem, and J. Isaac, which have also been cited herein. Readers should also note that the prices listed above are estimates based on 1994 extrapolations from comparative data in earlier published sources. One of the most difficult problems was to find out in Israel the true price of water paid by Jewish settlers in the Palestinian territories. Officials at the offices of the Water Commissioner, Mekorot, and Tahal all refused to give this author any figures. Other Israelis interviewed said they did not know, while Palestinians interviewed suggested extremely low figures but could not provide documentation for their estimates. The figures listed above are those which appear closest to the correct ones.

36. Interviews with Jad Isaac, Chair of the Palestinian delegation to the multilateral environmental working group and Director of the Applied Research Institute in Bethlehem, November 1993; and Ryiad El-Koudary, Chair of the Palestinian delegation to the multilateral water working group and president of Al-Azhar University in Gaza, December 1993.

37. Interview with Marwan Haddad, Palestinian water negotiator and professor of engineering at An-Najah University in Nablus, December 1993.

38. Ze'ev Schiff, 'Water Dispute Deferred', *Ha'aretz*, September 8, 1995, 1 (in Hebrew).

39. The above argument is based on H. Shuval, 'Approaches to Finding an Equitable Solution to Water Resources Problems Shared by Israeli and Palestinians Over the Use of the Mountain Aquifer', 51–7; E. Benevenisti and H. Gvirtzman, 'Harnessing International Law to Determine Israeli–Palestinian Water Rights: The Mountain Aquifer', *Natural Resources Journal*, 33 (July 1993) 557–62; and interviews with Elisha Kally, former Tahal official and currently Director of Be-Ezra Consultants in Tel-Aviv, December 1993, Avraham Katz-Oz, former Deputy Minister of Agriculture and chief of the Israeli delegation to the multilateral water talks, February 1994, and Jehoshua Schwarz, April 1994. The argument was supported by interviews with Avraham Katz-Oz, February 1994, and Eyal Benevenisti, law professor at Hebrew University, February 1994. See also E. Benevenisti and H. Gvirtzman, 'Harnessing International Law to Determine Israeli–Palestinian Water Rights: The Mountain Aquifer', 561.

40. At one of the multilateral water committees the previous year the Israeli delegates had agreed to use the term but had made it clear that this did not presume a formal recognition of legal rights. See Z. Schiff, 'Water Dispute Deferred', 1.

41. S. Rodan, 'Divided Waters – Part II', *Jerusalem Post*, September 1, 1995, who is also referred to in the following paragraph.

42. E. Fletcher, 'Israel, PLO make deal on West Bank water', *The San Francisco Examiner*, (21 September 1995) A-19.

43. Steve Rodan, 'Divided Waters – Part II'.

44. Communication with author from Gershon Baskin, Director of the Israel–Palestine Center for Research and Information, Jerusalem, July 1995.

45. BBC, November 22 1995.

46. 'Palestinians: Israeli water too expensive', *Jerusalem Post*, 29 December 1995.

47. Interview (April 1994).

9

Between Egypt and Jordan: Diverging Paths on Foreign Aid and Reform in the 1990s

Bradley L. Glasser

Scholars have long recognized the potentially negative impact of foreign aid on economic and political development in non-industrialized states. In the early 1990s, John Waterbury observed that infusions of external capital – including US foreign aid and donor contributions from the international community – had enabled the Egyptian government, for example, to forestall critical economic reforms in the late 1970s and early 1980s, a situation that continued throughout the 1990s and now on into the twenty-first century.[1] Subsequently, scholars of the development of 'rentier states' have argued that exogenous revenues, such as foreign aid or high levels of oil revenues (as in the Gulf states), insulated many Middle Eastern rulers from political opposition, enabling them to deflect pressures toward economic and political liberalization.[2] Among these are Michael Fields, who, in Volume I of this series, pointed out the converse observation that countries without oil resources or access to huge amounts of foreign aid, such as Morocco and Turkey, have pursued both economic structural reforms and political liberalization.

In the late 1980s and throughout the 1990s, tremendous shifts in provisions of foreign aid to select Middle Eastern countries had dramatic effects on those countries' economic and political lives. In Jordan, the collapse of foreign aid and remittance revenues prompted the monarchy to reinstate a parliamentary election process and to initiate an unprecedented political liberalization program. Meanwhile, in Egypt, an extraordinary increase in foreign aid receipts encouraged the Mubarak regime to crack down on opposition leaders in the country and to significantly scale back plural party movements, political liberalization, and further limit the electoral process.

In comparing these cases, this chapter underscores the obligation of donors to consider the effects of foreign aid on encouraging the process needed for building democratic participation and sustainable economic development. I seek to extend the conceptualizations of rentier-state literature (or 'rentier-by-proxy states' see Wright, Chapter 7) by arguing that foreign aid flows may well have a critical impact on parliamentary life. In concrete terms, foreign donor flows have contributed to the emergence in Jordan – and to the demise in Egypt – of a substantial opposition. In recent years, Jordan has moved toward establishing meaningful multi-partyism while Egypt has moved away from it.

In the late 1980s and early 1990s, Jordan and Egypt approached economic reform and relations with aid-granting governments, other international donors (UNDP, for example), and world financial assistance institutions (the World Bank, IMF, IFC, and so on) from dramatically different perspectives. During the 1970s, both Egypt and Jordan sought to avoid far-reaching economic reforms and were able to do so by relying on substantial exogenous revenues. They maintained liquidity via remittance revenues from the Gulf states and averted economic crisis. In the 1980s, Egypt became the recipient of massive US aid contributions because of the Camp David Accords, allowing it to further insulate itself from economic structural adjustment and political reform. But Jordan was not a beneficiary of this agreement. With oil pices and remittances declining by the late 1980s, most of Jordan's exogenous resources had nearly evaporated. In turn, the Jordanian state experienced a crippling fiscal crisis that compelled the monarchy to reach a sweeping accommodation with international financial institutions. Equally important, Jordan's more general economic crisis precipitated a powerful political crisis and forced it to reach watershed agreements with donor governments and international financial institutions (such as the World Bank and the International Monetary Fund). The government responded by extending significant political liberties and establishing a meaningful parliamentary process.

By contrast, in the late 1980s and early 1990s, Egypt had much greater exogenous resources and, therefore, averted the political and economic crises that rocked Jordan. Because it received extraordinary amounts of US and other foreign aid, the Mubarak regime had few incentives to engage in a risky economic restructuring, or to offer its population increased political liberties in exchange for its acceptance of budgetary austerity. Government-funded patronage employment is especially important in Egypt because the scale of it is several times larger than in Jordan. Its influence is even greater than Colton describes in her chapter on labor shocks in Jordan. Indeed, from a relatively secure position, the regime engineered the demise of the significant parliamentary opposition that had existed in the 1980s.

The contrast between the two countries' approaches to reform is especially interesting in that both have been grappling with painful economic reforms. For example, economic crisis has prompted Jordan to implement far-reaching political reforms. In the late 1990s, it significantly altered its trade regime structure, leading to the signing of a Free Trade and Investment Agreement with the US in 2000. Meanwhile, exogenous windfalls 'papered-over' Egypt's economic problems and left the Mubarak regime free to repress its opposition during a disruptive period of economic austerity. It avoided reforming its trade regimes, resulting in requests for embarrassing WTO extensions and a failure to reach a US Trade and Investment Framework Agreement.

Jordan: from economic crisis to political reform

The search for foreign aid contributions has long been a defining feature of Jordan's diplomatic and international relations agendas. For most of its existence, Jordan has relied heavily on grant-in-aid, bank loans and other forms of external budgetary assistance. Until the late 1980s, rather than expanding a resource-poor domestic economy, the monarchy used its geopolitical strategic position in the Arab–Israeli conflict to garner external assistance from the Gulf states. Therefore, observes Laurie Brand, the state 'gradually evolved as primarily a distributor or an allocator (of the rents collected from outside) rather than an extractor of resources from within'. In this sense, the state enjoyed 'relative autonomy from the input of societal forces'[3]. The royal government was thus able to maintain a highly repressive ruling order – at least as long as it provided its citizens with a relatively high standard of living through the distribution of external rent.

Accordingly, before the electoral opening of 1989, parliamentary politics had never developed in any significant sense in Jordan. By and large, when operative, the parliament was a 'rubber-stamp' institution that provided legitimacy to royal edicts by passing them into laws. However, it wrote little new or progressive legislation and had little influence on state policy. It certainly did not function as a meaningful forum for debate, effective dissent, or open political expression. In 1957, the regime banned political parties, leaving popular and professional interests with few avenues for political participation. The parliament was suspended in 1974 and was replaced in 1977 by an even more ineffectual National Consultative Council, whose members were appointed by King Hussein. In 1984, the regime reconvened the parliament. But by 1985, the perceived need for political repression increased – this time partly due to fears of Islamist resurgence in the electorate and partly due to growing quarrels with Jordan's Palestinian population. Elections slated for 1986 were indefinitely postponed. A government crackdown on remaining pockets of political pluralism, especially among the Palestinians, continued into 1988.

But recasting the Jordanian political landscape in 1988–89 was an economic crisis triggered by a steep decline in foreign aid sources, especially those provided by the Arab Gulf states. The result was – and arguably remains under King Abdullah – the Arab world's most promising and far-reaching political opening. Unfortunately, many of the reforms made during this period, most notably increased freedom of the press, were taken to task once again in 1997, with the passage of laws forbidding journalists to criticize government actions, oppose royal family members' views, and so on. Interestingly, this law arose only months after the US promised to substantially raise its aid contributions seemingly as a reward for opening more trade with Israel. The implication was that increased Clinton Administration aid contributions allowed the Jordanian government to backtrack on reforms it put into place earlier in the 1980s and 1990s.

In order to place these movements into more appropriate contexts, one must realize that, throughout the 1970s and the early 1980s, Jordan received roughly one-half of its revenues in the form of foreign aid grants and loans. The next highest source of funds came indirectly via remittance revenues from Jordanians and Palestinians working in the Gulf states. Such aid contributions and access to external financial resources – mainly from the Gulf states but also from Western allies – were unquestionably the state's most important revenue sources. For most of the 1970s and 1980s, foreign aid enabled the state to maintain high levels of growth, expenditures, and consumption. But by 1988, the Jordanian economy slipped into a severe crisis, as foreign aid receipts fell to roughly one-third of their 1980–81 levels. Guest-worker remittance levels also began to fall dramatically during this period. By 1989, external aid capital accounted for only about one-quarter of government revenues.[4] As a result Jordan began to borrow more money than it could afford. This situation created such a budgetary burden that the state was forced to reach an accommodation with the IMF and international creditors and to impose a relatively severe orthodox stabilization program in 1988 and 1989.[5]

This sudden shift toward austere macroeconomic policies triggered a political crisis. Brand's words, 'the budget could no longer bear the regime's part of the political acquiescence bargain',[6] meant that subsidy programs and widespread employment patronage policies had simply become too expensive for the state to fund. As the government's distributional capabilities declined, the population asserted itself, sometimes militantly. Severe civil disturbances rocked the country in April of 1989, as thousands of Jordanians took to the streets in protest at the government's economic policies and its reductions in social services spending. There were two primary responses to this conflict. First, the regime took decisive steps to quash the protests. Second, however, and facing much international pressure to do so, the government made the risky strategic decision to engage in unprecedented political reform. It provided limited political liberties, released and pardoned political prisoners, and, above all, held parliamentary elections in late 1989.[7]

In the elections that followed, the most significant since 1956, at least 877 475 voters were registered and 647 candidates competed for seats in the parliament. Even though parties were still banned throughout the process, groups supporting individuals' election campaigns were allowed to operate. The polling was free in most respects. Indeed, Islamist candidates won a stunning victory, becoming strident opponents of the regime. The Muslim Brotherhood alone captured 22 of the parliament's 80 seats – more than any other faction – and allied with ten independent Islamists to form an Islamic bloc. Leftist Arab and Palestinian nationalists won 11 seats and pro-government candidates won 35 seats. The consequence of this election seemed to be far-reaching and, to many observers, significantly positive. With the 1989 elections, parliamentary opposition emerged for the first time as a powerful force in Jordanian politics. In addition, the process established sweeping new political reforms and seemed to influence the government to make changes in other areas which had been primarily controlled by the King. In 1990, the regime abolished anti-communist legislation, freed political prisoners, repealed martial law and allowed the licensing of political parties. By September of 1991, authorities had officially approved about 90 parties.[8]

Jordan's parliament was seen as one of the region's most important emerging democratic institutions after the 'reformed' multi-party elections in 1993. Some 1.2 million voters registered, and 536 candidates and 20 parties participated. In addition, 4.7 percent increase in the turnout of voters seemed to reflect increased trust in the regime's democratization efforts. A change to a one-person, one-vote system also served to reduce the number of Islamist parliamentarians and to increase the number of independent or pro-regime politicians who won in the election. Despite the protests of some activists, the 1993 polling, for the most part, was considered an important step in Jordan's socio-political democratization process.[9] In sum, the parliamentary body had been endowed with genuine policy-making powers, had been able to support consecutive open and free elections, and had come to express a level of multi-partyism not seen before in Jordan.

Meanwhile, despite the revival of parliamentary life, the regime did not relent in its implementation of economic orthodoxy. In the early 1990s, Jordan's receipt of exogenous revenues remained at low levels and liquidity declined substantially following the Gulf War. In facing these declines, the regime had no choice but to adhere to macro-economic austerity (see Table 9.1). Indeed, the structure of Jordanian state revenues experienced a transformation in the 1980s and 1990s that was both dramatic and difficult to bear.

As can been seen from Table 9.1, Jordan's domestic revenues rose from 46 percent of total revenues in 1980 to 86 percent in 1993.[10] In short, in response to the collapse of Gulf states aid and remittances, Jordan was forced to increase its revenues from direct and indirect taxation, with receipts from income and profits tax more than doubling in 1990, and with an overall increase in tax revenue of 59 percent in 1992.[11] As the then Finance Minister Hanna Odeh noted, the regime was attempting to shift Jordan from a 'consuming to a producing society' that would be less vulnerable to vagaries in foreign exchange.[12] After persuading East Bank loyalists that the economic reforms were unavoidable, the government successfully defended its development program in the 1989 and 1993 elections, winning a majority in each.

There was, however, some gerrymandering, which did affect the outcome of both elections. Indeed, the drawing of electoral districts, which discriminated against the urban vote and helped get loyalists to the monarchy elected from rural areas, worked against Islamists who opposed the regime's new economic orthodoxy and prevented them

Table 9.1 The Jordanian central government budget of the 1990s: external *vs* internal revenues (%)

	1990	*1991*	*1992*	*1993*
Domestic	79	75	86	86
Foreign	21	25	14	14

Source: Monthly Statistical Bulletin of the Central Bank of Jordan, as cited in The Economist Intelligence Unit's 'Jordan Country Profile' (1994–95) p. 28.

from obtaining an absolute parliamentary majority in 1989.[13] In the 1993 elections, the regime's electoral manipulations improved the standing of pro-orthodox loyalists, enabling them to form alliances with other political forces so as to marshall a conservative parliamentary majority. As in other democratizing states, such manipulations represented a successful attempt on the part of the regime to reconcile the exigencies of political and economic reforms.[14] In sum, the 'Jordanian glasnost', as the former foreign minister Taha Masri termed it, expressed the regime's interest in obtaining an electoral legitimation of its new development policies.[15] It resembled the reform process in rent-poor Morocco in that the coincidence of political and economic crises generated a substantive process aimed at liberalization that has been sustainable until now. Powerful crises compelled the regime to seek far-reaching electoral legitimation.[16]

Egypt in the 1990s: limited economic reforms, increased repression and a deluge of exogenous revenue

The maintenance of social welfare provisions and the ability to fund widespread public sector employment were critical concerns for the Mubarak regime throughout the 1980s. Following a period of instability in 1979–81, which culminated in the assassination of President Sadat, Mubarak sought to reconsolidate the government's control over the Egyptian polity. At the same time, Egypt was also experiencing rapid economic growth – about 8 percent a year in the late 1970s and the early 1980s. This was fueled almost entirely by newly-found oil sales and increases in construction that were funded by foreign aid rents and revenues.[17] These seemingly favorable economic conditions enabled the insecure Mubarak regime to legitimate its ruling authority by increasing its populist and statist expenditures. Moreover, it allowed the regime to postpone economic reforms pressed by the IMF and other western donors and creditors – portraying itself as a populist defender of the Egyptian masses.[18] In parliamentary openings in 1984 and 1987, the regime underscored its populist positioning and, by doing so, ensured that its own National Democratic Party (NDP) won majorities in the house. However, most of these now-elected leaders opposed the espousing of right-wing and neoliberal economic policies. In addition, the Mubarak regime prevented left-wing parties (that is, parties to the left of the NDP) from gaining any meaningful representation in parliament.[19]

In the late 1980s, mounting debt, declining remittances, and the collapse of oil prices caused a precipitous decline in Egyptian growth rates. As the 1990 parliamentary elections approached, the regime realized that it had to scale back its populist expenditures and adopt a more-serious neoliberal reform program. Thus, for much of the 1980s, exogenous revenues (in the form of foreign aid, loans, oil revenues and Suez Canal tolls) accounted for between 40 and 50 percent of Egyptian budget revenues.[20] The state slowly moved toward reforming the economy in the late 1980s, as its debts mounted and its oil revenues declined.

Even so, by 1990, the Egyptian economy was not in any sense in the throes of a crisis. In fact, Egyptian GDP grew at an annual rate of 4.7 percent between 1986 and 1992.[21] In the fall of 1990, as the US solicited Egyptian participation in the anti-Iraq coalition, the Egyptian government engaged in intense negotiations with its international donors and creditors. Ultimately, bending to pressure from international lenders, Egyptian officials agreed to implement economic reforms in exchange for an unprecedented exogenous aid and debt relief. These were somewhat limited in scope, however.

But unlike other Arab states – such as Morocco in 1983 and Jordan in 1988 – Egypt did not experience a foreign-exchange crisis that would leave it in a weak bargaining position. Indeed, regional geopolitics enabled Egypt to obtain generous financial arrangements from the international donor community. The Iraqi invasion of Kuwait and the security interests of western and Gulf states eased Egypt's cash-flow problems as new aid from these sources eviscerated the Mubarak regime's interest in political reform. Foreign aid to Egypt tripled during the three years following the Persian Gulf War. Before that, in the period between 1980 and 1989, Egypt received between US $1.29 billion and $1.79 billion annually. Now it had commitments for roughly $5 billion per year.[22] Additional concessions from western donors and creditors, including massive debt relief, also dramatically increased the state's resources. For example, after the Gulf War, the US and several Arab governments (mainly the Gulf states) agreed to cancel $13 billion worth of debt that had been used to buy military equipment (see Zunes's chapter in this volume for more discussion of the implications of such policies). Soon thereafter, the Paris Club of creditor nations promised the eventual cancellation of $10 billion worth of loans to Egypt in exchange for a promise of economic structural reform. Egypt, in essence, had become the world's largest foreign aid recipient, claiming more than 10 percent of the $45 billion in overseas assistance, which is distributed annually among 150 nations.[23]

In its appeal for more international aid during 1990, Egyptian officials argued that the Iraqi invasion of Kuwait might create a potentially destabilizing economic crisis in Egypt – that the Gulf crisis had perhaps cost Egypt as much as $9 billion. Labor market shocks and huge losses of remittance revenues were expected from the mass expulsion of expatriate workers from Iraq. To a lesser extent, declines in tourism and Suez Canal traffic were expected to decrease foreign-exchange receipts. In reality, the recorded reductions in such revenues were considerably less precipitous. The decline of expatriate remittances from the Gulf states created a $1 billion drop in the balance of payments during 1990. The impact of disruption to tourism and the Suez Canal traffic was considerably less substantial. These latter two revenue sources returned to healthy levels in 1991.[24] Meanwhile, massive aid, loans and debt relief from the international community vastly outstripped the decline in state revenues from remittances. Consequently, despite the serious losses resulting from the war, Egypt's exogenous resources increased dramatically.

The US, Arab donors, and international financiers have closely co-ordinated their aid efforts in Egypt to achieve three aims. First, their foreign assistance has been a reward for Egyptian participation in the Gulf War. Second, western (and Arab) donors have used massive assistance to buy Egypt's implementation of limited economic reform. Third, the donors have been concerned with the regime's political stability and the threat of militant Islamist movements, in particular. In attempting to finance Egypt's economic revival and confronting its enduring poverty and economic inefficiency, the donors have sought to ensure the security of a regime that serves as the cornerstone of a pro-West regional influence.[25] Their concerns, notably, have not included substantial efforts to promote political liberalization or democratization.

Foreign Aid: obviating political-economic crisis

To this effect, massive foreign aid infusions from donors, especially the US, prevented the cycle of economic crisis in Egypt as well as the precipitous political liberalization which often comes as a result of economic trauma – such as, for example, the type that occurred in Jordan. In 1990, because of the regional geopolitical crisis, Egypt was in a relatively strong position vis-à-vis its donors and creditors. It eventually extracted unprecedented levels of aid from the international financial community on comparatively lax terms that alleviated its need for economic austerity. The key point here is that Jordan liberalized both economically and politically, largely because it lacked exogenous revenue, and it needed simultaneously to impress potential international donor governments and pacify an increasingly distraught local population. Extreme fiscal pressures created a political crisis that the regime sought to defuse through democratic liberalization.

By contrast, Egypt was not brought into a substantive reform process through a destabilizing political-economic crisis. Rather, the Mubarak regime agreed to very limited economic liberalization measures in order to obtain extraordinary levels of exogenous resources, namely, increases in the levels of international aid that were allowing it to avoid the very changes being sought by the IMF and others. From the regime's perspective, such resources would in fact obviate the occurrence of the political-economic crisis that rocked states like Jordan and Morocco. Like Guillermo O'Donnell and Philipe Schmitter, among others, who theorized about the causes of political opening, it is asserted here that a regime, especially one with a more-or-less autocratic power structure, only liberalizes politically and promotes democratization in order to deal with political or economic crisis, or social chaos.[26]

Of course, crises in and of themselves do not necessarily prompt an authoritarian regime to liberalize. Yet, during the last two decades, a far-reaching crisis and state fiscal crisis, in particular, or at least partially, as Wilson points out, brought about by the end of Soviet foreign funding to key regimes in the region – provided the most propitious context for initiating political liberalization in the Middle East. Indeed, in those Arab countries most keen to reform, like Morocco and Jordan, and to a lesser extent Tunisia, the evaporation of exogenous aid resources pushed implementation of orthodox economic restructuring programs and initiation of significant political reforms.

Why did political liberalization increase in rent-poor Middle Eastern countries, compelled to reach far-reaching agreements with the international financial institutions, but decline as the relatively aid- and rent-rich Egypt implemented its version of neoliberal economic reforms? The Egyptian case demonstrates the ability of foreign aid flows to shape – or as easily to disrupt – non-industrialized countries' political development and liberalization processes. In the case of the Mubarak regime, before the advent of economic crisis, it apparently calculated that the acquisition of massive aid would alleviate political pressures on the regime and obviate the need to cope with issues related to economic reform or political opening.

Above all, unlike other Middle Eastern regimes, the Mubarak state moved toward economic orthodoxy while its control over the political system was still relatively secure. Indeed, during 1990 and 1991, as Egypt drew closer to the international financial community and began finding new sources of foreign assistance, the Mubarak regime was, in the words of one observer, 'without any serious challenger'. The secular opposition remained badly fragmented, and the power of the Islamists, particularly the Muslim Brotherhood, had also waned, largely because of disarray in the Islamic investment houses. Furthermore, during and after the Gulf War, the regime enjoyed broad popular support for its handling of the crisis and its stance against Iraq (which for years had mistreated its two million Egyptian expatriate workers).[27] In turn, the aid enhanced its position, halting movement toward increased political liberalization which had been prominent during the 1980s.

In fact, a limited closing of the political-electoral system took place in 1990. In deference to supreme court rulings that the parliamentary electoral laws were illegal, Mubarak dissolved the People's Assembly which had been elected in 1987. But in drafting new electoral codes, the regime designed a single-member electoral system that disadvantaged the interests of the major opposition forces, especially the Wafd and the Muslim Brotherhood. Most of the opposition boycotted the elections (weakening their own position) and the NDP ultimately obtained 91 percent of the seats. Consequently, in creating an electoral system that was obviously unacceptable to the major opposition forces, the regime effectively constricted the political liberalization process. The coincidence of the narrowing of political space and the new deluge of foreign aid illustrates the rentier-state thesis: namely, high levels of exogenous revenues may well mitigate against processes of political liberalization and democratization. In the end, a rentier windfall worked to constrict the Egyptian polity, whereas resource gaps served to liberalize other Middle Eastern states.

Foreign aid and vital electoral factions

Stagnation was the key feature of Egyptian politics during the 1990s. Under Mubarak, the NDP retained its institutional structure, notwithstanding minor cabinet shuffles and shifts in the regime's attitudes toward reform. Unlike Jordan and Morocco, Egypt did not experience the emergence of vigorous parliamentary competition. Nor did the NDP attempt to reform or reorganize its own management or power structures in any substantive way. The regime made provisions for the political participation of center-right forces in the 1980s, but did so only within the context of the opposition, and through the Wafd and the Muslim Brotherhood, in particular. The regime's indulgence of the Egyptian opposition in the 1984 and 1987 parliaments dissipated in the early 1990s, as aid increases freed its hands. With one opposition party, the leftist Tagamu, winning six seats in 1991, the parliament no longer functioned as a locus of meaningful competitive party politics.

The regime seemed to reach an important milestone in 1994, when it began what was obviously a renewed campaign to suppress the Muslim Brotherhood. By June of that year, most Brotherhood leaders had been arrested and placed in jail on charges of incitement against the regime or for complicity in terrorist attacks. The government seemed to be returning the organization to an illegitimate status, branding it a terrorist group for the first time since Mubarak reopened the political system in the early 1980s. According to Said Issam al-Irian, a senior Brotherhood leader:

> This is the first time the government has linked us to terrorism. It is a wide move by the government to curtail all forms of democracy. By narrowing the opportunities for democratic participation, the government is creating more problems than it is solving.

Another Brotherhood activist noted that the repression would make the movement more, rather than less, extremist, because members who had moderated their political positions and wished to participate in the parliament in the 1980s, have now became increasingly disillusioned; he added, 'What do you expect?'[28]

In addition, secular opposition members, who had advocated parliamentary participation in the 1980s, became increasingly alienated and distrustful of government actions in the political sphere in the 1990s. One prominent member of the Wafd's old guard, for example, maintained that the parliament is nothing but 'a branch of the dominant party'. It is his observation that the party's participation in elections under the Mubarak regime is probably 'pointless'.[29] That Wafdists have such opinions is predictable enough, given the demise of oppositional politics during the 1990s. However, it is also a far cry from the optimism they displayed in the mid-1980s, when party leaders openly supported the democratic election process and predicted, if only for propaganda purposes, that the New Wafd would eventually come to dominate the parliament and the polity.[30]

Surely, both independent politicians and NDP members of the parliament became considerably more sanguine about the body's prospects. They, of course, still presumed that the existence of parliamentary life signified movement toward a truer process of 'democratization'.[31] Consequently, some members supported the continuing operation of the body and seemed to believe the parliament would eventually become representative and inclusive of a vociferous debating assembly. One highly-regarded independent member argued that pressure from the US and from a young generation of educated, restless, CNN-watching Egyptians, would ultimately force the regime into expanding the nation's electoral processes. Like other members of the Egyptian political elite, they believed that the US is responsible for, and would promote, democracy in Egypt. From this viewpoint, economic dependence on the US and other industrialized nations and the consequent liberalization of the country's economic institutions, should that actually happen, could lead to prompt and increasingly autonomous social forces pushing for real political liberalization.[32]

Naturally, dissidents of this political process have tended to present a more realistic evaluation of the impact of foreign aid on political life in Egypt. In their view, genuine Egyptian democratic activity has, in fact, withered as a result of increasing US aid, which they see as the opposite of what might have been expected. In addition, while not necessarily opposing the Egyptian government's acceptance of massive foreign aid payments, prominent human rights activists remain particularly sensitive to the fact that aid increases the ability of the regime to stifle movement toward democracy, sometimes in inhumane and violent ways.[33] Their gloomy predictions that political stagnation would persist in Egypt so long as the regime is subsidized by unprecedented levels of external aid assistance, appear sound for the foreseeable future. In fact, it seems increasingly true now, given Mubarak's apparent reluctance to liberalize either political or trade regimes during difficult economic adjustment periods, which seem to be persistent.

Therefore, in view of the western donors' poor record of promoting democracy in the Arab world, and indeed its propersity for subsidizing more restrictive governments, the insiders' and independents' claim that external forces will push Egypt to democratize in the near term seem fatuous. Furthermore, the regime's inability or unwillingness to undertake restructuring projects like privatization, seems to ensure that those powerful social forces clamoring for more democracy will not be unleashed anytime soon.

The 1995 elections: chaos and thuggery

The parliamentary elections of late 1995 only reconfirmed the regime's lack of interest in establishing any significant multi-partyism. The government seemed to begin its campaign with a pre-election crackdown on opposition groups early, when it renewed its harassment of members of the Brotherhood. On 23 November, 54 Islamist professionals, including parliamentary candidates, were sentenced by a military court to between three and five years in prison. The regime then closed the Brotherhood's Cairo headquarters and arrested dozens of members, some of whom were activists managing election campaigns. The Egyptian interior minister, Hassan Alfi, asserted that the Brotherhood was a greater threat to the secure re-election of NDP members than were the Islamist candidates, some of whom were radicals pledging to wage a bloody campaign against the state for several years.[34]

These heavy-handed tactics and the ominous political developments that followed in response precipitated the bloodiest elections in the history of modern Egypt. Forty people were killed and between 400 and 700 were injured in a polling process that was later said to have been dominated by fraud, vote-buying, chaos, intimidation and sectarian violence. On 7 December the NDP won 317 seats, independents won 113 and opposition parties won 14. But the next day, 99 independents rejoined the NDP, giving it 416, or 94 percent, of the seats. Denouncing the results as invalid, the opposition called for new elections and for the dissolution of the new parliamentary body. In short, because of the many irregularities in the 1995 election, parliamentary politics became increasingly irrelevant in Egypt. For example, after this ballot the Egyptian Human Rights Legal Aid Center warned of a 'political explosion because the chances of peaceful change seem to be non-existent.'[35]

Meanwhile, and although the Egyptian GDP growth rate slowed to 1.5 percent, the state retained its access to extraordinary exogenous aid flows. Indeed, by 1995 it had amassed $17 billion in foreign-exchange reserves, which made the regime, observers noted, immune to demands from international financial institutions to reform the economy, open its trade regime, or promote its commercial sector.[36] IMF complaints about Egypt were that it had not addressed its exchange rate, its high inflation problems, or its government-led structure of spiraling public-sector wages; that industrial subsidy dependencies had not been changed; and that there was an almost complete lack of progress on establishing the privatization, trade liberalization, and civil service reforms that were promised.[37]

In a report to the 1995 Amman Economic Summit, the IMF expressed its displeasure with the Egyptian government's sluggishness in implementing economic reforms while applauding Jordan (along with Tunisia and Morocco) for leading economic reform efforts in the Arab world[38]. IMF attitudes toward the two countries underscored the divergence of the Jordanian and Egyptian paths toward reform. Since 1988, lacking the nonconditional funding enjoyed by its neighbors, Jordan had not had much leeway in its dealings with the international financial institutions (at least not until it signed agreements with Israel). In addition, in becoming increasingly reliant on domestic revenue sources (that is, taxation), the royal family had no choice but to acquiesce to popular demands for democratization. Thus, in Jordan the parliament became a useful venue for a wide-ranging debate about the scope and meaning of economic reforms. By contrast, in Egypt, exogenous windfalls gave the regime greater freedom of action in its dealings with the international financial institutions. Moreover, nonconditional funding to Egypt augmented the regime's political latitude, forestalling any manner of parliamentary accommodation with the opposition forces calling for increased democratization.

Unfortunately, Jordan was not been a paragon of democratic development or an icon of freedom of speech, especially since the passage in June of 1997 of laws clearly meant to restrict the press as well as stifle academic and other expressions of debate and free speech. And, before that, stung by vitriolic criticisms of his rapprochement with Israel, and in the wake of the assassination of Israeli Prime Minister Yitzhak Rabin, King Hussein formulated stricter laws governing freedoms of associations and the press in December of 1995. Even so, King Hussein's government did not decide to directly attack the electoral process it had allowed to grow in Jordan. Under King Abdullah, it remains the leading example of political liberalization in the Levant.

Therefore, from a practical point of view, Jordanian efforts toward political liberalization and Egyptian moves toward political repression are starkly different. In Jordan, the parliament has remained a meaningful mechanism of popular political participation and expression, even as the government has had its way with the institution. For example, although the parliament ultimately ratified Jordan's austere 1996 budget, debate over the government's economic policies and its handling of poverty and unemployment was heated.[39] This is evidence of a dynamically developing system.

In sharp contrast, Egyptian parliamentary life stagnated in the 1990s. Being supported by unprecedented levels of exogenous aid revenues, Egypt took a gradualist and often inconsistent and poorly planned approach to economic growth and industrial restructuring. Moreover, it refrained from developing any kind of vital electoral factions. During the 1990s, as foreign aid obviated the need to impose a sweeping austerity, the NDP did not attempt to use the parliament as a serious venue for political discussion and participation. Attempting to incorporate the major viewpoints of both the right and the left during the 1990s, the

NDP was content with its domination of a Lilliputian parliamentary opposition.

What can been seen most clearly from these cases is that fiscal crisis compelled the Jordanian regime to tolerate – and to develop – increasingly sophisticated electoral coalitions. Having ensured the dominance of a coalition calling for an unpopular austerity, the regime was also obliged to tolerate the activities of opposition groups. But in Egypt no such toleration was granted to the opposition.

Concluding comments: multi-partyism and political liberalization, amid economic austerity: the importance of conditionality?

Multi-partyism represents the substantive and (for the regime) risky dimension of a political system which is beginning to reform. In the modern Middle Eastern context of liberalizing authoritarianism, it suggests a support of substantive democratic accommodation with opposition forces. Ideally, multi-partyism implies some kind of power-sharing, a system which curbs the power of the ruling party or regime and which enables opponents of the established polity to participate in some aspects of a country's policy-making process. Presumably, this process has the potential to evolve someday into a genuine democratization. Moreover, in the short term, multi-partyism enables opposition groups to protect newly-extended political liberties, including freedoms of movement, speech, petition, dissent and so forth. As such, the regime in power sanctions and institutionalizes a delimitation of its control over the political process and, although to a lesser extent, the economic development process as well.

Thus, substantive multi-partyism emerges, because the regime believes that it signifies the best strategy for forging some kind of democratic bargain with a citizenry suffering from the effects of economic crisis and fiscal austerity. Its development in Jordan followed the evaporation of its exogenous aid resources, the onset of economic crisis, and the regime's acceptance of far-reaching neoliberal reforms. Of course, such a crisis does not guarantee that political reforms will take place (Iraq being a key example), but it does provide a favorable context for the regime's implementation of serious political liberalization and reform. Typically, the nature and severity of the impending economic crisis dictates the extent to which regime elites are willing to permit liberalization and democratization. A manageable challenge tends to translate into more limited reforms. Intense pressure (the collapse of a key revenue flow, for example) limits the ability of the regime elites to control political openings that are demanded by populations and opposition forces.

Patrick Clawson has argued that difficult economic circumstances have enhanced the prospects for democratization in the Middle East.[40] Indeed, the disintegration of external sources seems to create a particularly compelling crisis, because state elites must extract more internal revenues and reach a more substantial parliamentary accommodation with leading opposition groups. Conversely, this line of analysis underscores the negative aspects of massive aid to authoritarian rulers. Of course, the realist understands that the industrialized world's aid to Middle Eastern countries has historically not been oriented toward democratic development, but instead toward the promotion of geopolitical stability and, most recently, toward support of an Arab–Israeli peace process.

Rather, in countries like Egypt, massive foreign aid has been used primarily to preserve decades-old statist and authoritarian structures. At the same time, donors have considered aid to Egypt and other Arab countries as vital to supporting the Peace Process and maintaining a pro-western geopolitical order. As Zunes' chapter illustrates, the intense levels of competition that make up the defining roles of how this order will actually be implemented and ultimately controlled. And, since such massive amounts of foreign aid effectively decrease reformist pressures on a regime, the promotion of peace and the promotion of democracy seem to contradict one another. This thesis does not stand alone as several chapters in this volume, especially those by Roy (Chapter 11) and Sullivan (Chapter 10), point out. Massive aid packages to the Palestinian Authority have not led it to institute measures toward significant political liberalization or market reforms. Nor has it opened up to civil society or social services development programs. One is therefore led to feel that aid funding and real reform are in opposition. Lisa Anderson offers the conclusion that this opposition, 'presents genuine and important dilemmas for policy makers, faced with hopes not only for peace and democracy but also for a stable, pacific and democratic world that is inexpensive to create and maintain'.[41]

It is also worth noting that much of Israel's resistance to privatization has also been facilitated by US aid programs which make much of the regime's budget fungible and therefore spendable on subsidies for government-owned firms. Thus, by definition, the dilemma over a poor country's need for economic assistance and the potential for a regime to use aid funding in ways that essentially repress the reform process, defy facile solutions. There are other precedents in the region. As I have stated elsewhere:

> In each minimally-rentier state polity, the regime adopted a neo-liberal development strategy, and then privileged a center-right bourgeoisie in the political system. Thus, in response to economic pressures, and despite the difference in regime type, critical commonalties have existed in the opportunities afforded for political participation in the Moroccan and Turkish cases. Here one should note that in liberalizing Arab states, parliamentary life has in general assumed unprecedented importance during the 1980s and 1990s. … [as an example] In recent years in Kuwait, oppositional forces have achieved unprecedented success at the polls, the policy-making powers of parliament have become increasingly important and that this body has become critical in defending various political liberties. In Morocco, multi-party and oppositional participation in the Parliament became increasingly institutionalized and effective.[42]

The link between crisis and reform is clear. This chapter identifies a basic incoherence in western policies toward facilitating economic and political reform in the Middle East. This incoherence flows from the nature of the conditionality imposed upon foreign aid contributions to Arab states. In fact, it is through conditionality that the international financial institutions have forced some governments in the Middle East to take steps toward economic reform; conditionality has been the driving force behind the adoption of neoliberal reforms in many developing nations both inside and outside the MENA region. Indeed, donors have not flinched from using the provision of conditionality in foreign aid packages to impose harsh economic austerity and restructuring programs.[43] But fearing political instability, they have refrained from demanding serious political reforms from their Middle Eastern clients. Indeed, the foreign aid projects have often only delayed such political reforms.

Thus, notwithstanding the official lip service paid to the promotion of democracy, the array of industrial-world aid to the region should be intended, above all, to foster a friendly geopolitical environment and the implementation of neoliberal economic reforms. If international donors are serious about promoting democracy in the region, they must consider linking foreign aid to a regime's adoption of political reforms and its respect for civil rights. Conditionality should provide the regimes with incentives to develop forms of meaningful multi-partyism. That prescription may sound radical to some practitioners. Yet the provision of foreign aid sometimes has been premised on reformist concerns in other areas. The Bush White House and Powell's State Department is perhaps already recognizing the need for increased leverage in the Egyptian case.[44] More generally, however, practitioners might object that such a conditionality defies the rules of Realpolitik. But humanitarianism aside, nonconditional support of decaying authoritarian regimes undermines western interests, undermines business relationships, constricts trade opportunities, radicalizes opposition groups, and precludes peaceful regime transitions. This situation exacerbates, rather than mending, the Peace Process' structural flaws and, in turn, underscores the reasons for many of its crucial failures.

Notes

1. J. Waterbury, 'The Soft State and the Open Door: Egypt's Experience with Economic Liberalization, 1974–1984', *Comparative Politics*, 24, (1991) 68.
2. H. Beblawi and G. Luciani (eds), *Nation, State and Integration in the Arab World: the Rentier State* (London: Croom Helm, 1987).
3. L. Brand, *Jordan's Inter-Arab Relations: the Political Economy of Alliance Making* (New York: Columbia University Press, 1994) p. 82.
4. See Brand for another discussion, as well as Jordanian state revenue tables in V. Lavy and E. Sheffer, *Foreign Aid and Economic Development in the Middle East: Egypt, Syria and Jordan* (New York: Praeger, 1991); or R. Satloff, 'Jordans Great Gamble: Economic Crisis and Political Reform', in H. Barkey (ed.), *The Politics of Economic Reform in the Middle East* (New York: St. Martin's Press, 1992) p. 131.
5. The Economist Intelligence Unit, 'Country Report: Jordan' (1993).
6. Brand, *Jordan's Inter-Arab Relations*, p. 291.
7. A. Amawi, 'Jordan', in F. Tachau, ed., *Political Parties of the Middle East and North Africa* (Westport, CT: Greenwood, 1994) p. 266.
8. Amawi, 'Jordan', 267.
9. Amawi, 'Jordan', 269.
10. Economist Intelligence Unit, 'Jordan Country Profile', 1994–95, 28.
11. Economist Intelligence Unit, 'Jordan Country Profile', 1994–95, 28.
12. Satloff, 'Jordan's Great Gamble', 136.
13. Satloff, 'Jordan's Great Gamble', 143.
14. See R. Kaufman, 'Liberalization and Democratization in South America: Perspectives from the 1970s', in G. O'Donnell and P. Schmitter (eds), *Transitions from Authoritarian Rule: Comparative Perspectives* (Baltimore, MD: Johns Hopkins University Press, 1986).
15. Satloff, 'Jordan's Great Gamble', 143.

16. See my discussion of Morocco in 'External Capital and Political Liberalization: A Typology of Middle Easter Development in the 1980s and 1990s', *Journal of International Affairs*, 49, (Summer 1995) 70; Also see M. Fields in Volume I.

17. *The Economist* (7 April 1984) 65.

18. See my discussion of Egypt in 'External Capital', 64–8.

19. R. Moench, 'The May 1984 Elections in Egypt and the Question of Egypt's Stability', in L. Layne (ed.), *Elections in the Middle East: Implications of Recent Trends* (Boulder, CO: Westview Press, 1987) p. 57.

20. See my discussion of Egypt in 'External Capital', 53–64.

21. *The Middle East*, (July/August) 1995, 28.

22. W. E. Schmidt, 'A Deluge of Foreign Assistance Fails to Revive Egypts Stricken Economy', *The New York Times*, (17 October 1993) 10.

23. Schmidt, 'A Deluge of Foreign Assistance Fails', 10.

24. The Economist Intelligence Unit, 'World Outlook' (1991) 102.

25. Schmidt, 'A Deluge of Foreign Assistance Fails', 10.

26. O'Donnell and Schmitter (eds), *Transitions from Authoritarian Rule: Comparative Perspectives*, p. 16.

27. The Economist Intelligence Unit, 'World Outlook' (1991) 102.

28. Quoted in C. Hedges, 'Egypt Begins Crackdown on Strongest Opposition Group', *The New York Times* (June 12, 1984) 3.

29. Personal interview with Muhamed Asfur February 1994.

30. I. D. Abaza, 'Congratulations, Wafd', *Al Wafd* (in Arabic), (June 7 1984) 3.

31. Conversation with Muhamed Al Tuwab Al Mohandis (former NDP member of parliament) February 1994.

32. Personal interview with Mona Makram Ebeid. February 1994.

33. Conversations with Dr Muhamed Mandour, Sabir Ahmed Mahmud Nayal (head of the Cairo division of Amnesty International), and Abdel Rahman Al Zein (Amnesty activist) (December 1993 and January 1994).

34. *The Economist*, 'Vote or Fight', 2 December 1995, 38–39.

35. Quoted by the Arab Press Service, Diplomat News Service (18 December 1994).

36. *Middle East Economic Digest*, 2 June 1995, 28.

37. *The Middle East*, July/August 1995, 28.

38. *Middle East Economic Digest*, 22 September 1995.

39. Xinhua News Agency, 4 January 1996.

40. P. Clawson, 'What's So Good about Stability?' in H. Barkey (ed.), *The Politics of Economic Reform in the Middle East* (New York: St. Martin's Press, 1992).

41. L. Anderson, 'Peace and Democracy in the Middle East: The Constraints of Soft Budgets', *Journal of International Affairs*, 49 (Summer 1995) 44.

42. Glasser, 'External Capital', 66.

43. B. Stallings, 'International Influence on Economic Policy: Debt, Stabilization, and Structural Reform', in S. Haggard and R. Kaufman (eds), *The Politics of Economic Adjustment* (Princeton, NJ: Princeton University Press, 1992).

44. *The Middle East*, 'Opposition Denounces Election Farce' (January 1996).

10
Between the Palestinian Authority and Palestinian Civil Society: International Aid and the Peace Process

Denis J. Sullivan

During the 1990s, international donors committed billions of dollars to the government of Israel and the Palestinian Authority (PA) in order to sustain and further promote the Peace Process.[1] In addition to the need to support both of these political entities, donors find themselves facing two separate entities *within* the Palestinian community, both needing substantial help and both being key to the success of the Peace Process with Israel. In the early 2000s donors remain caught between trying to support, sustain, and otherwise develop political institutions and governing structures in Palestine, or to promote PA legitimacy, while not undermining the sectors that are the primary agents of development in the area: non-governmental organizations (NGOs).

For years, long before the Gulf war, NGOs have received hundreds of millions of dollars from donors – Arab, European, North American, and Asian – to fund their development work. However, since Israel and the PLO signed the Declaration of Principles donors have focused their attention and thus their funding on the PA. This means donors gave hundreds of millions of dollars directly to the PA so that it could pay the salaries of police and civil servants as well as pay for construction, research, feasibility studies, development and other projects necessary for the resuscitation (or actual *creation*) of an economy and infrastructure suffering from 28 years of occupation.[2] Unfortunately, the decision to support the newly established PA came at the expense of *Palestinian NGOs* (PNGOs) – which is to say donors robbed Peter to pay Paul by cutting down on or eliminating the funding provided to Palestinian NGOs in the past and transferring those funds to the PA.

In the early 1990s, PNGOs received between \$170 and \$240 million annually in development assistance, the vast majority of which came from bilateral and multilateral donors. These enormous sums indicated several things:

1. the extent of the need by Palestinians living under military occupation and economic abandonment;
2. the acknowledgment by the international community that Palestinians deserved *some* (however insufficient) restitution for the great injustices being done to them, often with complicity from some of the same donors;
3. the ability of Palestinians to work together in their own NGOs, to absorb huge amounts of money and put it to use in appropriate development, welfare, and reconstruction projects; and,
4. the trust these donors had in PNGOs to put their aid to adequate, if not exemplary, use.

This chapter analyzes the complexity of international donor interaction with elements of a would-be Palestinian civil society and the emerging institutions of a would-be Palestinian state. Notice, however, that in making this assertion Israel is not included in this diagram, even though its power over both the PA and PNGOs is significant. Ironically, Israel also has a voice because it is one of the donors to the PA (see Table 10.1). Rather, each of the three actors in this uneasy triangle influences the others. This chapter illustrates how each entity has its own locus of power even when theoretically committed to the same goal – Palestinian prosperity and development.

The function of NGOs in Palestine

Without a functioning state or independent economic system, for years Palestinians relied on their own ingenuity for delivering a wide array of relief and developmental services. NGOs are the institutional face of those efforts. These generally

> operate on the principle of voluntary social actions through which individuals and groups work together within a local framework, in many instances free of charge, to promote the welfare of society. They embody a strong element of political pluralism, for the members of these groups are of diverse political persuasions and come from different class origins and religious backgrounds.[3]

Table 10.1   Donor commitments to Palestinians in the West Bank and the Gaza Strip (US$ 000)

Donor	Pledges 1994–98	Commitments 1994	Disbursements 1994	Commitments 1995	Disbursements January–July, 1995
European Union	600.00	101.94	45.46	80.10	33.50
United States	500.00	73.13	69.23	83.85	61.32
Japan	200.00	84.04	57.04	40.00	21.75
Saudi Arabia	200.00	100.00	30.00	100.00	17.50
Norway	150.00	34.42	27.07	13.51	8.60
World Bank	140.00	30.00	2.00	20.00	8.87
Italy	80.00	15.06	5.26	18.48	4.13
Israel	75.00	4.00	1.50	6.50	5.00
IFC	70.00	3.80	3.80	15.00	0
Turkey	52.00	2.00	2.00	0	0
Netherlands	47.59	31.92	16.55	9.80	0
Denmark	43.25	42.90	15.25	0	4.37
Sweden	40.00	12.21	10.22	18.22	5.00
Switzerland	40.00	25.97	11.19	0	2.43
Germany	31.17	24.07	10.68	7.10	6.78
Arab Fund	30.00	30.00	0	0	0
France	25.68	13.36	3.68	11.58	1.46
Kuwait	25.00	25.00	8.00	0	13.00
United Arab Emirates	25.00	5.00	5.00	10.00	10.00
Others	172.77	93.68	65.08	76.90	10.64
Total	2547.46	752.50	389.01	511.04	214.35

Sources: AHLC & PECDAR, July 1995 (via InterAction, December 1995).

PNGOs began largely as welfare organizations in the 1920s and 1930s and developed into a full-blown sector after the Israeli occupation in 1967. This third sector developed further during the Intifada, which began in December 1987. By 1997, there were as many as 1500 PNGOs delivering health care, education, agriculture extension, housing, human rights and legal aid, charity/welfare, culture, as well as technical assistance and research.[4] In addition, there were some 200 International NGOs (INGOs) providing similar services to Palestinians, usually in co-operation with PNGOs. The NGO sector employed between 20 000 and 30 000 workers and their work directly or indirectly benefited hundreds of thousands of Palestinians annually. The American Near East Refugee Aid (ANERA) has the most extensive, but still incomplete, database of PNGOs available. They have located at least 800 PNGOs based on data they collected at workshops throughout Palestine, but they recognize that many did not participate in the workshops. ANERA's database, which also provides information on the regional NGOs, is summarized in Table 10.2.

While over 40 percent of PNGOs are headquartered in the Ramallah–Jerusalem–Bethlehem area, many provide services to communities and refugee camps throughout Palestine. Around the start of the Peace Process, the PNGO sector 'accounted for 60 percent of primary health care services, nearly 50 percent of hospital care, and 100 percent of disability care'.[5] Two PNGOs provided nearly 100 percent of all agricultural extension, research, and training; and about 30 percent of educational services were in private and/or charitable group hands. Kindergartens were almost all run by NGOs. Social welfare functions were provided by the vast majority of NGOs, including *Lijaan al-Zakaat* (Islamic 'tithing' committees), church organizations, *Jam'iyaat Khayriya* (charitable associations), women's committees, health clinics, and so on.

While the work of NGOs is, now and then, generally positive and important to sustaining Palestinian development, PNGOs can exhibit negative attributes. Many NGO members criticized their colleagues for lacking professionalism and sometimes poor planning. Factionalism was and is a significant problem facing NGOs and PNGOs. For example, too often if an NGO supportive of the Democratic Front for the Liberation of Palestine were established in a given village or town, Fatah would establish a similar NGO in order to maintain its relative support within that community. This tended to promote a plethora of NGOs in communities, some of which duplicated services and in some cases exacerbated funding problems.

Despite this factionalism, there remains considerable cooperation between NGOs providing similar services as well as across services.

Table 10.2   Distribution of PNGOs by region

District/Region	Minimum no. of NGOs	Approximate percentage of total
Gaza Strip	146	18.55
Hebron	100	12.71
'Middle' West Bank: Jerusalem, Ramallah, Jericho, Bethlehem	340	43.20
'North': Nablus, Jenin, Qalqilia, Tulkarem	201	25.54
Total	787	100.00

Source: ANERA (1994).

Solidarity is alive and well as the large number of networks and unions attests, as does the fact that NGOs continually demonstrate mutual support by joining forces on particular development projects. These unions and networks include, but are not limited to: eight unions for women's activities, two for education, two for agriculture, five primary unions for health care, one primary network for providing care to the aged, one also for providing services to disabled persons, one for conflict resolution, and one dedicated to monitoring local electoral processes. In addition, there are general unions, including the Palestinian NGO Network, established in 1994, with more than 40 members, and the General Union of Charitable Associations in Palestine, with nearly 400 members or approximately one-third of all PNGOs. Member organizations of these unions provide extensive services in literacy, financial aid (grants and loans), sports clubs, orphanages, day care centers, health clinics, and vocational training. The General Union, and its regional branches in Jerusalem, Hebron, and Nablus, has been increasingly active at co-ordinating these activities and traditionally has been a primary conduit of economic assistance from the PLO and Arab donors to their members. Despite extensive networking and cooperation among NGOs, divisions persist and the Peace Process has probably exacerbated some of the problems they face. As noted by Mustafa Barghouti, a leader in NGO health care delivery and research, with the signing of the Gaza-Jericho agreement in 1993, it was

> inevitable that there will be some polarization and differentiations in this broad-based sector [NGOs], especially in that some of the activists in this movement perceive their role as temporary and are waiting for the establishment of a Palestinian authority. Consequently, a proportion of what are considered NGOs today will be transformed into government organizations or will become part of the authority's structure.[6]

As the PA moved toward autonomy, the expectation was that it would take over many of the functions that NGOs have traditionally provided. For example, the Health Services Council ran as many as 62 clinics throughout the West Bank and the Gaza Strip until 1994, after which it agreed to merge its services base and its resources into the structure of the PA. In the process, its director joined the PA as Deputy Minister of International Cooperation. This is one example of the way in which the PA has absorbed PNGOs into its ruling structure.

However, while several dozen NGOs have joined ranks with the PA, the majority have not. Some have offered to give up their services and allow their new government to assume these functions. PA officials, however, generally declined such offers, telling NGO leaders that they would attempt to learn from the NGOs first before attempting to do what the NGOs have been doing successfully for years.[7] NGOs would continue to uphold the vast majority of relief and development work for the foreseeable future and thus were in further need of the donors' financial support. Even more so, they needed the PA's political support because it granted permits and operating licenses. Therefore, the PA and its agencies provided financial support as well as sagacious largesse, or, if it should choose to, the PA could remove NGOs (as some PA officials continue to say must occur) or approve draconian laws like it proposed in 1995 (see below). Or it could severely restrict the PNGO community's financial mobility and make its activities difficult to sustain. Beyond their vital contribution to social and economic development, NGOs – in Palestine as in most societies – were critical to political development, specifically as this pertained to promoting civil society, democratization, and popular participation.

Civil society

The term civil society encompasses a variety of concepts, including civility as well as citizenship, civil liberties, and *civisme*, a participant culture of activism, reason, and political engagement.[8] The term also suggests to many the notion of secularism. There is some concern whether civil society is an appropriate concept and framework of analysis to apply to Arab politics and societies. Some Arab scholars reject the concept as a western, and thus alien, notion.[9] Some western scholars have a similar concern about the applicability of this term, and democratization literature more generally, to the Arab World. Carrie Rosefsky Wickham suggests that

> recent developments in [several] Arab states do not fit comfortably within the democratization paradigm. [Rather] they suggest an alternative trajectory, one that reveals the specificity of the democratization model and challenges its utility as a general model of political change. . . . [C]ivil society is not merely a sphere outside government but rather one endowed with a legally mandated autonomy, involving legal rights and protections backed by the law-state.[10]

Eva Bellin, on the other hand, provides sound reasoning why the term should be used and, indeed, embraced:

> because it focuses our attention on despotism in all its incarnations and because it captures an ideal that Middle Easterners are actively struggling over (and for) themselves. . . .By retaining the term civil society we will combat the tendency toward Middle East exceptionalism and invite comparative, cross-regional analysis of this dynamic process.[11]

Moreover, the term civil society conjures up positive sentiments, at least in the minds of western audiences.[12] If western publics can somehow connect with Palestinian and other Arab publics because they can relate to feminist movements, business associations, human rights organizations, labor unions, professional associations, charitable works programs, religious activities, student organizations, and so on, so much the better. If civil society is useful in conceptualizing these non-governmental, non-violent, social, political, and economic activities, it should indeed be utilized, regardless of the cultural context. Norton and his collaborators provide sound scholarship on various Middle Eastern societies to demonstrate that civil society is not just an acceptable term, but is also a realistic (if still distant) objective for many states in the region. As Norton notes:

> [c]ivil society is more than a mixture of various forms of association, it also refers to a quality and civility, without which the milieu consists of feuding factions, cliques, and cabals. Civility implies tolerance, the willingness of individuals to accept disparate political views and social attitudes. . . . Unfortunately, civility is a quality which is missing in large parts of the Middle East. . . . The absence of civility counsels skepticism about the short-term prospects for democracy in the region; however, if the art of association, as de Tocqueville called it, can be learned, then the promotion of civil society is no less than the creation of the underpinnings of democracy.[13]

The absence of civility leading to factionalism and worse is unfortunately relevant to Palestine, especially as NGOs were forced to struggle against one another for dwindling aid dollars and against the PA for legal rights. This factionalism, however, need not overshadow the critical role the PNGO community as a whole has played in sustaining service provision and development for Palestinians throughout the West Bank and Gaza Strip.

In this increasingly uncertain and evolving climate, especially in the absence of an established state (normally seen as a prerequisite for building civil society), it has been difficult to define civil society in Palestine, but it is easy to acknowledge that PNGOs constitute an essential foundation upon which a developed Palestinian civil society could be built. Thus, autonomy for Palestinians along with the establishment of the PA, is a double-edged sword for PNGOs, which faced new and somewhat unexpected opportunities and challenges after the Peace Process changed the structure of aid. The two biggest challenges facing PNGOs were: (i) that their rights as legitimate organizations were being threatened as the PA decided how to govern, regulate, and contain the extensive NGO community; and (ii) that aid dollars were being threatened as donors switched from funding NGOs to funding the PA directly.

NGOs, the PA, and international donors

As the Peace Process evolved, NGOs faced drastic changes to their mandates, resource bases, activities, and legal status. Since the signing of the Oslo Agreement in September 1993, NGOs working in the territories have experienced significant cuts in economic assistance, 'from $170–240 million at its peak in the early 1990s to barely $100–120 million' by 1995.[14] Of the latter figures, up to $90 million of that money came from international donors; up to $30 million came from local Palestinians and perhaps some from the Palestinian diaspora. As this funding continued to decline, PNGOs lost their ability to serve the communities that had come to depend on them, especially since the PA seemingly remains unable to replace those services. The PA became even more hard-pressed as it confronted the inevitability of taking over UNRWA-managed projects, which many officials assumed would see significant cuts and perhaps even be eliminated by the end of the century.[15] (See Table 10.3.)

NGOs had already had to reduce or eliminate services and lay off inordinate numbers of employees. Hatem Abu-Ghazala, the president of the Society for the Care of the Handicapped in the Gaza Strip, says the Society had to dismiss 180 employees and cut its Early Intervention Program services to 2500 children as a result of a US aid reduction amounting to $1.5 million in 1995; that aid was given instead to the PA. The president of the General Union of Charitable Associations claims his and many other organizations began collapsing as a result of the decline of Arab and private Palestinian donations. As an example, the Culture and Free Thought Association of Khan Younis in the Gaza Strip ran a Children's Center, a Teen Center, and a Cultural Center. The EC was its biggest donor but, following Oslo, it shifted its aid contributions to the PA. This meant a loss of 60 percent of this NGO's budget (over $200 000/year). For example, 39 employees went without salaries

Table 10.3   Palestinian socio-economic data, as of December 1994

	Gaza Strip	West Bank
Population	875 000	1 395 455
Unemployment	50%	30–40%*
No. of registered refugees (RR)	666 343	512 434
RR average anual growth (%)	6.0	4.9
RR as % of area population	76.2	36.7
RR in camps	370 849	131 532
UNRWA EXPENDITURES (US$)		
– Education	41 560 000	24 888 000
– Health	14 683 000	14 579 000
– Relief & social services	10 611 000	5 862 000
Income-generating loans provided by UNRWA (US$)	4 435 397	1 202 483
Illiteracy % (16–60+) age group	M 15% F 29%	M 16% F 26%
Infant mortality/1 000 (est.)	34	44

Source: UNRWA, December 1994.
*Near East Council of Churches places the unemployment rate for the Gaza Strip at 60–65 percent as of October 1995.

for several months. As NGOs throughout the Palestinian communities faced similar fates, demands for services only increased, especially given the high levels of unemployment and poverty. Whether and how the PNGOs and the PA would work together to solve these mounting problems remains a fundamental and nagging question.

Examining the PA's actions toward PNGOs is important for two reasons. First, the PNGOs are indispensable for the continuing development of the territories. Second, the way in which the PA has dealt with NGOs is an indicator of whether it will support civil society, democratic governance, and popular participation over the long term. A key example here relates to early attempts by the PA to place legal constraints on NGOs. During 1995, the PA began drafting, and in some cases approving, new laws concerning NGOs, elections, political parties, trade, the environment, freedom of expression and association, and so on. These drafts and laws were received with a chorus of rejection by interested Palestinian groups who felt that their years of struggle were being scorned as a new Authority imposed its will and drafted legislation without consulting the people most concerned. When there was consultation, it was often in the form of *Mukhabaraat* (secret police) seeking information from and about individuals and groups, information that was used to monitor, control, and/or subvert grass-roots, charitable, and developmental activities, not to encourage and support their expansion.

The PA needed to achieve a balance between regulating, policing and governing Palestinian society while trying to avoid their proclivities to control and thus stifle that society. However, competition within the PA between various ministries and other agencies often put the NGO–PNGO communities in the middle of bureaucratic and political turf wars.[16] NGOs were often uncertain of which ministry they should report to and register with. With the establishment of a ministerial steering committee to coordinate NGO activities and regulations surrounding them, PNGOs struggled to understand which ministry or ministries had ultimate responsibility for their activities. Potential overlords included the ministries of Health, Justice, Social Welfare, Education, Interior, Planning and International Cooperation, Culture and Information, and Transportation. Beyond the competition between ministries, the PA's police and security units also entered the fray.

In addition to oversight by the Ministry of Social Welfare, NGOs were being monitored by *al-mukhabaraat al-'aama* (general intelligence). Two questionnaires were distributed by the secret police and general intelligence squads in 1995. The first was a fairly innocuous one asking general information about NGOs and their board members. The second, however, was especially intrusive into the personal affairs of individual members associated with NGOs. For instance, the second questionnaire asked the following:

(1) Name of mother; her profession, social status, address.
(2) Individual's passport number, profession, height, color of skin, eyes, hair, blood group, distinguishing marks.
(3) Name of wife (before and after marriage); name of second wife; third wife; their mothers' names.
(4) Name of father, his occupation, other family income.
(5) Names of brothers, their professions and addresses.
(6) Names of sons and their professions.
(7) Other relatives' names.
(8) Names of three important friends (professions and addresses).
(9) Have you ever belonged to any Palestinian organization? Mention date and reason for leaving.
(10) Have you ever been a member in a political party? Name and Date.
(11) Has any of your family been charged with spying? Name and Date.
(12) Does any of your family members belong to a political party? Name of family member and name of party.
(13) Have you ever been imprisoned for political reasons or others?
(14) Write a personal report about events in your life.

Moreover, this questionnaire was not made public. Rather, the *mukha-baraat* threatened any organization that leaked its existence. This type of heavy-handed approach to governing NGOs in Palestine is one of many reasons why the PNGO community is so concerned. In addition to *mukhabaraat* monitoring, NGOs would be regulated by the Ministry of Social Welfare. To formalize this regulation, a draft law was prepared and nearly approved by President Arafat and his Council of Ministers.

Formulating the Draft Law concerning NGOs

That Palestinian NGOs would have to be regulated was never in doubt. This is a common procedure in most countries and it enables better coordination and management. How and when such regulation would occur, what form it would take, under which ministry, with what rights and responsibilities accruing to NGOs – these and other questions are still being considered within the emerging PA. The back drop for these talks began in May 1995, when formal contacts were made between the PA and the PNGO Network. The Network held workshops aimed at writing proposals for regulating NGOs. But in response, the Network received word that a draft law had already been written, by three men from the Ministries of Social Welfare and Justice. This was done without input from either local or foreign NGOs. The PA would not even show PNGO leaders a copy of the proposed legislation, making it the only draft law to date not made available to the public.[17]

What was soon discovered, however, was a draft law that sought: to restrict an individual from participating in more than one NGO; to prohibit an NGO from local and foreign contributions without prior approval of the Ministry; to prohibit an NGO from holding bank deposits in excess of one month's expenditures; to restrict an NGO from co-operating with any organization outside the jurisdiction of the PA; to grant the Minister of Social Welfare the right to dissolve any NGO, cancel permits, and initiate any type of regulation she/he sees fit to execute this law.[18] What was particularly frustrating about this restrict-ive draft law was that it came at a time when Israel had ordered the closure of three Palestinian NGOs based in Jerusalem. PNGOs, as well as the Palestinians they served, felt under siege from both Israel and the PA.

Fortunately, other agencies of the PA were more open to PNGOs and sought to establish cooperative relationships. Officials from PECDAR offered their own draft on how PNGOs should be governed. These officials, however, had a much different law in mind than did their counterparts in other PA offices. PECDAR distributed a working paper discussing principles that would indeed govern – in other words, regulate but not control – the NGO community in Palestine. PECDAR's draft made a point of praising the role of PNGOs in sustaining Palestinian society under Israeli occupation. It gave NGOs rights to establish, raise funds, and operate in ways NGO leaders chose, rather than in ways dictated by the Ministry of Social Welfare (as the previously mentioned draft insisted). But PECDAR's proposal was not seriously considered by the rest of the PA. Instead, the Ministry of Social Welfare wrote its own draft law. When PECDAR officials received a copy of the draft, their lawyers rejected it and concluded it would be better for NGOs to 'close up shop' than to live under this law.[19]

Prior to the establishment of the Legislative Council, laws were made by decree from the Office of the President, usually in consultation with the Council of Ministers. Laws could be changed, of course, once the Council took office. Rather than wait for this uncertainty, the PNGO community mobilized members and campaigned against the draft law on NGOs. As one of the organizers explained:

> We wrote papers, put ads in *al-Quds* [an Arabic daily paper], wrote a newsletter with a translation [English] of the law and an analysis of it, we asked friends in the international community to complain, some of us called ministers and asked them to reject this. Finally, Um Jihad [Minister of Social Welfare] called me and said to 'cool down, be patient, and stop your campaign against the law'.[20]

By mid-October 1995, a second draft law was distributed by the Ministry of Justice. Among the positive changes (in the view of many PNGOs and some international donors) of this second draft was introduction of a right of appeal by NGOs against the Minister of Social Welfare should the Minister decide not to allow an NGO to register; a right explicitly not allowed in the first draft. The right of appeal is especially significant, since otherwise the Minister of Social Welfare had the final say in allowing an NGO to register and provide services. The right of appeal gives the judicial branch a check on the power of the Executive Branch. More than anything, PNGO members were relieved that the draft had been delayed until further discussion. Their goal was to have the elected Palestinian Council decide on this important legislation.[21] The PNGOs were especially displeased, however, that they now had to get the approval of the Minister of Social Welfare to accept foreign assistance – rather then simply reporting such assistance to the Minister, as had previously been the case. PNGO members wondered why their own boards could not decide whether or not to accept money from a particular group. An official with the Ministry of Social Welfare (MOSW) responded: 'because we don't want Iran or other certain groups or countries sending money into Palestine to undermine us, the government and the society.'[22] Having received significant sums from foreign sources in the past, Hamas-supported NGOs have been the primary (but not the only) target of PA efforts to monitor and restrict grass-roots activism.

The effect of international aid on civil society, and democratization

The PA had its own international supporters. Foreign donors generally were supportive of PA efforts to control Palestinian society, curb violence, and develop the economy. Supporting such control may well have been diametrically opposed to supporting democratization, especially given the nature of the PA and its President, Yasser Arafat. Arafat walked a political tightrope as he attempted to prove to Israel that he could stop violence against Israeli targets while not alienating his populace so much that they shifted their anger toward him and his governing authority.

Yet, Arafat and the PA were already being compared to the numerous other authoritarian Arab regimes whose main efforts were directed to limiting the freedoms and stifling the ambitions of their populations. Part of this presumption of authoritarianism was Arafat's own tendency toward assuming total control and concentrating power (including an unwillingness to delegate responsibilities), following his experience of nearly 30 years as leader of the struggle for the liberation of Palestine. This assessment was partly an expectation by some Palestinians that, since other Arab regimes were too often dictatorial (albeit to varying degrees), this regime too would assume strict methods of rule.[23] It was also true that 'twenty-seven year occupation has naturally made Palestinians distrustful of authority' – *any* authority.[24]

Even more to the point was the practice of the PA while in power and especially of its various subunits – ministries and multiple police units, including the *mukhabaraat*. As these entities attempted to impose their will, their authority on the population of the West Bank and Gaza Strip, they consistently offended and often outraged the people who actually carried on the resistance to Israeli occupation for 28 years. Many of these new governors were returnees from PLO headquarters in Tunis and other offices, who were often dismissed as people who came in to reap the benefits of someone else's daily struggle against oppression and subjugation. This comment, from a PNGO leader, is characteristic of the views expressed at the time:

> If NGO existence is not recognized or supported by internationals, who will protect them? Not this Authority, not with this [proposed] law [governing NGOs]. We are willing to share the responsibility of laws with the PA. We are willing to build civil society. Arafat can have the power. No one from the opposition wants it! We want to, *need to*, build civil society and not go the way of traditional Arab systems![25]

Donors could and did act as a source of pressure on the PA, especially given their collective aid pledges of $2.5 billion (1994–98). The World Bank coordinated this aid from over 40 donor countries; the US pledged $500 million of this total (see Table 10.1) and raised the ante several years later at Wye. Given the PA's dependence on this aid, it was perhaps inevitable that international pressure became a factor in PA policy making. At the Donor Conference in Paris in October 1995, donors were prepared to criticize strongly the NGO draft legislation, which donors had criticized to NGO leaders and PA officials alike. Before donors could make this criticism official, the PA announced its plans to suspend further consideration of the draft law governing NGOs and said it would start over, this time in consultation with PNGOs.[26]

The demand side: field interviews on the need for foreign assistance

Perhaps even more pressing on PNGOs than the PA's proposed method of regulating them (they had, after all, survived Israeli occupation) was the PA's confiscation of financial resources. Leaders of most of the NGOs studied said they depended on aid for 80 to 100 percent of their budgets.[27] PNGO representatives were generally worried, even distressed, over the certainty of funding cuts from traditional supporters – INGOs and church groups, bilateral donors, UN and other multilateral agencies, and even individual philanthropists (primarily Palestinian business people). Of the $262 776 897 given in external assistance to the Palestinians in 1993, roughly $15 000 000 went directly to PNGOs in health care, education, agriculture, and social services development; indirect support for PNGO activities in these fields was substantially more. Overall, approximately 66 percent of this external assistance went to the social sector (education, health, social development and humanitarian aid), while less than 15 percent went to agriculture, employment, industry and trade.

Of the US $1 462 billion in donor pledges to the West Bank and Gaza, through June 1995, commitments to Palestinian NGOs accounted for only $51 million. Of this, $36 million (from the EU) was to pay for running costs of universities and community colleges. Of the total $51 million, $37 million was already fully accounted for. As universities, colleges, and hospitals continued to account for the bulk of support to NGOs, this left very little money for most smaller NGOs – health clinic NGOs were affected especially harshly. In 1993, according to the Health Development Information Project (HDIP) in Ramallah, there were 132 NGO clinics in rural West Bank communities. Two years later, there were less than 50. Mustafa Barghouti of HDIP said the reasons so many NGOs closed were, first, the shifting of funds from NGOs to the PA and, second, the move by some NGOs into the PA's structure.

In addition to the existing PNGO infrastructure facing overextensive downsizing, there were at least two other aspects of relief and development needs in the Palestinian community that required international support. The first was the UNRWA activities. As the world community promoted the development of Palestinian governance, there was an assumption, indeed an expectation, that UNRWA activities would be taken over by the PA. Just as the PA was in no position for the next few years of taking over the extensive activities of NGOs, so was it unable to replace the elaborate and extensive activities of UNRWA, especially in education and health care. Indeed, if UNRWA programs were downsized, their functions would likely be taken up by NGOs-PNGOs. If these groups were not sustained through international support there would be no capable set of institutions to attend to peoples' needs.

Exacerbating the problem of PA inability was PA inattention. As the PA negotiated with Israel on the status of the West Bank, the Gaza Strip, and Jerusalem, the PA's brand of autonomy was developing. However, while in power, its officials were in no position to replace NGOs as service providers, relief workers, development officers, and agents of change, in general. In some cases, NGO leaders had offered to turn their activities over to PA officials only to be politely or otherwise rebuffed by PA officials. According to Constantine Dabbagh, the Executive Secretary of the Middle East Council of Churches, one of the largest NGOs in the Gaza Strip:

> The PA was not yet in a position to take over the services NGOs provide. We tried to hand over our projects to them and they refused it flatly. We tried to give our 3 health clinics to the Minister of Health. He refused. He said he can't consider replacing us for the

next 3 years at least. It's the same story with the Ministry of Labor –
we tried to hand over our Vocational Training Centers. No way! We'd
be pleased to hand over our projects to the PA, but they cannot
handle these yet. (Ibid.)

The bottom line of the relationship between the PA and the PNGOs
was that the PA was in need of at least three to four years more to learn
the ropes of service provision – especially in health care, education,
social welfare, and agricultural extension – if they intended to provide
them at all. It also needed time to develop a cooperative relationship
with those NGOs that continued to provide the bulk of these important
developmental services. In the case of agriculture, for instance, many if
not most Ministry of Agriculture employees had worked for the Israeli
administration's Department of Agriculture. But they were not allowed
to carry out agricultural extension, land reclamation, veterinary services, and so on. Instead, those and other jobs fell to two principal
agricultural NGOs – the Palestinian Agricultural Relief Committees
(PARC) and the Union of Agricultural Work Committees (UAWC).
These NGOs continued to do 90 to 95 percent of extension and other
services. At the same time, they had to teach employees in the Ministry
of Agriculture tasks they had been doing for at least 10 years.

And yet, these NGOs suffered severe cutbacks in foreign assistance at
this time. UAWC has had to endure a cut from $550 000 in foreign aid in
1992 to less than $200 000 in 1994. Its representatives were worried that
UAWC would not survive until the year 2000. The failure of this one
NGO would represent a loss to the Palestinian agriculture sector of at
least 40 percent of important services, services that the Ministry of
Agriculture is unable to provide, now or in the foreseeable future. In
addition to the need for continuing the funding levels for agriculture
and education and health care, PNGOs were in need of additional
resources because, despite the Peace Process, the Palestinians' standard
of living declined throughout the 1990s. This was certainly true in Gaza,
where formal sector unemployment was estimated at 60 to 75 percent or
more by 1997/8. It was at least half this amount in the West Bank.

The supply side: a shift away from NGO support

Even as the demand for foreign assistance continued to grow, the supply
side of service provision shifted away from NGOs in an equally significant way. Governments and multilateral agencies began shifting
resources to support the PA and to avoid supporting NGOs for various
reasons, explained below. One main reason was the need to support the

Table 10.4 EU Assistance to Palestinian NGOs in selected fields, in ECUs

	1992	1993	1994	1995*
Agriculture	740 324	228 879	5 914	0
Health/emergency aid**	994 804	1 043 439	465 919	0
Education***	1 042 642	551 118	1 396 921	0
Environment/water	17 702	27 573	0	0
Women	337 269	92 297	32 396	163 521^
Total	3 132 741	1 943 306	1 901 150	163 521

* By 1995, EU assistance to Palestinians was channeled either through European NGOs or directly to the PA or to Universities, Hospitals, and other institutions (but not NGOs, as defined in this report).
** hospitals have been disaggregated.
*** universities have been disaggregated.
^ indirectly to PNGOs via European NGOs.
Source: EU.

PA as a means of demonstrating the benefits of the Peace Process. Related to this is the traditional relationship between donors and governments. When there was no Palestinian government, there was no question that PNGOs were the best alternative to receive foreign aid. Now that there is a Palestinian Authority in place, some agencies have made the decision to support the PA simply because it was an official governing body – not because it was seen as more capable than NGOs.

Traditionally, the EU had been a strong supporter of PNGOs. Yet, as of 1995, PNGOs no longer received direct assistance from the EU (with the exception of universities). Instead, PNGOs were forced to seek funding from European NGOs which propose projects or respond to proposals from their governments. Then, PNGOs found themselves competing not only with one another but with NGOs globally as these organizations also requested more support from European NGOs from the same funds. Changes in the level of EU support for PNGOs can be seen in Table 10.4. Still, even as overall international assistance increased markedly, the level of assistance to PNGOs declined and shifted from one recipient (that is, PNGOs, INGOs) to another (that is, the PA). More unfortunately, these funds were not redistributed to NGOS as they should have been. Additional aid is directed to the PA rather than divided between the governing authority and the grass-roots, social-developmental, and/or charitable organizations.

In a recent interview, an official from UNDP explained this trend:

Our top management is pushing us to work with the PA and no longer with NGOs. UNDP's mandate is to work directly with governmental authorities; we are an inter-governmental agency. But, before there was no government so we dealt directly with Palestinian NGOs. Now that there is a government, we are constantly under pressure by our bosses to give our money to the PA. But the employees are not happy about this because we've worked closely with NGOs, we know what they can do. And we know the PA can't replace NGOs. Now that we work with the PA, we see they know nothing about grass roots organization or development. UNDP funding has jumped from less than $10 million before 1994 to around $40 million this year. But 67 percent of this money is from Japan, so if this one nation decides to give money directly to the PA [which it is expected to do], we'll lose all that. For now, Japanese and other donors trust us more than they do the PA. But the PA won't stand for this. They'll get the money soon enough.[28]

A USAID official dealing with NGOs in the territories acknowledged that

> our percentage of aid to NGOs has gone down. State [i.e. the US State Department] is pushing for high visibility projects such as water to villages and other infrastructure projects. There is considerable pressure to spend the $75 million [USAID's current level of support to WB/GS] on infrastructure – 'demonstration projects' – not on NGOs. Our support of NGO activities ends in 1997 and there is no certainty about where we'll spend the money after that.[29]

Acting as conduits of assistance, International NGOs also had to decrease funding to PNGOs, but for different reasons. Since 1983, the Welfare Association had sent money to Palestinian NGOs (primarily) as well as to municipalities (somewhat). Between 1985 and 1995, such aid approximated $44 million (a figure that does not include the administrative costs of their operations in Geneva or the territories). Most of the money came from wealthy Palestinian businessmen and from Gulf states supporters of the Palestinians. Annual expenditures were around $5 million until the last three years. (In some years, due to emergency needs, the total was $8 million.) By 1996–98, because of the loss of support for Palestinians from the Gulf states, the Welfare Association provided only about $2 million annually to NGOs and municipalities in the PA-controlled territories.

Prior to the drop in aid, the Welfare Association supported projects in the fields of health care, education, culture, social and economic development. Post-1995, health care and economic development projects were no longer supported due to the lack of funds. The Association received scores of applications for support from Palestinian charitable associations and other NGOs but was able to fund less than 20 percent of those requests. This cut in aid from a traditionally important international NGO, albeit with considerable backing from the Palestinian diaspora, represented the loss to the PNGO community of up to $3 million annually for the last three years and for the next few years as well. The supply of foreign assistance to Palestinian NGOs thus shrank rapidly. This was a result of: (i) donors shifting their assistance to the PA

Table 10.5   Funding levels to Palestinians in the West Bank and the Gaza Strip, by type of donor (US$)

	1992	*1993*	*1994*^	*1995*^ ^
UN agencies*	116 161 576	48 598 321		
Multilateral**	15 249 000	75 486 214		
Bilateral	42 437 482	138 692 362		
Total	173 848 058	262 776 897	389 010 000	511 040 000

* UNRWA, UNDP, IFAD, UNCDF, UNICEF, UNFPA, WHO, ILO, UNESCO, UNIFEM, FAO, UNCTAD.
** EU, AFESD, AGFUND, Islamic Development Bank, NECC.
^ UN agencies treated as conduits of assistance after 1994.
^ ^ Commitments. Pledges were $667 330 000; Disbursements as of July were $214 350 000.
Sources: UNDP (1992 to 93); PECDAR (1994 to 95).

Table 10.6   Donor funding levels to selected sectors in the West Bank and the Gaza Strip (US$)

	1992	*1993*	*1994–95**
Education	69 215 934	79 570 830	78 500 000
Health	44 064 714	72 485 646	104 500 000
Social Welfare	25 547 451	33 722 969	0
Agriculture	4 149 364	8 425 117	5 000 000
Total	142 977 463	194 204 562	188 000 000

* PECDAR did not separate statistics for these sectors by year; rather, it discusses pledges and commitments to three new categories – Investment, Technical Assistance, and Start-up and Recurrent Costs. These figures were determined from charts, not precise numbers. No money was earmarked for social welfare.
Sources: UNDP, PECDAR.

and to INGOs/PVOs from their own countries; and (ii) the reduction in aid from many private and some governmental donors (such as some Arab Gulf leaders and states) as bilateral and multilateral support for the Palestinians – meaning the PA – increased.

Tables 10.5 and 10.6 demonstrate the trend in increased support for the PA coupled with the declining support for key development sectors, the principal domains of PNGOs. What is striking about these figures is that even as international assistance increased dramatically in the last two years, financial assistance to key development sectors actually dropped. Hundreds of millions of dollars have been redirected to housing, water, sewage, urban/municipal development, and so on. Social welfare did not even appear on the charts detailing the commitments of donor resources, although it was unlikely that this sector would be eliminated entirely. It was certain that agriculture, education, and health, in total, received less per year in 1994 and 1995 than they did in 1992 and 1993. This was further evidence of what NGO representatives had been saying individually and collectively – even though financial support to the Palestinians increased in 1994 and 1995. Donors were shifting their money away from NGOs in general and key development sectors in particular, toward the PA, and at a net loss to the community.

Conclusion

Funding levels to and expenditure levels by PNGOs have decreased substantially since the PA was recognized as a governing authority. Historically, the PNGO community had been dependent upon international assistance for the vast majority of their revenues. As they faced cuts from these sources, PNGOs attempted to develop more income-generating projects at home, but these could not entirely make up for the millions of dollars lost. Donors confirmed that there were more cuts to come. PA officials also acknowledge that, even with the increased resources now available to them, its ministries would not be in a position to provide the level of services that the NGOs had for the past decades. Because PNGOs have been severely restricted in their activities due to a combination of PA regulations and/or lack of resources, the social and economic situation of Palestinians has deteriorated. There remains a great need, perhaps a desperate need, for sustained support for PNGOs at this crucial and uncertain stage of political, social, and economic transition. There is also a political importance associated with the PNGO community. As Barghouti succinctly expressed, if the Peace Process's supporters 'want a civil society in Palestine, we can't have it without NGOs'.[29]

The economic and social dislocation that arose because the activities of PNGOs were severely limited was probably avoidable, had international support been maintained and expanded. International assistance was and is a necessary but not sufficient factor in achieving a prosperous future for Palestinians. These people also needed to develop a social contract between state and civil society in order to move beyond the mutual suspicion and distrust that was clearly evident between PA officials and members of society. International donors may pretend to be either uninterested or uninvolved in the development of this contract; the reality, however, has proven to be quite the opposite.

Among the three entities most committed to the development of a Palestinian economy – the international donor community, PNGOs, and the PA – the evidence from this research indicates that no one actor has been more powerful or significant than the others. The PA is in no position (now or even several years hence) to take over the development role of the PNGOs, but it has been in a position to thwart the latter's activities. PNGOs are not an alternative to the PA because they are not state institutions, but they can continue to provide essential public services indefinitely, or at least until the PA develops its own capacity. Donors have significant clout and the potential for pressure on the PA to promote certain policies, but donors' plans for the development of the West Bank and Gaza Strip will continue to come to nothing without the cooperation of the PA and PNGOs. In short, this troika of actors has tremendous potential to achieve its collective goal of socio-economic development as long as they remain mutually supportive. Similarly, if one of the three attempts to limit or undermine the power of another, the ultimate objective will be lost.

At present, international donors have demonstrated support – through substantial financial and technical assistance – for both the PA and PNGOs. But do PNGOs still accept the legitimacy of the PA and support the PA in its difficult task of governing Palestinians? Is the PA a cooperative third partner, with donors and NGOs, for development? PA policies to date would suggest that it is not, that it attempts to stifle PNGO activities, thus destroying a crucial partner for peace and development. Not only would economic development be prevented, but policies that aim to undermine PNGOs would, by definition, undermine attempts to develop a civil society in a future Palestinian state. If Palestine continues to be threatened with a restrictive and undemocratic regime (though no such claims are being made at present), the NGO community is in danger of having its laudable past forgotten, and of having its future discounted because of a regulatory environment that severely limits its freedoms and gives a new Palestinian government extensive powers over its activities.

This heavy hand of government was not inevitable, but there was a conflict of philosophy between donors and the constituents that has yet to be resolved.[30] The hope for the future state of Palestine comes especially from the leadership that has been involved in establishing, running, or working for NGOs: community centers, human rights groups, schools, health clinics, women's centers, charitable organizations, cooperatives, popular committees, and youth groups. This socialization is what must be continuously encouraged and developed if Palestine is to become a democratic state much as it tries to develop into a democratic society.

Notes

1. US aid to Israel amounts to between $3 billion and $4.5 billion annually. This economic and military assistance is often justified as being essential to keeping Israel a secure US ally, as it makes the difficult decisions for peace with its Arab neighbors.
2. See S. Roy, *The Gaza Strip: The Political Economy of De-Development* (Washington, DC: Institute for Palestine Studies, 1995).
3. M. Muslih, 'Palestinian Civil Society', in A. R. Norton (ed.), *Civil Society in the Middle East*, Vol. I (Leiden: E. J. Brill, 1995), p. 257.
4. Catholic Relief Services puts the number of NGOs at 1200, including unions, cooperatives, and clubs. The PNGO Network estimates there are 800 NGOs, excluding unions, cooperatives, and clubs. The Palestinian Center for Micro-projects Development puts the figure at between 1200 and 1500. The real figure is difficult to determine given the previous Israeli monopoly on statistics, and because there are a considerable number of 'licensed service providers' that are not registered as NGOs but whose work constitutes NGO activity.
5. 'Toward Middle East Peace and Development: International Assistance to Palestinians and the Role of NGOs During the Transition to Civil Society', by J. Zaucker, A. Griffel, and P. Gubser (Washington, DC: InterAction Occasional Paper, 1995) 17.
6. M. Barghouti, 'Palestinian NGOs and Their Role in Building a Civil Society' (mimeo, 1995).
7. Interview with Constantine Dabbagh, Director of Near East Council of Churches, Gaza, (27 November 1995).
8. Eva Bellin, 'Civil Society: Effective Tool of Analysis for Middle East Politics?' *PS* (September 1994) 510.
9. Egyptians especially have had much to say on this matter. Gehad Auda has shared with me his concern about the concept at a meeting in New York, March 1993. M. K. Al-Sayyid discusses other scholars' similar concerns in 'A

Civil Society in Egypt?', *Middle East Journal*, 47 (Spring 1993) 228–42. See fn. 7. S. Zubaida discusses contrasting views of 'civil society' in 'Islam, the State, and Democracy: Contrasting Conceptions of Society in Egypt', *Middle East Report*, 22 (November/December 1992) 2–10. Certainly there are Egyptians and other Arabs who have no difficulty using a civil society construct. Saad Eddin Ibrahim, of the Ibn Khaldun Center in Cairo, promotes the study of civil society both in Egypt and the Arab world through his publication of *al-Mujtama' al-Madani* (*Civil Society*).

10. 'Beyond Democratization: Political Change in the Arab World', *PS* (September 1994) 507–8. See also C. Rosefsky Wickham, 'Are the Islamists in Egypt part of Civil Society?' *Proceedings: American Political Science Association Annual Meeting* (Washington, DC 1993).

11. Bellin, 510.

12. 'Political culture' is another 'neutral' term that provides a useful framework, even if it occasionally gets applied in negative fashion against Arab and/or Islamic culture. See E. Kedourie, *Democracy and Arab Political Culture* (London: Frank Cass, 1994). For an assessment of how the Islamic movement has become an institutionalized process in Egyptian politics, see G. Auda, 'The Islamic Movement and Resource Mobilization in 'Egypt: A Political Culture Perspective' in L. Diamond (ed.), *Political Culture and Democracy in Developing Countries* (Boulder: Lynne Rienner Publishers, 1993).

13. A. R. Norton, 'Introduction', *Civil Society in the Middle East*, Vol. I (Leiden: E. J. Brill, 1995) pp. 11–12.

14. Zaucker et al., 20.

15. UNWA is the principal international agency working to provide assistance to Palestinian refugees throughout the West Bank, Gaza, and in the Middle East region.

16. The Palestinian Economic Council for Development and Reconstruction.

17. Interview with Rana Bishara, Coordinator of PNGO Network, Beit Hanina, 17 October 1995.

18. PNGO *Newsletter*, I, IV (September 1995), 2–14.

19. Interview, October 1995.

20. Interview, PNGO member, 24 October 1995.

21. Interview, PNGO member, 24 October 1995.

22. Interview, Ministry of Social Welfare, Gaza City, 18 October 1995.

23. I reject the cultural determinism explanation. Still, there is something to be said for socialization that perpetuates a *political* culture. For Palestinians, socialization has tended to be pluralist and democratic-populist because they have consistently strengthened the notion of solidarity in the face of repression. This 'culture' of struggle and popular participation is something the PA must either rein in or let loose as it seeks to work with (or against?) the community it now co-monitors with Israel.

24. A. K. Wing, 'Democracy, Constitutionalism, and the Future State of Palestine: With a Case Study of Women's Rights' (Jerusalem: PASSIA, 1995) 11.

25. Health Clinic Founder, supporter of Popular Front for the Liberation of Palestine, (one of various sub-groups that constitute the Palestine Liberation Organization). Interview, Bethlehem (27 October 1995).

26. Interview, Fritz Froehlich, Society for Austro-Arab Relations, 1 November 1995.

27. My research was conducted in October and November 1995 and involved distribution of a survey to, and interviews with, members of the PNGO Network as well as the General Union of Charitable Associations in Palestine. Of the 23 surveys I distributed to members of the PNGO network and the General Union of Charitable Associations in Palestine, six were returned. Interviews were conducted with: representatives from 26 different PNGOs; officials from various donor agencies (UNDP, USAID, EU, UNRWA); officials of the PA (Ministries of Social Welfare and Justice; PECDAR; Office of National Establishments/Institutions); representatives of international PVOs/NGOs (the Welfare Association of Geneva, ANERA, CRS, Society for Austro-Arab Relations). This research also involved collecting data from numerous sources and compiling a series of tables/charts that serve as 'answers' to several of the points you asked me to investigate.
28. Interviews in Ramallah, 27 November 1995.
29. Interviews in Ramallah, 27 November 1995.
30. Khalil Shikaki, Director of the Center for Palestine Research and Studies, made a similar point in a BBC news interview, 19 January 1996.

11

Between Hamas and the Palestinian Authority: Islamic Movements and Palestinian Development in the Gaza Strip[1]

Sara Roy

The dangers arising from Islamic fundamentalism in the Gaza Strip and West Bank are obvious: bombings and commitments to continue the armed struggle against Israeli occupation despite the signing of the Oslo agreements. The problem was true before the new Intifada of 2000 and it has heightened impact now. I will not address this except to say that the new conflict, at least in part, comes out of a social services structure that has crumbled over the past decade. The fundamental problem is that during the course of the Peace Process more people have become disenfranchised. This has led to more violence and radicalism, not less. The historic structure of 'fundamentalist terrorism'[2] has led to the idea that Islam and the West are somehow irreconcilably opposed to each other, resulting in what is referred to as the clash of civilizations, which assumes the Middle East and the West are two homogeneous entities lacking permeability, diversity, or nuance. No viewpoint could be more misleading.

In the Gaza Strip, where the Islamic movement is over four decades old, religious activism has been varied and complex, with a tradition of social, charitable, and development work within the Palestinian community that long predates the emergence of political Islam. Throughout, the work of the Islamic movement has been implemented through institutions engaged in the provision of social and economic services. Among the best known are *zakat* (alms giving or tithing) committees to which every Muslim should contribute; revenues collected are spent on a range of services for the needy. The *waqf* (religious endowment), another well-established Islamic institution, owns 10 percent of all real estate in the Gaza Strip, including hundreds of shops, apartments, and public buildings, which it rents. In addition, the *waqf* owns 2000 acres of agricultural land, portions of which are leased to farmers, and it employs people ranging from preachers to grave diggers.[3] These institutions are among the oldest and most effective Palestinian groups, promoting moderation and stability, not violence and disorder. They need to be distinguished from Islamic political and military organizations such as the often-mentioned Hamas (itself more diverse than portrayed).

Despite the disproportionate attention paid to the rise of political and militant Islam, the strength of the Islamic movement in the Gaza Strip has not resided in the work of political and military institutions, but in the work of their social and economic counterparts.[4] During the 1990s, Gaza's economy deteriorated and the business society became more fractured. Islamic social services and community development work has, therefore, assumed new significance in the post-Oslo period. Hamas may arguably be the Islamic movement's least important arm, especially now. The power of Islamic militants and the threat of a radical-Muslim takeover in Gaza has been consistently and grotesquely exaggerated by western governments and media; political Islam and its military wing in particular have never been less popular then they are today.[5] The uprising in 2000 was also in part due to frustration over how these groups have been treated.

Islamic social and economic institutions have been under serious threat for some time. Since Yasser Arafat came to power, he has been under considerable pressure from Israel and the US to suppress radical Islamic groups, notably Hamas, the largest of Gaza's Islamic political factions. His strategy seemed to be to divide the political from the military wing of Hamas; to weaken and possibly co-opt the political wing and eradicate the military wing; and undermine those Islamic institutions, including universities and charities, he regarded as sources of radicalism.[6] This last component represents an official change in policy; earlier Arafat practiced almost total non-interference in the affairs of Islamic social and economic organizations.[7]

Unlike attacks against the political and military leadership of the Islamic movement by the Palestinian Authority (PA), which growing numbers of Gazans no longer oppose, an attack against mainstream Islamic social and economic institutions would not be readily tolerated. Popular opposition to such state-sponsored attacks was increasingly widespread, fueled by those who either depended upon the services they provide or who perceive their work as crucial. Most critically, given the religious nature of Islamic institutions, any move against them was often perceived as an attack against Islam itself. The mass base of the Islamic movement in Gaza, as opposed to its political and military leadership, has been neither ideological nor radical. As Arafat's policies have been implemented, however, the results have led to greater fragmentation and disunity.

The consistent representation of all supporters of Gaza's Islamic movement as radical militants and of Islamism as monolithically subversive and terroristic has been a dangerous distortion of reality. In Gaza, and elsewhere, the relationship between Islamic institutions in the social-economic sphere and those in the political-military sphere was not nearly as ineluctable as believed. Despite certain cross-cutting ties of membership and affiliation between the two spheres, there have been important differences among those individuals who belong to the Islamic movement, especially with regard to the work they do, the clientele they serve, and the beliefs they hold. Could an unqualified political role be attributed to Islamic societies in Gaza as part of a feared Islamic design for seizing political power as argued by Israel and more recently by the US? Upon closer examination, the research strongly suggests that Islamic societies and social service institutions, and their developmental branches in the Gaza Strip, have been stabilizing forces. They are less dogmatically Islamic than has often been assumed (particularly the Islamic economic organizations) and their clientele belong to varied social classes having a wide range of political outlooks. They have never acted collectively in support of radical Islam. Finally, since the Intifada's end, and response to social and economic disintegration which has followed the implementation of the September 1993 Oslo Accords, the balance of power between the institutional forces of political and social Islam appears to have shifted toward the latter, as we see today, particularly at the grass-roots level, where most people interact with the movement and where need is most acute.

Features of the Palestinian Islamic Movement

Islamism is generally defined as the political expression of the Islamic movement. An Islamist is usually defined as a devout Muslim who seeks the establishment of a political order based upon the Quran (that is, the shari'a) and the sunna, which makes no distinction between religion and state (*din wa dawla*).[8] Here, the term Islamism is used to describe an Islamic movement that is not only political but social and economic as well, and an Islamist as anyone belonging to such an Islamic institution. Contrary to western notions that there is a universal Islamic conspiracy,

Islamism is not a monolithic phenomenon but is very much context-specific. Palestinian Islamism shares some characteristics with Islamic movements elsewhere in that it arose in response to adverse socio-economic-political conditions – in the Palestinian case generated by an Israeli military occupation that left the Gaza Strip impoverished and de-developed, as well as socially and politically fragmented.[9]

The resulting dislocations have produced frustration, low achievement, personal alienation, and continued powerlessness. Their inability to challenge, let alone defeat, the occupier – even during the Intifada – led to calls among a disillusioned segment for religio-cultural authenticity (i.e. religion as politics), that is, for a strategy of turning social defeat into moral victory, where inclusion was guaranteed and control assured. Unlike other post-colonial Islamic movements, Palestinian Islamism evolved in the absence of a sovereign entity. Therefore, 'transition from *umma* to state', difficult and forced though it was for other modern Arab nations, has not yet occurred in the Gaza Strip and West Bank.[10] The hegemonic system imposed by Israel did not disappear with the implementation of limited self-rule, although an amorphous and constrained political mode and the installation of the PA in the Gaza Strip, have taken its place.

Diminished expectations continue to shape attitudes in Gazan society, but harsher perceptions appear to be fueled by new realities that may have important implications for the role and appeal of the Islamic movement. First, while the existence of an independent state does not in itself guarantee democratic practice or political inclusion, it is a necessary precondition for them. Yet, for growing numbers in Gaza, the possibility of establishing a nation, and the state institutions this requires, seems as remote as ever since the new PA-led order appears painfully similar to the old one. The sense of shock and betrayal among people is palpable.

Second, before the implementation of the Oslo Accords, the distinction between those ruling and those being ruled – the occupier versus the occupied – was clear. After Oslo, the distinction became blurred. To which category does the PA belong? To Israel, it remains among the ruled; to Palestinians, it is another ruler. In this context, who or what is being opposed? What forms should (and can) this opposition take?

Third, the political culture of Gaza has been characterized by the striking absence of nationalist ideology, a reality without precedent. The PA is increasingly seen as corrupt and inefficient, with interests lying in securing political control, even at the cost of national liberation.[11] In the absence of a unifying secular political ideology, nationalism can no longer be measured by support for Palestinian self-determination, but for an expanding security apparatus and patronage structure with little political legitimacy. By contrast, support for Islam (but not necessarily for political Islam, which also suffers from weak political legitimacy) has increasingly been seen as support for family, community, morality, development, and social order. This distinction is extremely important to understand in a situation of acute economic deprivation, social fragmentation, and psychological confusion.

Fourth, with the beginning of limited autonomy, new (sub)categories of exclusion have been introduced throughout the Palestinian community. When Israelis ruled directly, almost every Palestinian was the victim of exclusion. Today, under the security strictures and patronage structures created by Yasser Arafat, some Palestinian groups greatly and clearly benefit over others. The excluded include not only Islamists but also many people who depend upon them for support, people with no access to the system's resources because they are poor and demobilized. Gaza's ever-widening social divisions attest to this formidable exclusionary process, which is most keenly felt at the individual and community levels, where Islamic institutions operate.

In the Gaza Strip, the key Islamic groups are the Muslim Brotherhood (al-Ikhwan al-Muslimin), the Islamic Resistance Movement (Harakat al-Muqawama al-Islamiyya) or Hamas, and the Islamic Jihad (al-Jihad al-Islami), which collectively represent Islamic social, economic, political, and military institutions.[12]

The political revival of Islamic forces in the territories began with the Intifada and the organization of Hamas, the political wing of the Muslim Brotherhood. Before that, the Brotherhood, whose formal inauguration in Palestine took place in Jerusalem in October 1945, dominated the Palestinian Islamic movement. Although the Brotherhood did have a political position vis-à-vis the Palestine question, its activities were mainly dedicated to advancing Islamic socio-morality rather than forcing political reform.[13] Between 1948 and 1967, the Brotherhood in the territories, linked to parent organizations in Egypt and Jordan, promoted social and religious agendas by building a decentralized network of charities, schools, youth and sports clubs, nurseries, and kindergartens. After the 1967 war, the Brotherhood continued to pursue Islamic re-socialization programs despite a changed political environment, in which resistance and national liberation were the dominant trends.[14]

The failure of the Muslim Brotherhood to participate in the nationalist resistance movement limited its development as a popular force. The Brothers were not part of the armed struggles against the occupation that peaked in the late 1960s and early 1970s, which cost them many supporters, many of whom defected and joined the secular nationalist Palestine Liberation Organization (PLO) and its largest faction, Fatah.[15] During the 1970s, however, three events occurred that strengthened the Brotherhood's position in the territories. First, in 1973, Sheikh Ahmad Yasin, a Muslim Brother who later became a dominant figure in Hamas, established the Islamic Center (al-Mujamma' al-Islami) in Gaza, which centralized and coordinated the activities of all Brotherhood organizations. Second, the Palestinian Muslim Brotherhood underwent a restructuring in which the Gaza, West Bank, and Jordanian branches were merged into a single entity based in Jordan. Third, the 1979 Islamic revolution in Iran, coupled with the PLO's continued failures, renewed popular interest in the Islamic movement, which the Brotherhood exploited.[16] Their anti-PLO stance, and the fact that the Brotherhood did not pursue armed resistance, allowed them to operate relatively unencumbered by Israel, enabled it to expand its organizational network. With funds from Jordan and Saudi Arabia, the Brotherhood built orphanages, health clinics, and libraries, which strengthened its social service infrastructure and helped it gain increasing control of the *waqf* and of many mosques; by 1986, the Ikhwan controlled 40 percent of Gaza's mosques.[17]

Still, the Brothers' non-involvement in fighting an increasingly repressive occupation frustrated many of its members, some of whom left in 1980 and formed the Islamic Jihad (which was more strongly influenced by the militant Egyptian Islamic Brotherhood).[18] The founders of the Islamic Jihad also believed in establishing an Islamic state, but rejected the notion that the Islamicization of society must precede political action. It claims to be a military strike force comprised of mainly small and underground cells.[19] Unlike the Brotherhood, it is not interested in building visible institutions because doing so constrains its operational capabilities.[20] During the 1980s, the Islamic Jihad conducted several military operations, some in conjunction with Fatah.[21] It was never as large as the Muslim Brotherhood, but the Jihad contributed greatly to the psychological preparation for the Intifada, though Israel's successful campaign against Jihad cells led to its declining political influence.[22]

The outbreak of the Intifada was a turning point for the Brotherhood because it became clear that they could no longer avoid political involvement in the conflict and also maintain and expand their popular mass. The strength of secular nationalist forces and growing support for the tiny but more militant Islamic Jihad threatened to rob the Brotherhood of its political legitimacy. The leadership was therefore forced to find ways of participating in the uprising without placing its social services programs at risk. The result was the formation of the Islamic Resistance Movement, Hamas, which played an active role in the Intifada and for a time challenged the PLO as a viable opposition force. In addition, second to Fatah, its popular support enabled it to win local elections, call labor strikes, organize demonstrations, and conduct armed actions. Its filial link to the Brotherhood gave the parent organization legitimacy in a dramatically changed political context. But its distance from it enabled Hamas to attract non-Brotherhood supporters, activists who did not necessarily feel the Islamicization of society was a priority over political reform.[23]

The movement's goals, a nationalist position couched in an Islamic idiom, were identified in the Hamas charter, a political manifesto strong in racist polemics and weak in strategic vision, which, not surprisingly, paid less attention to the reformist aims, and more attention to the goal of uprooting the occupier through *jihad*. Yet, unlike other Islamic political movements, Hamas has consistently demonstrated greater political pragmatism and flexibility, often achieved by taking contradictory positions on issues like participation in legislative elections. This has allowed Hamas to keep channels open and widen its political space.[24]

Hamas's organizational structure has become somewhat complex. It has a political wing with its own bureaucracy and a military wing, the 'Izzal-Din al-Qassam Brigades. The political wing has a reputation for greater moderation than the military wing. It has participated with some success in local elections and in professional associations, student organizations, and labor unions. In 1991 and 1992, for example, Hamas captured between one-third and one-half of all votes cast in various local elections in the occupied territories.[25] Hamas's extreme factions, the Qassem Brigades, who still conduct armed attacks against Israeli targets, were highly indoctrinated radicals. They are small in number – no more than 100 members divided into five or six cells – and are believed to operate independently not only of the political wing but of one another, and are subject only to the authority of a senior military chief.[26]

In fact, Hamas's real strength was the subject of intense speculation. However, what was clear was that Hamas became a barometer of public discontent, because it functioned as a 'nationalist alternative' whose popularity (vis-à-vis Fatah) changed depending upon the political circumstances.[27] For example, when the 1991 Madrid Peace Talks seemed to falter, public opinion began to favor Hamas. With the signing of the Oslo Accords and the expectations that accompanied it, support for Hamas declined rapidly, and several years later remained low.[28] What was also clear was that Hamas's legitimacy is the product of 'nationalist activity, and not of a greater receptiveness among a more militant and desperate Palestinian generation to their religious message'.[29]

Since the Intifada, Hamas has dominated the territories' Islamic movement, overshadowing the Muslim Brotherhood. The relationship between them now remains close. Some observers even claim the Brotherhood social service programs have been ipso facto Hamas-controlled institutions, used for proselytizing and recruitment. Many officials of Islamic social service organizations reject this supposition. There can be no question that Hamas works within the framework of Islamic institutions and that there are linkages between Hamas and the social and economic institutions created by the Brotherhood. But it is far more questionable whether automatic connections exist between Hamas and these groups, whether these links are inherently subversive or whether such institutions promote radicalism.

The post-Oslo context

In order to understand Islamic social and economic groups' roles, one must discern the context in which they function. As others in this collection make clear (especially Diwan and Walton, Wright, and Colton), the most urgent problem in the territories is continued unemployment which, throughout much of the Peace Process has been in excess of 70 percent in Gaza. Between 1987 and 1996, the number of Gazans working in Israel fell from 80000 to less than 7000.[30] The resulting economic damage was due to Israeli measures taken during the Intifada. Border closures have become the most detrimental, however. They restrict the movement of all people and goods into Israel from the territories, as well as movement within the West Bank and other areas. Between 1995 and 1997, over 20000 Gazan jobs in Israel were eliminated, costing Gaza's economy at least $25 million per month in wages and related services. When calculated according to 1987 employment levels, the monthly wage loss is almost $44 million. Gaza's per capita GNP is now $750, half its 1987 level, and well below the average for all less-developed countries, which stands at $950. Between 14 and 25 percent of the entire Palestinian population lived at or below an absolute poverty level of $500 to $650 per capita per year, the highest percentages of which were found in the Gaza Strip. The hardest hit were the poor and refugee camp populations.

While the Gaza Strip has long been poor, basic survival was seldom a problem. This was no longer the case. The number of families who could not adequately feed their children rose daily. In May 1995, for example, one hundred babies in Gaza City and the Jabalya refugee camp were suffering from marasmus, an extreme form of malnutrition. The situation was so bad that detainees in the Ansar 3 detention center in the Negev desert regularly smuggled food out of the camp to their relatives.[31] This unprecedented hardship had few immediate solutions, which left people dependent on salaries earned in Israel and through employment in the PA. In March 1995, the PA employed close to 40 000 people; nearly half were police and security officials. By May 1996, this number increased to 70 000, and at the end of 1997 over 80 000. While state salaries are critical, their economic impact, compared to wages earned by workers in Israel, was largely non-productive with salaries too low to live on. In addition, the PA's growing bureaucracy was financed largely by international donors who were increasingly insistent on structural reforms which would decrease the level of patronage jobs. These situations make aid funding an increasingly tenuous source, as Sullivan points out.

For some time, Gazan society has been deteriorating, a result of unabated economic dissolution and political repression. The erosion of critical support structures such as the extended family, the school, the political faction, and the traumatization of the society, particularly among the young, who grew up during the six years of Intifada, have weakened and damaged social relations. The emergence of new social divisions – rich–poor, refugee–indigenous, camp–non-camp – and the decline in participatory behavior are seen by the lack of community consensus. These fractures have only grown worse under limited self-rule. Similar to the situation Sullivan describes in the West Bank, the PA has further impinged upon Gaza's already troubled civil society by introducing some new dynamics: militarism, institutional disempowerment, and increasing alienation and confusion among the population.[32]

That Gaza has been associated with violence is indisputable. That this violence was a direct outgrowth of economic decline and social fracture is equally indisputable. But this has not been entirely the local population's fault, nor is it attributable solely to the poor employment perspective. For example, rather than offer job-development programs as a means for combating conflicts in Gaza, the PA has installed a military court system with no independent judiciary and deployed police and security forces. Perhaps the most alarming aspect of the militarization trend was the growing and increasingly rapid absorption of Gazan youth – some 500 young men per month – into the PA's security apparatus. By absorbing young men into the security structure, the PA not only asserted control but created inefficient dependencies among an increasingly vulnerable population. Recruits received status and identity, which should not be underestimated in a traumatized society, but their positions caused increased confusion as to their loyalties.

Other implications for institutional development were similarly disturbing. First, given that power was being centralized in the president, there was very little real authority among civil servants, which usually left people poorly trained for making managerial or strategic decisions. Second, there was increasing concern among local services directors that the PA was using its institutions as channels for patronage employment, effectively eroding its viability. Third, as the PA's secret police infiltrated associations, their autonomy was limited. Fourth, as Sullivan reveals, the PA grew increasingly hostile to Palestinian NGOs, the very institutions that historically formed the backbone of economic development and service delivery in the territories. As a result, growing inter- and intra-factional competition over increasingly scarce resources contributed to continual decline in the political order. And, because the PA failed to negotiate an end to persistent Israeli border closures, making them an economic fact of life, its political philosophy became largely devoid of meaning. The resulting loss of this mediatory structure, in a time of acute social and economic distress, significantly weakened the social order.

The implementation of the Oslo Agreement did little to reinvigorate the political process. On the contrary, the emergence, in effect, of a Palestinian police state and a one-party system opposed to dissent, marked the end of any viable political dialectic capable of commanding and sustaining popular support. The smaller secular factions have ceased to function, leaving Fatah and Hamas as the primary players. Hamas's political vision has limited utility. The establishment of an Islamic state in Palestine is as irrelevant to popular needs and aspirations as is the presence of 30 000 Palestinian security agents. The terrorist attacks, perpetrated by the Qassem Brigades, and the suicide bombings in 1997, were unpopular because they accomplished nothing politically and imposed greater social and economic suffering.[33] Hence, political life in Gaza was characterized far less by ideological conflicts between Fatah and Hamas, as was commonly portrayed, than by the lack of any political ideology, let alone one that was shared. The resulting void was filled by bureaucratic power plays, the hoarding of budgetary resources, sporadic violence, and rising social tensions.

Characteristics and services of Islamic institutions

Long before Hamas, the Ikhwan established a vast social service network in Gaza consisting of associations supporting orphanages, schools, day care centers, health clinics, libraries, sports clubs, youth clubs, women's centers, and economic development programs. Experience, commitment, and largely religious-based funding allowed them to become some of the most effective service-delivery institutions in Gaza. In the social sector, these institutions' largest members included the al-Salah Association, the Islamic Society, the Islamic Committees, and the Women's Islamic Association. A common focus of these institutions was children's programs, especially for orphans, and the families of collaborators.[34] In 1975, there were between 7000 to 10 000 orphaned children in the Gaza Strip who received support from various Islamic associations. Through their many committees and branches in the refugee camps, villages, and towns, Islamic groups identified children facing exceptionally difficult circumstances. If a case was approved, an orphaned child would receive support of 100 Israeli shekels (IS) ($33) per month through the age of 16 years. Hence, Islamic associations were spending between $2 772 000 and $3 960 000 annually on orphan support. Clothes and basic school supplies were also provided for school-aged children, as were food rations, when needed. Some Islamic charities had programs through which sponsors and needy children were connected.

Islamic committees continue to work in each of the Gaza Strip's eight refugee camps, where approximately 35 percent of the population lived. In the Nuseirat camp, for example, the Islamic committee had five branches, each with a staff of ten people, typically consisting of a teacher-director, an administrator, a social worker, a secretary, an accountant, and teachers. The Islamic committees ran five kindergartens (three of five housed in mosques) for 1200 boys and girls who attended school from 8 to 11 in the morning in classes of 35 to 40 children. The curriculum consisted of reading and writing in Arabic and English and recitations from the Quran. Any child, regardless of a family's political affiliations, could attend. An annual fee of IS 120 ($40) per child was charged, or IS 170 ($57) with transportation. These fees, which were used to buy supplies and pay salaries, are high for impoverished camp residents (though they are often subsidized by individual contributors), but people seemed willing to pay them since the kindergartens had a reputation for quality and discipline. Parents in the camp requested that two more Islamic-group-run kindergartens be established, while the kindergartens run by the secular political factions in Nuseirat were forced to close due to low enrollments. Only one kindergarten run by the government survived.

Another reason for the popularity of Islamic committee services is that they have traditionally included volunteer efforts, which has tended to build community commitment. For example, at camp kindergartens parents were often involved in the educational process: mothers met monthly to voice concerns and some were asked to evaluate teacher performance. In the Nuseirat camp, 100 children in grades 5 through 12 received tutoring in math and English from volunteer teachers who usually taught in government and UNRWA schools. Some Islamic associations both inside and outside the refugee camps provided computer courses for nominal fees. Some offered teenage boys and young men extra-curricular sports (such as soccer and table tennis) usually in or through the mosques. A sports center was being built at one mosque by volunteer masons, carpenters, and painters. There were also programs for blood donation and dispensing medicine and health care. The al-Salah Association had also arranged for children with Intifada-related injuries to be treated in France, Germany, and the United Kingdom with funds from foreign donors.

Other Islamic committee activities were oriented toward home care and occupational development. Many programs focused on counseling, training, and cost-effective household management. These programs were staffed almost entirely by female volunteers. As of March of 1995, 300 of the volunteers in Nuseirat camp worked with the Islamic women's committees.[35] Many of their programs combined training with religious instruction. The Women's Islamic Association in Gaza city, for example, offered courses in skills such as knitting, sewing, and secretarial work so that women could earn an income and help their families. A six-month sewing course cost NIS 120 ($40) and a four-month knitting course cost NIS 100 ($33). The poor were exempted from tuition fees. The director of one branch insisted that market studies be made so that women could be trained in areas for which there was sufficient demand. A result of the study was to offer computer courses. In one interview, a mother explained: 'We need more computers. If our children are going to compete in the 21st century, they [we] must be computer literate.'

The role of Islamic social and economic institutions

Obviously, the work of these Islamic committee projects have had an economic impact, whether by broadly raising the skills level of the workforce, or by directly providing aid to families. However, purely Islamic economic institutions are a relatively new phenomenon in Gaza. Most of the beneficiaries of these institutions' programs were small to medium-sized firms, usually retailers (such as clothing, housewares, electrical appliances, and grocery sellers).[36] According to committee officials, their programs were designed to create opportunities for profits beyond those available in Gaza's constrained (and un-Islamic) economy, and to channel these opportunities to lower socio-economic groups with little access to financial assistance.

Islamic investment companies adhere to certain Islamic rules, such as not engaging in interest-based lending and setting aside a percentage of their profits for *zakat*. Beyond this, however, Islamic commercial enterprises tend to support free-market operations. Islamic investment companies, like their secular counterparts, were often involved in the purchase and sale of land and real estate, a risky but profitable endeavor in Gaza City. Profits are not guaranteed and losses may occur, although no company had claimed any losses. Some claimed they broke even, while others boasted profits of between 29 to 43 percent annually over a two-year period.

One company, a well-known Islamic enterprise, had four partners (one of whom was Christian). When asked whether women could become partners, one director said they could if they were professionally qualified and observed the shari'a. The firm was started in 1993 with a working capital of $320 000. Two years later, the working capital had grown to $1.6 million. The minimum investment was $1000 and the maximum $60 000. The average investment was $3000 to $5000, meaning that there were many small investors. According to company officials, the majority of small investments came from women, who typically sold their gold jewelry (their only asset in most cases) to raise the cash needed to invest. These women generally were between the ages of 25 and 35 and came from the poorer, lower, and middle classes. Eighty percent lived in Gaza City, the remainder in the Strip. Anyone could invest, although women were targeted for funds because they had fewer opportunities.

A common assumption about Islamic social and economic institutions in Gaza was that they received funding from Hamas, but representatives from both sets of institutions emphatically denied this link, although several said that they would vote for Hamas candidates. Local funding typically came from religious, not political, groups and there were contributions from Israel, US, and European associations. Several people interviewed evinced irritation over contentions that they were used by Hamas for political and military recruitment. One angrily asked, 'Is every Catholic charity in Ireland funded by the IRA?' Islamic businessmen insisted their capital derived from private and commercial sources, not political nor necessarily religious ones.

Whether or not Hamas was their funding source – which cannot be known for certain – the far more important role Islamic social and economic institutions played concerned services provision at the grass-roots level, especially in Gaza. In addition, a key role of Islamic social institutions was in their focus on the Arab family,[37] which was, perhaps, the only institution to have withstood the dislocating effects of the occupation and the combined impacts of the Intifada, the Gulf War, and Israeli border closures. In their work with orphans, youth, the families of collaborators, women, widows, and the poor in general, Islamic social and economic institutions dealt with problems at the individual, family, and community levels. In so doing, they restored control to family networks by helping them to better provide for their children. Most importantly, given the PA's bureaucratic disorder and corruption, and the lack of control among many PNGOs, Islamic institutions' abilities to deliver basic services reliably, quickly, and equitably, and to create new, albeit limited, economic opportunities, stood out. In a context in which renewed popular expectations remain unmet, their capacity to respond to disenfranchised social classes is not only recognized, but forms, perhaps, the only basis around which community consensus is built. The danger, of course, was that this occurred in non-regulated spheres.

By working within a religious and cultural framework, Islamic social and economic institutions worked to restore community self-reliance, especially important in a context in which the PA has given public space a distinctly bureaucratic patina; Islamists imparted a moralist hue on the community.[38] In so doing, they responded to sensed marginalizations that were not only political, but also social, economic, and psychological. Thus, Islamism became a component of a religio-cultural or religio-social personal identity,[39] and an arena for building consensus (much as the church does in rural America). Its attention to community values was further supported by an extensive social services infrastructure.

A particular strength of Islamic institutions, especially in the post-Oslo period, came from the clarity and consistency of their message.

Arafat's message has been fluctuating and contradictory, and hardly relevant to the difficulties of everyday life. The Islamic message, however, has been clear, unchanging, and attainable: a moral and ordered life can be created and sustained through Islam. The importance of this fact should not be underestimated in a social and economic order as fractured as Gaza's. Although the Islamic message is limited and sometimes problematic – its local actors offer something both intimate and social and does so in a way that is tangible, practical, and reproducible.

The Islamists, like the PA, understood the importance of working with Gazan youth. Their strength, however, lay in the services they provided. The PA primarily absorbed young men into the security apparatus, providing a source of employment and identity. Islamic programs, by contrast, while not providing employment per se, used religious and cultural frameworks that built community and promoted economic inclusion. The result of this latter approach was a sense of personal identification, grounded in civic work – an infrastructure of cooperation, as it were – not simply bureaucratic positioning. Perhaps this is why the rate of volunteerism in Gaza was and remains so high. Thus, Islamic institutions created workplaces and provided a stable environment where gradualism was possible and accountability and trust were perceived to be high. And, since they focused on areas where frustrations over unfulfilled promises have led to the lowest expectations, their role as 'alternative provider' is increasingly significant.[40]

However, Islamic institutions also suffered from a lack of vision – although no worse than the PA – which was partially rooted in Islam's lack of theory on state economics or institutional management.[41] But it is also true that groups like the Muslim Brotherhood 'did not produce a modern applied theory for economic and social organizations, or a comprehensive educational approach, which led the people in charge of such agencies to revert to borrowing'.[42] This borrowing was dually characterized by Arab hostility toward western values and by what Malcolm Kerr referred to as a 'passive, uneasy [and] ineffectual acceptance of European institutions and social practices'.[43] Similarly, François Burgat and William Dowell defined Islamism as a

> recourse to the vocabulary of Islam, used in the post-colonial period to express within the state, or more often against it, an alternative political program that uses the heritage of the West as a foil, but allows nevertheless the re-appropriation of its principal references.[44]

As a result, Islamic institutions may be able to meld social contradictions, but they cannot resolve them. Yet, given the loss of secular political factions as mediators in Gaza, they may be well-positioned to address crucial failures and fill voids in the current structure of events.

If there is no applied theory for Islamic social and economic organizations, what makes them Islamic? What features define them as such? Can these features be used as support and recruitment forces for radical Islam? Can political or subversive roles, therefore, be attributed to Islamic social and economic institutions?

In fact, Islamic social institutions shared certain characteristics, such as the segregation of the sexes, Muslim dress, religious instruction and Qur'anic memorization, prayer services, contributing to *zakat*, proselytizing, and working with families. Therefore, is it unreasonable to assume that the Islamism of certain social programs emanates from Islamic practice rather than an Islamic theory of social (or political) change?

In fact, it is not ideology per se that makes Islamic institutions Islamic, but it is certain visible patterns of behavior. Institutions, furthermore, are only as powerful as their clients. In Gaza, the majority appeared to be poor and from lower socio-economic groups. They used Islamic-based services primarily because they needed the services provided. Some clients were Hamas supporters or members, and others were not. What these clients had in common was not a shared political ideology but, rather, shared needs and frustrations with the PA. But these factors alone were not enough to encourage united or sustained action in support of political or radical Islam. Furthermore, although Islam does not forbid revolt, Islamic social institutions do not appear to be engaged in revolutionary behavior. If anything, they seem to spurn dramatic change, preferring to work at the piecemeal rebuilding of a status quo rather than destroying it. If anything, Islamic social and economic institutions are more reactionary than radical, encouraging moderation instead of instability. Moreover, Palestinians have not traditionally supported religious fundamentalism; even today most of them want a secular state. In addition, strong divisions found within and between Gazan social classes mitigate the possibility of any singular movement.

In the economic sphere, Islamic institutions also collectively emphasized practices aimed at Islamicizing the economy – for instance, eliminating the use of interest from finance, pursuing profit-sharing instead of usury, collecting and distributing *zakat*, and improving the allocation of wealth.[45] But beyond upholding these basic tenets of Islamic law, Islamic economic associations appeared to be motivated by the same commercial interests as any other business (even if that means having non-Muslim partners) and demonstrated a similar commitment to private-sector development.

Some questions remain. First, do the owners of Islamic economic enterprises belong to an emerging native commercial bourgeoisie or to the Islamic movement? That is, were Islamic businessmen traditional capitalists seeking the legitimizing symbols of Islam, or were they activists genuinely trying to reform the economy according to Islamic law? Did Islamic economic institutions, therefore, represent rising local capitalism with a Muslim coloring? Were they the economic wing of an Islamic political movement? The available data strongly suggested the former, particularly in the absence of any organizing theory of Islamic economy.[46] Hence, the Islamism of certain economic institutions may have been tied more to the Islamic identity of institutional owners, managers, and staff than to any ideological or intellectual program of economic reform. Within this framework, material interests would more often than not conflict with ideological interests and consequently override them.

Second, how similar or divergent (if not contradictory) were the class interests of the owners and clientele of Islamic economic institutions? What was the basis for bringing these social classes together? Were they joined by their mutual support for political Islam or by shared economic interests that are expressed symbolically in a common Islamic idiom? Again, the available data pointed strongly to the latter, further limiting a political, let alone subversive, role for Islamic economic institutions.

The relationship between Hamas and Islamic development institutions

That a relationship existed between Islamic social and economic institutions and their political and social association counterparts was undeniable.[47] Yet, the nature of this relationship was not necessarily as automatic or as evil as portrayed. The relationship between Islamic development and political institutions could be understood largely in terms of membership or support. Typically, Islamic social and economic institutions were considered Hamas institutions because members of management or staff may have been Hamas sympathizers.[48] While this was true of some institutions, it was not true of others. In fact, there was little hard evidence to support any of these allegations.

In contrast, the interviews revealed that the philosophy of Islamic development institutions and their clients was very different. Their doctrine was one of service to individuals and communities. Their purpose was to plant and nurture the seeds of a future. They were oriented toward life, not death. Similarly, the discourse of militant Islamists is utopian while that of social Islamists is practical, pragmatic, and, increasingly, technocratic. Because of this, Islamic social institutions now appeared to have a greater capacity for mobilizing people than their military or political counterparts. In Gaza, legitimate Islamic social movements were even as non-combative and aimed at serving needs and creating possibilities, not destroying them.

Conclusion

As reviewed here the Islamic structure in the Gaza Strip was not unified, homogeneous, or monolithic. It varied by institutions, leadership, and clientele. Islamic institutions also appeared to differ in their Islamicness, with economic institutions being the least faith-oriented, but important service providers no less. What seemed to define social and economic institutions as Islamic – the practice and propagation of Islamic laws and ideas – was not enough to mobilize people in support of political or radical Islam. Indeed, Hamas's shift from the political to the social realm may have reflected its declining political status as well as the central importance of Islamic social institutions.

While many Palestinians, perhaps the majority, rejected the political theology associated with political and militant Islam, the Islamic organizations played an increasingly important developmental role in the Gaza Strip, providing badly needed services and economic relief in an already fractured society. Western powers should differentiate between radical and moderate (and productive) Islamic forces and actively assist the latter.

The fundamental problem in Gaza, as in many other places, is that the majority of people are disenfranchised and poor, having no power, access, or future. Radical Islam emerged not because people were opposed to developmental change but because they were unable to attain it.[49] Of all the problems facing Palestinian society today, Hamas is low on the list. In Gaza, the ruling elite that refuses to guarantee civil liberties or human rights and does not create legitimate channels for political dissent and/or economic growth is at the core of the problem.[50]

The key question in the Gaza Strip, as elsewhere in the Arab world, is not whether Palestinian society will be religious or secular, but whether people will eat, develop, and progress. In all these respects, Islamic institutions have an increasingly critical role to play. They have provided for critical needs that remain unmet because of persistent structural flaws, some of which were present before the Gulf War began, but many of which have emerged as a result of failures in the Peace Process. This makes the Islamic committees inextricable and important parts of the local economic, political, and social development equations in the Gaza Strip. New methods must be found to incorporate them into the process. Any attempt to eliminate them will surely fail and may incite more violence.

Notes

1. This chapter is a slightly amended version of an article that first appeared as 'Beyond Hamas: Islamic Activism in the Gaza Strip', *Harvard Middle Eastern and Islamic Review*, 2 (1995) 1–39. Reprinted with permission.
2. A. Perlmutter, 'The Israel–PLO Accord Is Dead', *Foreign Affairs*, 74 (May–June 1995) 68.
3. Z. Abu-Amr, *Islamic Fundamentalism in the West Bank and Gaza: the Muslim Brotherhood and the Islamic Jihad* (Bloomington: Indiana University Press, 1994) p. 15.
4. J. L. Esposito, *Islam: the Straight Path* (New York: Oxford University Press, 1991) p. 218.
5. Several polls and surveys conducted in the Gaza Strip and West Bank confirm this point. For example, see W. K. Levitt, 'Islamistes palestiniens, la nouvelle generation', *Le Monde Diplomatique* (June 1995) 5; and Gaza Community Mental Health Program (GCMHP), 'People's Opinion of the Palestinian Authority and Their Political Attitudes' (Gaza City: Research Unit, GCMHP, February 1995).
6. Based on interviews with officials of Hamas, the PA, and the US State Department, Gaza Strip and Jerusalem, (March 1995).
7. Based on interviews with officials of several Islamic social and economic organizations, Gaza Strip (February–March 1995).
8. For different approaches see, N. Ayubi, *Political Islam: Religion and Politics in the Arab World* (London: Routledge, 1991); J. L. Esposito, *The Islamic Threat: Myth or Reality?* (New York: Oxford University Press, 1992); M. Juergensmeyer, *The New Cold War? Religious Nationalism Confronts the Secular State* (Berkeley, CA: University of California Press, 1993); O. Roy, *The Failure of Political Islam* (Cambridge, MA: Harvard University Press, 1994); and B. Tibi, *The Crisis of Modern Islam: a Pre-industrial Culture in the Scientific-Technological Age* (Salt Lake City, UT: University of Utah Press, 1988).
9. See S. Roy, *The Gaza Strip: The Political Economy of De-development* (Washington, DC: Institute for Palestine Studies, 1995). For an analysis of Gaza's social and political sectors, see S. Roy, 'The Seed of Chaos, and of Night:

The Gaza Strip After the Agreement', *Journal of Palestine Studies*, 23 (Spring 1994) 85–92.

10. See Ayubi, *Political Islam*, p. 220.

11. See S. Roy, 'Report from Gaza: Alienation or Accommodation?', *Journal of Palestine Studies*, 24 (Summer 1995) 73–82.

12. In addition, there is the Islamic Liberation Party and the Islamic Jihad Movement (Bayt al-Maqdis) that have limited political influence. See A. al-Jarbawi, 'The Position of Palestinian Islamists on the Palestine–Israel Accord', *The Muslim World*, 84 (January–April 1994) 127–34. There are several detailed works on the Islamic movement in the West Bank and Gaza. For example, Z. Abu-Amr, *Islamic Fundamentalism in the West Bank and Gaza*; idem, 'Hamas: a Historical and Political Background', *Journal of Palestine Studies*, 22 (Summer 1993) 5–19; A. Rashad, 'Hamas: Palestinian Politics with an Islamic Hue', Occasional Papers Series No. 2 (United Association for Studies and Research, October 1993); M. K. Shadid, 'The Muslim Brotherhood Movement in the West Bank and Gaza', *Third World Quarterly*, 10 (April 1988) 658–82; J-F. Legrain, 'The Islamic Movement and the Intifada', in J. R. Nassar and R. Heacock (eds), *Intifada: Palestine at the Crossroads* (New York: Praeger, 1990) pp. 175–89; 'A Defining Moment: Palestinian Islamic Fundamentalism', in J. Piscatori (ed.), *Islamic Fundamentalisms and the Gulf Crisis* (Chicago: American Academy of Arts and Sciences, 1991), pp. 70–87; and M. Jubran and L. Drake, 'The Islamic Fundamentalist Movement in the West Bank and Gaza Strip', *Middle East Policy*, 2 (1993) 1–15.

13. Shadid, 'The Muslim Brotherhood Movement', 668–70.

14. Abu-Amr, 'Hamas: a Historical and Political Background', 5–7. See also J. O. Voll, 'Fundamentalism in the Sunni Arab World: Egypt and Sudan', in M. E. Marty and R. S. Appleby (eds), *Fundamentalisms Observed* (Chicago: University of Chicago Press, 1991) pp. 345–402.

15. Rashad, *Hamas: Palestinian Politics with an Islamic Hue*, pp. 2–3.

16. Abu-Amr, 'Hamas: A Historical and Political Background', 7.

17. G. Usher, 'The Rise of Political Islam in the Occupied Territories', *Middle East International*, 25 (June 1993) 19; Abu-Amr, 'Hamas: a Historical and Political Background', p. 8, notes that between 1967 and 1987 the number of mosques grew from 200 to 600 in Gaza and 400 to 750 in the West Bank.

18. Abu-Amr, 'Hamas: a Historical and Political Background', 8.

19. Al-Jarbawi, 'The Position of Palestinian Islamists', 130.

20. 'The Islamist Movements in the Occupied Territories: an Interview with Iyad Bargouthi', *Middle East Report* (July–August 1993) 10.

21. Abu-Amr, 'Hamas: a Historical and Political Background', 10; *Islamic Fundamentalism in the West Bank and Gaza*, pp. 93–104; Legrain, 'The Islamic Movement and the Intifada', 177–9; and Jubran and Drake, 'The Islamic Fundamentalist Movement', 5.

22. Rashad, *Hamas: Palestinian Politics with an Islamic Hue*, p. 4.

23. Abu-Amr, 'Hamas: a Historical and Political Background', 10–11.

24. Al-Jarbawi, 'The Position of Palestinian Islamists', 136. In addition to the sources cited in note 14, a detailed description of Hamas's organizational structure can be found in Israel Information Service Gopher, *Hamas: the Islamic Resistance Movement*, Information Division, Israel Foreign Ministry, Jerusalem (January 1993).

25. Al-Jarbawi, 'The Position of Palestinian Islamists', 137.

26. The level of separation is unclear. Some observers believe this is a deliberately circulated rumor which helps the political wing to maintain tactical distance from the military wing.

27. Hamas has lost many of its cadres through deportation, imprisonment, and execution. After the Tel Aviv bus bombing in October 1994, for example, Israel arrested at least 1500 Hamas activists, followed some months later by a PA crackdown in which several Hamas leaders and 500 Hamas supporters were imprisoned (including Mahmud al-Zahar, Sheikh Ahmand Babar, and Sheikh Salama al-Safadi). The July and August 1995 suicide bombings led to the arrest of at least 30 military cadres and the February and March 1996 attacks in Israel led to another crackdown. See, S. Schmemann, 'Israel Captures Arab Gang Linked to Two Bus Bombings', *New York Times*, 24 August 1995, A1. In August of 1997 another dual suicide bombing sparked new rounds of arrest of Palestinians by the PA and Israel.

28. In a poll conducted one month after Oslo, only 13 percent of respondents said they would vote for Hamas in elections, compared to 45 percent who would vote for Fatah; A. al-Jarbawi, 'The Position of Palestinian Islamists', 141.

29. M. Budieri, 'The Nationalist Dimension of Islamic Movements in Palestinian Politics', *Journal of Palestine Studies*, 24, (Spring 1995) 93.

30. This section is derived from Roy, 'Report from Gaza', 73–7, where there is a detailed discussion of the economic situation; and S. Roy, 'Economic Deterioration in the Gaza Strip: Heightened Closure and PA-controlled Monopolies', *MERIP* (Summer 1996).

31. Roy, 'Report from Gaza', 75. Cited in N. Patrick, *Middle East International*, 12 May 1995, 18. This situation was also discussed in an interview with Amira Hass, correspondent for *Ha'aretz*, Gaza Strip, March 1995.

32. This section is based on Roy, 'Report from Gaza', 77–80; as well as my articles, 'The Seed of Chaos', 92; and 'Separation or Integration: Closure and the Economic Future of the Gaza Strip Revisited', *Middle East Journal*, 48 (Winter 1994) 11–23.

33. See, for example, Joel Greenberg, 'Arabs Say Attacks Hurt Them Too', *New York Times*, 25 July 1995, A3.

34. I conducted interviews with these and several other smaller organizations, Gaza Strip, February–March 1995. The following data is derived from interviews and site visits.

35. Given an average of eight people per family, and approximately Nuseirat camp 5000 families, each volunteer would have to work with 17 families to cover the whole camp.

36. The sample consists of five Islamic business establishments (further study is planned); access was very difficult and those institutions that participated asked not to be identified.

37. See N. Ayubi, 'Rethinking the Public/Private Dichotomy: Radical Islamism and Civil Society in the Middle East', *Contention*, 4 (Spring 1995) 89.

38. See Ayubi, 98, for a similar but diverging interpretation.

39. E. W. Said, 'The Phony Islamic Threat', *New York Times Magazine*, 21 November 1993, 64, writes, 'Being an Arab, even for a non-Muslim, means being a member of what the late scholar Marshall Hodgson called an Islamicate world or culture.'

40. Ayubi, 'Rethinking the Public/Private Dichotomy', 98.

41. Ayubi, *Political Islam*, p. 230. See also S. Abed-Kotob, 'The Accommodationists Speak: Goals and Strategies of the Muslim Brotherhood in Egypt', *International Journal of Middle East Studies*, 27 (August 1995) 326–7. For a fascinating discussion of the problem at a broader theoretical level, see M. Kerr, *Islamic Reform: the Political and Legal Theories of Muhammad 'Abduh and Rashid Rida* (Berkeley, CA and London: University of California and Cambridge University Press, 1966).

42. Ayubi, *Political Islam*, p. 57. Original citation: Zakariyya S. Bayyumi, *Al-Ikhwan al-muslimun was al-jama'at al-islamiyya* [*The Muslim Brothers and the Islamic Groupings*] (Cairo: Wahba, 1979) p. 321.

43. Kerr, *Islamic Reform*, p. 221.

44. F. Burgat and W. Dowell, *The Islamic Movement in North Africa*, Middle East Monograph Series (Austin, TX: University of Texas, 1993) p. 41.

45. Similar characteristics are described by A. M. Lesch, 'The Muslim Brotherhood in Egypt: Reform or Revolution?' in M. C. Moen and L. S. Gustafson (eds), *The Religious Challenge to the State* (Philadelphia, PA: Temple University Press, 1992) p. 201. Also see J. T. Cummings, H. Askari, and A. Mustafa, 'Islam and Modern Economic Change' in J. L. Esposito (ed.), *Islam and Development: Religion and Sociopolitical Change* (Syracuse, NY: Syracuse University Press, 1980) pp. 25–47.

46. Ayubi, *Political Islam*, pp. 186–95, addresses these and other questions with respect to Islamic enterprises in Egypt.

47. For example, Imad Faluji, the former head of Hamas's military wing, is now associate director of the Al-Salah Association. Interview, Gaza City (February–March 1995).

48. Y. M. Ibrahim, 'Arafat's Forces Push Crackdown on Gaza Radicals', *New York Times*, 10 July 1995, A8.

49. See I. Pappe, 'Moderation in Islam: Religion in the Test of Reality', *Palestine–Israel Journal of Politics, Economics, and Culture*, 2 (Spring 1994) 11–25; and F. Halliday, *Islam & the Myth of Confrontation* (London: I.B. Tauris, 1996), especially pp. 107–32.

50. In this regard, see S. Erlanger, 'Intelligence Experts Meet to Combat Mideast Terrorism', *New York Times*, 30 March 1996, in which a senior French official stated, 'Terrorism will be over when Palestinians feel they have their rights recognized'. Also see E. Beilin, 'Civil Society and the Prospects for Political Reform in the Middle East', Conference Report (New York: Civil Society in the Middle East Project, New York University, 1994) 12; Belin, 12 and Pappe, 'Moderation in Islam', 16–19.

12
Between Capitalism and Jewish Voters: Electoral Economics in Israel, 1977 to 1997

Shimson Bichler[1]

During the past decade several researchers have convincingly argued that, as a developed democracy, Israel exhibits a fairly clear pattern of electoral economic cycles. This chapter questions some of the fundamental assumptions and political anthropology underlying this approach. Specifically, it points to the crucial impact of long-term economic restructuring and power realignment on the nature and outcome of electoral politics. The significance of these processes has become apparent mainly since the 1970s, with the transition from a growing economy, dominated by a social-democratic government, to a stagnating market dominated by large business groups. Thus, when there emerges a consensus of discontent among key business and labor coalitions, the government is dethroned. Due to limitations in the available data, this study must be regarded as preliminary. The hypothesis is tested against two major electoral shifts, 1977 and 1992, and again in an epilog on the 1996 election. An alternative political-economic approach to Israeli social development, as opposed to political and economic paradigms, is also presented.

Background to the study

There is a considerable body of academic literature dealing with Israeli politics. This writing can be divided roughly into two types. One approach emphasizes political structure and institutions, as well as patterns created and transformed since the time of the British Mandate over Palestine. According to this view, the old dominant political center was undermined and eventually replaced by a competitive system in which shifts of voters and parties along the ideological axis determine the outcomes of elections and the formation of coalition governments.[2] The second approach is more behavioral, stressing the electoral characteristics of voters. The focus in these works is on demographic, ethnic and cultural change and the way in which political parties are able to adapt themselves to the voters' will.[3]

These approaches are founded on a paradigm that has developed in the Israeli social sciences since the 1950s.[4] This paradigm may be summed up in two postulates: (i) the primordial sin of Israeli politics is rooted in the authoritarian socialist or statist political culture of the East-European founding fathers, who created a rigid political center and a dominant party, and then seized control of the economy and diminished competition and private enterprise. In this way, a statist economy developed, consisting of heavy government intervention in key industries, and in capital and labor markets. This process was further enhanced by the Israeli–Arab conflict; (ii) Israeli society is a *sui generis* case, meaning the historical determinants common to other developed societies do not apply to its experience. It is a class-less society that never experienced a ruling class and did not pass through the stages of capitalist development.[5]

The social-class perspective is therefore neglected in academic political analysis, which instead sees the political system as autonomous and contingent mainly on electoral choice and party alignment. On the one hand, the prevailing notion is that the current democratization of Israeli society, especially the growing competitiveness of the party system, strengthens the sovereignty of the voters and their capacity to influence politics. On the other hand, the economy is undergoing a process of liberalization and emancipation from government control. Thus, the regime's power to influence elections declines, while the impact of civil society grows.[6]

The purpose of this study is not to confront these traditional approaches directly, but rather to suggest an alternative, broader analytical perspective. The argument develops along two main lines. First, I focus on electoral economic cycles. This direction is taken in order to break out from this narrow niche toward a more comprehensive concept of Israel's political economy. Second, rather than stressing macroeconomic or behavioral indicators, I concentrate on the changes occurring within the dominant groups controlling politics and the economy. Without blurring the complex nature of these issues, I hope to offer an alternative analysis emphasizing the political-economic aspects that have generally been ignored in most discussions of the subject.

Electoral economic cycles

In 1975, Ben-Porath published a short article in *Kyklos*, claiming that, using simple macroeconomic indicators – particularly changes in private consumption per capita – one could identify in Israel what he called a political business cycle. 'Presumably', he wrote, 'if this cyclical behavior is induced by a desire to generate a feeling of well-being before elections, then private consumption is an indicator of what the politicians are indeed trying to affect.'[7] This alleged link between elections and government-induced macroeconomic fluctuations was endorsed by subsequent writers. Levi, for example, pointed to cyclical patterns in real GNP per capita, employment and real wages as policy indicators; Doron and Tamir focused on public spending as a policy tool to generate a feeling of well-being among voters; Ben-Hanan and Temkin emphasized exchange rate policy and the government's impact on the real prices of subsidized commodities as a means of achieving similar ends.[8]

Several fundamental assumptions seem to characterize much of the literature on electoral economic cycles. First, most of these studies adopt the hedonic-rational framework, wherein a government that endeavors to maximize its votes and spoils stands against voters who seek to maximize their consumption of private and public goods. The common presumption is that, because voters are short-term optimizers, they tend to suffer from amnesia and myopia, and thus become susceptible to electoral economic policy. In the industrialized democracies, where the underlying parameters of scarcity and demand are relatively stable, this setting usually creates a permanent cyclical pattern of government-induced expansions and contractions. Second, this literature has a fairly rigid separation between economics and politics. The economy is seen as a self-contained organism, with government as an external force and generally regarded as the main cause of economic distortion. Third, most observers in this area, in Israel and elsewhere, tend to concentrate their attention on aggregate economic indicators. This preoccupation with overall macroeconomic performance pervades the descriptive and analytical literature.[9]

Unfortunately, these basic perceptions are potentially misleading. First, while the focus on short-term goals may be useful in explaining the re-election of a ruling party, it is not as revealing when dealing with dramatic electoral shifts, such as the ones occurring during the 1977, 1992, and 1996 elections in Israel. This inherent limitation is acknowledged by Ben-Hanan and Temken, who found a progressive shortening of pre-election economic upswings and wondered whether the 1977 elections marked the 'end of the electoral economic cycle in Israel'.[10]

Although their answer was negative, they also argued that there was most likely a broader transformation underlying the electoral economic cycle, which gradually altered the political rules of the game. Long-term economic and political changes slowly undermined the dominant party system, leading to a more intense multi-party competition and a forced shortening of economic cycles. Second, a shortcoming of the electoral economic cycle approach lies in its formalistic treatment of power. The emphasis is almost entirely focused on the relationship between the voter and the government. Elections are viewed primarily as a competition over the rational votes of sovereign political consumers; since elections are seen as the ultimate essence of politics, it seems only natural to concentrate on the individual voter as the most basic unit or even the building block of political research. In a way, this disregard of effective power relations resembles the choice of many neoclassical economists who, in a world of giant oligopolies, remain preoccupied with individual rational consumers.

A similar problem arises when, in the larger context of economic coalitions, one continues to view the government as the ultimate focus of power. In Israel, this view endows the government with an immense ability to intervene and distort economic performance. The socialist tradition, it is often argued, generated a bureaucratic-collectivist political culture, which instituted the supremacy of the political orientation over the business orientation,and thus propagated the domination of politics over economic affairs. Electoral economics are then taken as evidence for the demonic power of the Israeli government, which works to harm economic performance and undermine its democratic basis. Unfortunately, this view may not be very adequate for the Israeli case, at least not since the 1970s.[11] As I see it, the neoclassical notion of market-life interactions between autonomous voters and omnipotent politicians diverts attention from a different, and perhaps far more important relationship. The crucial political determinant may not be the preferences of political consumers, but rather the underlying structure of political-economic power. From this perspective, electoral politics is only part of a wider struggle raging among the main power groups within the economy.

According to Ferguson, there is an increasing need for research along these latter lines. In his view:

> it is high time to begin developing a different approach – a fresh account of political systems in which business elites, not voters, play the leading part; an account that treats mass party structures and

voting behavior as dependent variables to be examined in a context of class conflict and change within the business community.[12]

Challenging Downs' emphasis on individual utility and Olson's focus on group benefit, Ferguson suggests an 'investment theory of political parties', an alternative approach that analyzes changes in political hegemony as part of a more fundamental transformation in the structure of economic power. The central issue is not how politicians interact with voters, but the changing role of government in the wider context of power coalitions. Instead of focusing on the way in which political parties sway the masses, we should look for those long-term economic processes that transform the structure of political power and, later, the relative position of government within that structure.

This leads us to the third weakness of the electoral economic cycle approach: its exclusive reliance on macroeconomic indicators. The difficulty with aggregate or average variables such as private consumption, government spending, taxes or subsidies is that they do not tell us much about the underlying processes of restructuring. For example, a rise in real private consumption per capita may serve to conceal a redistribution of income that makes one part of the population better off at the expense of another part. Similarly, an increase in government spending may be the outcome of a decline in orders from one group of firms, coupled with a larger increase in procurement from remaining contractors. Disaggregated indicators are thus necessary for gaining understanding of long-term restructuring.[13]

In order to grasp the realignment of political power, we must start by looking into matters like distributions of income and wealth, allocations of public spending, relative tax burdens, and differential flows of subsidies. The nature of these structural changes may then help explain major shifts in the ideologies, creeds, and sentiments of ruling elites, whose general mood trickles down through the various mass media and is assimilated by the voting population.[14] At the same time, one should not ignore all aggregate indicators, particularly those related to the labor market. Indeed, the very ability of the government to affect real wages and overall employment is, to a large extent, an indicator of its legitimacy and support among the key economic power groups. Given the crucial impact of these sentiments on voting behavior, our task then is to explain their structural origin. To do that, we will first explore those long-term political-economic processes which, since the early 1970s, have altered the dominant ideologies and policies in the western countries, and then examine the relevance of such changes for the Israeli case.[15]

From political business cycles to political trends

The term 'political business cycle' was first coined by Michael Kalecki, in his 1943 article on the 'Political Aspects of Full Employment'.[16] Explaining the role of democratic rule in advanced capitalist economics, he observed a fundamental transformation from the prewar period. Contrary to early experiences, which emphasized particular business needs, the Great Depression convinced many governments of the need to actively regulate economic activity. The main difficulty in achieving this goal arose from the objections of large companies. While industry leaders may agree to use expansionary policies as means of preserving the legitimacy of a regime, they strongly oppose government attempts to maintain full employment. Kalecki pointed out that, although higher employment may lead to higher profits, a commitment to full employment serves to undermine a far more important credo: the ideological hegemony of business enterprise.

The crux of the matter, which big business leaders know all too well, is that their own dominance can be sustained only in the absence of any alternative method for efficient economic organization. Discipline in the factories and political stability are more appreciated by business leaders than profits. Their class instinct tells them that lasting full employment is unsound from their point of view and that unemployment is an integral part of the normal capitalist system. As it turns out, then, governments in the postwar era were far from being autonomous. Caught between their conflicting needs to maintain political legitimacy and for capital accumulation, these governments were inevitably driven toward a political business cycle. In a slump, either under pressure from the masses or without it, public investment financed by borrowing will be undertaken to prevent large-scale unemployment. But if attempts are made to apply this method in order to maintain the high level of employment reached in the subsequent boom, a strong degree of opposition from business leaders is likely to be encountered. As has already been argued, lasting full employment is not to their liking. The pressure of all these forces, and in particular of big business, would probably induce a government to return to an orthodox policy of budget cutting. A slump would follow in which government spending policy would come again into its own.[17]

Kalecki's theory of a political business cycle was satisfactory during the relatively prosperous period of the 1950s and 1960s when, in the context of overall growth, western governments tended to follow counter-cyclical stabilization policies. Since the early 1970s, however, there seems to have been a profound change in direction. Writing some 35 years after his friend Kalecki, Josef Steindl observed that in the course of the 1970s we entered a new era, dominated by the conviction that in the future the long-term rate of growth was going to be much lower – or that it should be lower or must be lower – a belief which in the nature of things carries a great deal of self-fulfillment within it.[18] While this end of prosperity was affected by a combination of factors, it was mainly the result of two related developments: the increasing internationalization of the advanced capitalist economies and the growing concentration of large-scale business enterprises. Together, these fundamental changes augmented the power of the large multinational corporations and weakened the relative efficacy of domestic government policies. With their progressive loss of vitality, governments became less committed to stabilization and welfare policies. The growing power of large corporations was accompanied by a consistent decline in their relative share of tax payments. Labor was now burdened by an increasing share of the tax bill, combined with a continuous deterioration of public services. To Steindl, the business opposition to full employment policies, which Kalecki had so vividly described in his analysis of the political business cycle, gathered more and more strength toward the end of the growth period.[19]

However, it seems to have a more persistent and lasting character than suggested in Kalecki's political cycle, so that we might rather speak of political trend. By this, Steindl refers to the gradual abandonment of stabilization goals in favor of stagnation, or at best a stunted growth policy, limited social spending and persistently high levels of unemployment. In other words, during the 1970s the old postwar order of political business cycles gave way to a new regime. Instead of active fiscal policy and an ideology that saw government as a central actor, monetarism and the free marketeers called for an end to government intervention. The notion of an overloaded government was accompanied by a resurgence of free market ideologies demanding abolition of the welfare state and acceptance of a natural rate of unemployment. A somewhat similar political-economic transition was also evident in Israel. In my view, it was this structural transformation which destabilized the electoral scene and led to the dramatic electoral shifts of 1977 and 1992.[20]

The restructuring of Israel's political economy

At the risk of some oversimplification, Israeli history may be characterized as a transformation from a growing economy dominated by a social-democratic regime, to a stagnating economy dominated by business elites. During the 20-year period between 1952 and 1972, Israel enjoyed a rapid average growth rate of 9 percent per annum. Much of this growth was induced by a substantial inflow of cheap capital, due mainly to unilateral transfers of reparations from Germany and from Jewish fund-raising organizations. The bulk of this capital inflow was channeled through the government, enabling it to control the pace and nature of gross investment and capital formation. This, together with the expansion of government spending, particularly military expenditures associated with the Israeli–Arab conflict, made the Israeli government the country's pivotal economic power. In the Israeli political literature, this regime has often been characterized as a dominant party system, a party state, corporatism or simply the Mapai system. This latter term denoted much more than the electoral superiority of the Mapai (Labor) Party. More broadly, it reflected the cohesiveness, self-confidence and spiritual hegemony of the ruling elites.

At the time, the Israeli elites promoted social-democratic ideologies that had prevailed in Eastern Europe at the turn of the century, but the concrete historical context in which they operated involved a combination of a postwar welfare state and a managed war economy of military Keynesianism. This modern institutional context of government intervention has slowly altered the structure of the Israeli economy. The growth of public spending and the expansion of the private sector were accompanied by a significant redistribution of income and concentration of wealth. Following the financial mergers of the 1950s and the industrial mergers of the 1960s, there emerged in Israel a big economy of corporate conglomerates and large firms, increasingly linked together through complex ownership ties, reciprocal business dealings and mutual relationships with the government. The heavy recession in the mid-1960s intensified the concentration process and enabled the emerging core group to diversify their holdings and increase the integration of their component parts.[21] After the 1967 war, the recession was replaced by economic boom. The Israeli market suddenly expanded to include one million new consumers from the occupied territories. Moreover, the postwar years, roughly until 1973, saw a very rapid increase in the number of Palestinian employees working in Israel (about 70 000), and a consequent increase in purchasing power. This resulted in the further development of the corporate core, which by the early 1970s already dominated all of the country's key industries and much of its financial sector.[22]

To a large extent, the process of corporate concentration was accelerated by the pattern of capital allocation. In its selective channeling of capital inflows, the government acted to promote certain business groups that were considered conducive to employment growth and long-term economic independence. These preferences created a structure of intricate systems of mutual inter-relationships among the political, business and military elites, which eventually manifested themselves in a new, more polarized pattern of income distribution.[23] The backlash against this latter development was increased labor militancy; this culminated in a wage explosion and, since the late 1960s, began to undermine the Mapai system. With the unions' support no longer guaranteed, the government shifted toward a business orientation in an attempt to break the autonomy of organized labor.[24] The decline of the unions and the public sector was further accelerated by the rapid integration of Palestinian workers into the Israeli economy after 1967. Thus, business restructuring was accompanied by a parallel segmentation in the labor market.

The first to analyze this segmentation was Farjoun, who described the growing dichotomy between the primary and secondary labor markets. With the 1967 occupation of the West Bank and Gaza Strip, and the concurrent militarization of the Israeli 'big economy', writes Farjoun, 'came a growing need for a cheap mobile labor force, with no social rights, a free labor force in the classical meaning of the term'.[25] This was achieved by the proletarianization of the Palestinian population, which was rapidly becoming the main labor pool for a growing number of small economy sectors, such as agriculture, construction, services and low-technology civilian manufacturing. The other side of this process was that the big economy, particularly its financial and military branches, came to rely solely on a Jewish, unionized labor force, with relatively extensive social security and wage rates twice as high as those earned by the Palestinians. This injection of cheap labor boosted the small economy and promoted the ideology of free enterprise against Keynesian intervention.

The early 1970s were marked by the oil crises and the 1973 war, but these events merely served to conceal the dawn of a new historical phase. Since the early 1970s, the political economy of Israel has been characterized by two principal developments: (i) the progressive consolidation of the dominant core corporations accompanied by the ongoing weakening of the government and the decline of the public sector; and (ii) growing dependency on the United States and increasing subjugation of Israeli culture to the American capitalist ethos. These developments are associated primarily with the evolution of the military and financial sectors in Israel. Indeed, much of the early emergence and subsequent consolidation of the large core corporations was due to the expansion of military spending and the closely related increase in inflation.[26] This process of concentration simultaneously reduced both excess capacity and competition, which in turn helped to maintain and even increase profit margins on lower volumes.

In addition, the decline in the industrial offset to savings diverted funds to the stock and bond markets, causing a rapid speculative increase in the volume of financial assets. With the prices of these assets rising even faster than the prices of goods and services, the ratio of stock market capitalization to GNP rose from less than 8 percent in 1973 to 99 percent in 1982. This process of corporate concentration and income redistribution slowly diminished the government's economic power.[27] During the earlier phase, the government assumed a leading role in agricultural planning, industrial policy, research and development, residential construction and civilian public services. With the rise of the big economy, however, it gradually retreated, initially into a position of a mere catalyst for venture capital and, eventually, into the role of a virtually passive financier. The 1977 rise of the Likud Party, with its nationalist military orientation and ardent opposition to economic planning, seems consistent with these tendencies.

The second characteristic of the new, post-1970 phase arose when, following the end of the Vietnam War, the Middle East became the focus of attention for leading business interests in the US, particularly those associated with petroleum and arms. During the 1970s and 1980s, the Israeli government became increasingly dependent on US assistance, partially civilian, but mainly military. This support served not only to keep Israel at the forefront of American strategic interests in the region, but also to provide much-needed contracts for the large US-based corporations. Reagan administration policies led the US to become increasingly dependent on arms-related production.[28] The growing dependence on the US, together with the drastic restructuring of the Israeli economy, altered not only the economic role of the Israeli government but also the country's dominant ideologies. Much as Steindl described in 1979, the leading business groups in Israel and the US began to demand that the Israeli government adopt a deliberate stagnation policy. The combination of stagflation, declining investment, growing domestic and foreign debts, expanding military budgets and restricted welfare services, which first appeared in the early 1970s, became since the mid-1980s the accepted, and to some extent even desirable order.

Under the combined pressure of the large Israeli corporations and the US administration, Israeli governments, both those led by Likud and those run by a national unity government of Likud and Labor, embarked on a systematic drive to cut wages, revert to regressive taxation, reduce civilian public spending, and abandon the capital market in favor of the large conglomerates. Particularly illuminating are the recent trends toward deregulation and privatization. For example, in relaxing the investment rules for pension funds, the government revoked its commitment to workers' pensions in order to allow the large conglomerates that manage those funds to use them as a source of financial leverage. At the same time, recent governments appear determined to maintain very high rates of interest in order to support the large banks. These banks almost collapsed in 1983 under the burden of their own speculation, and their ongoing bail-out worked to undermine the very survival of many industrial and agricultural concerns. Finally, despite the backdrop of deteriorating public services and alarming increases in poverty, governments during the 1980s continued to subsidize doubtful ventures in military technology, poured resources into the occupied territories, and started (partly under pressure from the US) to privatize their extensive holdings.[29]

Political power shifts: when do they occur?

We now turn to several key questions. How did this broad transformation from the early era of economic growth and dominant social-democratic government to the subsequent regime of stagnation and dominant business elites affect the course of electoral politics? What was its impact on the pattern of election outcomes? How can it explain the sharp electoral reversals of 1977 and 1992? In general, the long-term growth of the 1950s and 1960s ensured the dominance of the Labor Party. With cheap capital inflows, rising civilian (and, since the mid-1960s, military) spending, subsidized housing and an interventionist industrial policy, the cultural and political hegemony of the Mapai government went practically unchallenged. In this context, 'stop–go' electoral economics was a feasible and effective policy; it was accepted by the various elites and helped secure their continuous dominance.

All of this started to change in the early 1970s, with the precarious combination of stagnation and restructuring. On the one hand, the polarization of income and growing unemployment tended to alienate the large unions while, on the other hand, the fiscal crisis of the government and the ensuing stagnation made it increasingly difficult to sustain the increases in profits that the large conglomerates had come to expect.

Under these antagonistic conditions, the labor and business coalitions began to lose some of their self-confidence and question their commitment to existing institutional arrangements. Different groups pulled in different directions, which made the government's political juggling ever more delicate and the electoral outcome increasingly uncertain. However, when these negative sentiments happened to coincide – that is, when there emerged a disappointment consensus among both the key labor unions and business elites – the government lost power.

I believe this is what happened when the Likud first came to power in 1977, and then, later, when it was defeated by Labor in 1992. This hypothesis is not easy to substantiate with the available Israeli data. Ideally, we would need to relate the temporal course of electoral politics to key disaggregated variables that reflect the relative positions and moods of the various elites. Unfortunately, such data rarely exist. For instance, the relative position of the large conglomerates is greatly affected by changes in their institutional arrangements with the government; but how can these arrangements be assessed when even their most rudimentary aspects, such as the size and distribution of taxes, subsidies or government contracts, are not publicly known? Also, unlike in many other developed countries, Israel's Central Bureau of Statistics does not estimate the national accounts from the income side. As a result, we have no official statistics on the size distribution of profit, and even the overall magnitude of business income is estimated only indirectly. Similarly, if we are to observe shifts in the labor arena, we need information on net (as opposed to pre-tax) wages, as well as on the distribution of labor income; again, unforeseen, these data do not exist in Israel.[30]

In spite of these difficulties we may identify three important similarities between the 1977 defeat of the Labor government and the 1992 fall of Likud. First, in both cases the pre-election years show a marked deterioration in the profit position of the major companies in the Israeli economy.[31] Prior to the 1970s, when the economy was still dominated by a Keynesian government, the large corporate groups were only at their formative stage and their profits were still relatively low. From the 1970s onward, however, these large firms started to emerge as a leading economic power and their net profits began to grow rapidly, in both absolute terms and as a share of total business income. This rapid growth ended in the mid-1980s and then reverted to a decline, which continued into the early 1990s. From 1974 to 1976, profits of the large holding groups declined by approximately 9 percent annually. This cessation of GNP growth was the first since 1966. Between 1984 and 1991 there was a persistent decline in profits of the big economy, especially in the years 1990–91. These last years were experienced with particular severity by the business elite, whose expectations had been temporarily raised in 1989 by a brief spurt of growth.

From this follows the second similarity, involving domestic military purchases. With the emergence of chronic stagnation since the mid-1970s, the profits of the big economy became increasingly dependent on financial activity and military production.[32] Domestic military procurement grew rapidly from the mid-1960s until its peak in 1974, a period that also saw the most rapid consolidation of the big economy. Between 1969 and 1974, domestic military procurement grew at an annual rate of 14 percent. As a share of GNP this indicator stood at about 3 percent in the early 1960s, and reached a peak of 13 percent during the 1973 war. The subsequent period, until the 1977 dethronement of the Labor government, witnessed a sharp decline in these expenditures, at an annual rate of 8.5 percent.[33] Since 1977, however, under the new Likud regime, domestic military procurement resumed its upward trend, which continued until the 1982–83 war in Lebanon. From 1984 to 1990, real arms purchases remained at a more or less steady level. But overall military sales continued to rise with the growth of heavily subsidized military exports. Since 1991, however, military exports began to decline, and a serious concern arose among the elites regarding the somber prospects for world military sales.

At the same time, the relaxation of superpower rivalry, the demise of the Soviet Union, and the outcome of the Gulf War, which excluded Israel from the winning coalition, have signaled the diminishing importance of Israel's strategic position to the US. These factors have all converged to generate a sense of apprehension in the Israeli military-industrial complex. The apparent downward rigidity of military spending throughout the 1980s and early 1990s, a rigidity that persisted despite growing public calls for cutbacks, serves to demonstrate the pivotal political position of the large corporations. At the same time, the pressures to curtail the military economy, together with the decline of inflationary speculation, bore heavily on the profits of the big economy. During the late 1980s, many leading firms, and most notably, the country's largest industrial concern, Koor, started to crumble, and that must have undermined the self-confidence of the business elites. Although the government was increasingly attuned to the demands of big business, its ability to further increase this sector's profits was evidently limited. Moreover, during that time, the business elites grew anxious about Israel's deteriorating relationships with the US, as highlighted by repeated revelations such as the Pollard affair, the Iran–Contra scandal and the Dotan affair. Over the years, the large Israeli conglomerates became increasingly dependent on US military and civilian assistance, as well as on the intricate set of business relationships with the large armament corporations – a dependency that was increasingly endangered by the inflexibility of Likud's foreign policy.[34] The souring of relations with the US also ran counter to the long-term assimilation of American values by Israeli elites, particularly the business ethos.

This reference leads to the third similarity, since in both 1977 and 1992 there was growing uneasiness about Israel's relationship with the US. The 1974–77 Rabin government first clashed with the Ford Administration over the peace talks with Egypt, and then with the Carter Administration over proposals for Palestinian self-rule. This latter conflict even led to an American re-evaluation of its military assistance to Israel.[35] However, for these negative business sentiments to affect the electoral outcome they had to coincide with a broader atmosphere of discontent in the labor market; indeed, both electoral reversals were preceded by severe setbacks for the labor unions. The 1960s were marked by a period of relative prosperity, supported first by the German payments and then by the post-1967 War boom. Since the mid-1970s, however, Israel entered a period of stunted growth. The Rabin government of 1974–77 adopted a contractionary policy aimed at increasing exports and improving the balance of payments. The policy included cuts in government capital formation, an effort to reduce real wages and a move toward more regressive taxation. The outcome was clear: unemployment rose 50 percent between 1973 and 1977. Real wages stopped rising after a long period of continuous increase going back to the beginning of the 1960s (between 1969 and 1973 real wages had risen 3.4 percent annually).[36]

The Begin government, which came into office in 1977, embarked on an expansionary policy of inflationary finance and foreign borrowing; this lowered the rate of unemployment and increased both profits and labor income. These developments were short-lived, however. Since the early 1980s, there has been a persistent tendency toward higher unemployment, and this was further augmented by wage erosion, which intensified during the 1989–91 period because of the massive immigration from the former Soviet Union.[37] The stagnation became particularly severe after 1985, when the unity government of Likud and Labor launched its stabilization policy. The plan included high real rates of interest (up to 40 percent), cuts in civilian spending and transfers (particularly social programs), reductions in marginal tax rates for high-income earners and a growing reliance on indirect taxes and levies, privatization, and support for foreign investment. Subsidies for agriculture were cut back and the income of the whole sector, cooperative (Kibbutzim and Moshavim) and private, declined drastically. The sword of privatization hung over the head of key large government firms, especially the Israel Aircraft Industry (the biggest Israeli arms producer), Bezek (the communication giant), and Israel Chemical (the leading Israeli exporter).

These trends had generated growing anxiety among the unions, especially given the rapid increase in the rate of unemployment since 1987, and the decline in real wage rates since 1989. New immigration from the Soviet Union, which might otherwise have acted as an economic stimulus, only contributed to a further rise in unemployment and stronger downward pressure on wages. The adverse evolution of unemployment and real wages again points to an important similarity between the fall of Labor in 1977 and the defeat of Likud in 1992. In particular, both elections were preceded by a few years of adverse trends in the key variables of the labor market. In other words, prior to these two elections there arose a consensus of discontent among the various elites. For the business coalitions, lower profits, falling military sales, and an antagonistic foreign policy signified a challenge to their leading role, while for the big unions, permanent high unemployment and lower wages spelled mass discontent and the loss of authority.

In this context, it is necessary to consider the impact of the Palestinian problem and the Intifada, which first broke out in the occupied territories in 1988. Contrary to conventional wisdom, both leading parties, Likud and Labor, and actually most of the Zionist parties, including the major parts of the current Meretz, have not recognized the Palestinian right to an independent state. As a matter of fact, the Palestinian question had never been a direct issue in electoral campaigns until the peace process debate was propelled into the Peres–Netanyahu election in 1996. The difference between the two major parties concerning the Palestinian question was merely tactical. The occupation itself was economically profitable, while its costs were relatively negligible (involving the maintenance of a small army and 'Shabak', General Security Service, force with minimal legitimation expenses). However, since the 1990s, the Israeli elite has started to lose its self-confidence, because it has become apparent that the occupation authorities have lost control and that terrorist activities have been spreading and endangering personal security within the green line. The elite's despair rapidly shifted the collective mood and led to a search for a noncontroversial authoritative figure who represented 'old' values. The combined weight of these sentiments projected itself forcefully onto the voting population and likely contributed to a change of government.

Conclusions based on the 1992 election process

In this work, I have argued that the customary approach of electoral economic cycles may not be sufficient to explain sharp political reversals, such as the 1977 defeat of the Labor government, or the 1992 dethronement of Likud. Belief in a sovereign, rational, utility-maximizing voter does not seem consistent with observed behavior, such as the fact that, despite a 400 percent rate of inflation, rising unemployment, the loss for many people of lifetime savings in the stock-market crash and the costly military entanglement in Lebanon, fully one-third of the voting population still chose to vote for Likud in the 1984 elections. Moreover, since the 1970s, Israeli governments have found it increasingly hard to run effective election economics campaigns, a fact that further diminishes the explanatory power of electoral economic cycles. My own approach in this chapter has been to focus not on cases of re-election, but on those instances in which a government lost power. These drastic reversals point to fundamental processes of political-economic restructuring, processes that are often ignored in the electoral literature but have a profound impact on political outcomes. Specifically, I have argued that the two cases in which the Israeli government failed in a bid for re-election arose from a coincidence of discontent among the business elite and key labor unions.

These reversals, however, became possible only since the 1970s, after the culmination of some important changes in the underlying structure of the Israeli economy. Israeli history involved a profound structural transition from a regime of economic growth with a dominant Labor government, to an era of stunted growth in which business elites assumed the leading role. The first period, lasting roughly until the early 1970s, was marked by growing population, rising real GNP per capita, expanding public services and rising military spending.[38] With the inflow of cheap foreign capital, the Labor government enjoyed a considerable degree of autonomy and cultural hegemony; this enabled and legitimized an effective 'stop–go' economic policy before and after elections. This process, which resembled Kalecki's political business cycle, began to disappear with the growth of the big economy in the early 1970s. The rise of the large conglomerates, together with the increasing dependence of Israel on the US, undermined the relative power position of the government and brought about a substantial change in dominant ideologies.

In the political literature, this change is often described as a shift from a dominant party system to a competitive party system.[39] The traditional notion is that this transformation arose when demographic, ethnic, religious or nationalistic changes altered the political preferences of the voting population. By focusing solely on the electoral form of the system, this view fails to recognize the profound change in its political-economic essence: the decline and de-legitimation of the political elite itself and the ascendancy of a political power alignment that established a new political order. It is noteworthy that proponents of this view overlook what might be called the democratization paradox, according to which the increase in the level of competition among political parties has taken place side by side with the monopolization of the economy. In other words, a reverse tendency exists between increasing economic concentration, on the one hand, and the decline of the dominant party system and the end of Labor hegemony, on the other.

This evaluation implies that Israel is perhaps not a special case after all, and suggests that an alternative theoretical perspective emphasizing social class and the process of capitalization may go a long way toward explaining its political development. Since the 1970s, Keynesian interventionism has given way to the 'new-old' ideology of free enterprise, including acceptance of a natural rate of unemployment and stunted growth. Under these conditions, the political arena becomes increasingly unstable and competitive. Although the government is called upon to take its hands off the economy, it must still respond to the plights of the various power coalitions. This need to both promote accumulation in the big economy and maintain legitimation with the labor unions involves a very delicate balancing act, which is made even more difficult by the weaker economic position of the government. The Rabin government of 1977 and the Shamir government of 1992 failed in that task. Both governments faced growing discontent among all the important elites and key unions and, with these negative sentiments projected forcefully through the various mass media, they both fell.

Here, we come to discussions concerning the structural change taking place in the 1990s. The Israeli elites have faced the reality of the new world order. The globalization of big business and the increase of world competitiveness cast doubt on the expediency of a state of permanent war economy for Israel's big economy. More importantly, the international market for armaments has entered a new period of contraction and cut-throat competition in which Israeli companies will find it hard to gain or even retain market share.[40] Those who want to survive must realign themselves with international investors, who see Israel as a springboard for regional business. Also, the Israeli conglomerates discovered that the international market, especially the emerging countries, offers great potential, but this depends upon removing the Arab boycott; which in turn is considerably dependent upon settling the Palestine–Israel conflict. In short, war has become an economic burden, both to the multinational corporations seeking to enter the region, and to their domestic counterparts who wish to ride the tide.

Thus, with the rise of the Rabin regime, the so-called peace dividend process began. This process, while largely stimulated by American intervention in the Middle East, encouraged the Rabin government to settle the Palestinian–Israeli conflict, which had become a burden, and to move toward a competitive economy integrated into the rest of the Middle East. This kind of integration in the new capitalist order led the Rabin regime to confront both the unions and the nationalistic right. The Rabin government took drastic measures in order to cut wages and social services, to maintain a high rate of unemployment and to destroy the unions. However, the government received support from the merchant elites and from the business sector at large, which profited from the recent upward trends in the stock market and tax-free capital gains. The three main centers of opposition most injured by this demilitarization-oriented neoliberal policy – the unemployed and low-wage workers; the clerical right and the settlement movement; and the unions representing employees of large industrial firms – are unlikely to be able to unite against this trend. Thus, as long as Rabin hoped to maintain solid relations with the US, integrating Israeli business into the Middle Eastern Pax Americana (see Zunes), he would not have needed to implement any drastic measures, aside from formulating a short-term electoral economics policy before the coming elections.

Conclusions based on the 1996 election

This chapter was originally written in 1993, before the Oslo Agreement between Israel and the Palestinians. Since then, the political picture has been changed by three successive events: first, the murder of prime minister Rabin in November 1995; second, the dethronement of his successor, Shimon Peres, by Benjamin Netanyahu and the Likud Party in May 1996; and third, by the terrorist bombings. Subsequently both Ehad Barak and Arial Sharon have come to power running on peace and security platforms. Both Netanyahu's and Barak's tenures were short and Sharon's is likely to be similarly brief. More important than speculating about this in understanding the basis, confusion if you will, that has caused these short-term swings in power. This takes us back to the events in 1995 and 1996 that combined to bring Netanyahu to power.

These events were part of a right-wing nationalist movement in Israel and similar trends among the Palestinians against the new trends in the Middle East. The Israeli masses discovered that peace was not necessarily synonymous with personal security and rising standards of living. For example, although unemployment declined from its 1991 peak of 11 percent, down to around 6 percent in 1995, job security – a traditional hallmark of Israeli labor relations – deteriorated rapidly. The main reason was the disintegration of the unions, primarily the Histradrut, which lost much of its earlier control over the labor force. The arrival of over 70 000 new immigrants from the ex-Soviet Union intensified competition in the labor market, and guest-workers from the former Eastern Europe, Latin America and Asia, numbering over 200 000 (9 percent of total employment), practically bar Israeli Jews from most manual jobs; by extension these workers bar Palestinians. The consequence was that the 1990s were marked by growing income disparities between rich and poor, professionals and laborers and between Muslims, Christians, and Jews. Despite rapidly rising GDP per capita, average real wages stagnated and most workers saw their real incomes fall: according to surveys, real wages of managerial and professional occupations actually grew by 18 percent between 1990 and 1995, while those of the bottom third of the labor force fell by between 9 and 18 percent.

The economic policies of the Labor government, which initially seemed supportive of capital-intensive programs, instead benefited the big conglomerates and foreign investors. The increasing openness of the Israeli economy enabled its large conglomerates to extend their global influence by floating equity issues on the New York Stock Exchange to raise capital, by increasing exports to the emerging markets in the East, and by raising the level of direct and multinational investment outside the country. Direct investment in Israel climbed to over $2 billion in 1995, up from next to nothing a few years earlier, and strategic alliances between foreign and local conglomerates have multiplied dramatically. The Labor government has also privatized many public assets, selling the bulk of these institutions to the local conglomerates, who are often backed by investors. In addition, the six largest Israel core conglomerates were partly or wholly merged with foreign transactional corporations.

In sum, Israel underwent, in a relatively short period of time, a significant restructuring, interlocking its business elite into global capital. For the small business sector, where the majority of voters earn their living, the New Middle East Order has become more a curse than a boon. It should be noted, however, that it was not Palestinian imports that have closed these businesses, but rather it was Rabin's policies. This segment of the Israeli business sector was the primary victim of repeated closures of the Palestinian territories, because these closures prevented Palestinian workers from selling their services to weaving and finishing contractors. Labor border-closure policies also caused significant losses in agriculture, construction and services, which, in the end, have caused inflationary pressure in Israel.

More generally, the acceptance of the Washington consensus in Jerusalem required a modified high-interest-rate regime in order to counteract over-heating (although inflation has actually declined since the early 1990s). The principal losers were the small businesses who, unlike the large conglomerates, could not borrow abroad. Moreover, after hitting an all-time high in 1994, the Israeli market crashed, causing many firms to lose a significant part of their capital base. Many small-time investors suffered very heavy losses, and with the central bank's restrictive monetary policy preventing the stock market from recovering, the sense of betrayal among such investors intensified. The final straw for many Israeli voters was an unprecedented wave of terrorist attacks in Israel. For the first time many Israelis lost their sense of personal security. These apprehensions have not been eased.

Given the particular path of the Peace Process, the wave of terrorist attacks since 1996 and the recent militant movements should not be that surprising. The agreements reached at Oslo, Paris, and Hebron have each promised too little to the Arabs. For many Palestinians, these pacts are increasingly perceived as sell-out schemes accepted by the Palestinian Authority (PA) to the Israelis' benefit. Relative to the period before the Intifada, the economic and political reality in the territories has deteriorated. Because of the border closures and the importation of guest-workers to replace Palestinians, unemployment in the territories has soared to 40 percent or more and the daily wage rate has dropped below \$10. With few internal resources, a trickle of international aid and no independent fiscal and monetary policy tools, and even less hope of foreign direct investment, the PA has been unable to alter the situation.

Moreover, the leadership of the PA has been constantly humiliated by Israeli officials throughout the negotiations. Arafat has managed to gain partial independence (without sovereignty) in a mere 4 percent of the occupied territories. The Israeli government continued its policy of administrative arrests, land seizures and settlements, particularly in the so-called Greater Jerusalem and, in the negotiations over the Hebron redeployment, they fought for the right of pursuit into PA territories. This would be unacceptable to Arab locals, who would fear Israeli police incursion, and whose police would not have reciprocity should they want to chase Israeli settlers into Israeli-controlled parts of Hebron.[41] According to the *Nekuda*, a religious/nationalist newsletter with strong fascist overtones, the number of Jewish inhabitants in the occupied territories has risen by over 40 percent over the past five years, and government spending in these areas has doubled relative to the golden days of the Begin and Shamir governments. Under these circumstances, there is little wonder why opposition to Arafat and the Peace Process has intensified among the Palestinians.

And so, although the core coalition between the Labor government, the large local conglomerates, foreign investors, the US administration, the EU and the international financial institutions has remained intact, the popular belt which supported it in 1992 was getting progressively thinner. The assassination of Rabin temporarily boosted the Labor Party's popularity, but their lead proved insufficient in the face of a massive bombing wave just before the 1996 elections. However, the new government found it had only limited room to maneuver. Judged by his education (ten years in the US) and his supposed espousal of neoliberal ideologies, Netanyahu was portrayed as being the first all-American prime minister of Israel. This, together with pressure from the domestic conglomerates, foreign investors and the US Administration, suggested that he would continue the liberalization and regional integration policies of his Labor predecessors, all the while, however, remembering that serving the corporate elites' profit-maximizing agendas would serve Likud well.

Therefore, the Peace Process continued to concentrate on the pro-US axis of Turkey, Jordan, Egypt and the Gulf states. The Palestinians were restricted to a quasi-state, criss-crossed with Israeli settlements, with declining water resources, no direct access to the sea and forced economic dependence on Israel. From this point of view, the structural change which has taken place in Israeli society since the 1970s succeeded in securing its positions. By 1997, Israel neither constituted a unique case in social research nor in any research regarding electoral politics, rather, it served as a typical example of a semi-peripheral state in the age of global corporate capitalism.

Notes

1. This chapter first appeared as the article 'Political Shifts in Israel, 1997 and 1992: Unsuccessful Electoral Economics or Long Range Realignment?' *Science and Society*, 58 (Winter 1994–95) 415–39. It has been updated and revised for the 1996 elections, but is reprinted with the *Journal*'s permission. I want to thank the editors for their cooperation.

2. D. Horowitz and M. Lissik, 'Democracy and National Security in a Contentious Conflict' (in Hebrew), *Yahdoot Zemanenu*, 4 (1978) 27–65; and Yonathan Shapiro, 'The End of a Dominant Party System in Israel', in A. Arian (ed.), *The Election in Israel, 1977* (Jerusalem: Jerusalem Academic Press, 1980) pp. 23–38.

3. A. Diskin, 'Polarization and Volatility among Voters', in D. Caspi, A. Diskin, and E. Gutmann (eds), *The Roots of Begin's Success* (London and New York: St. Martin's Press, 1984) pp. 113–40.

4. The essentials of this paradigm are to be found in manuals on Israeli political sociology and economics. See, S. N. Eisenstadt, *Israeli Society* (London: 1967); R. Ben-Porath (ed.), *The Economy of Israel Maturing Through Crisis* (Cambridge, MA: Harvard University Press, 1986). For a critique, see U. Ram, *The Changing Agenda of Israeli Sociology: Theory, Ideology and Identity* (New York: State University of New York Press, 1995).

5. Two primary studies have been devoted to examination of electorate behavior from a class-consciousness perspective; both are in Hebrew and deal with the 1960s. See G. Yatziv, 'The Class Basis for Party Association – The Example of Israel' (Jerusalem: Department of Sociology, Hebrew University, 1979); and A. Zloczower, 'Mobility Patterns and Status Conceptions in an Urban Israeli Settling', Unpublished PhD Dissertation (Jerusalem: The Hebrew University, 1968). These works predicted the decline of the Labor movement, but did not analyze objective power relations development between capital and labor. These studies challenged the predominantly American functionalist theories and the 'end of ideology' concept that prevailed in the Israeli social sciences.

6. R. Y. Ben-Porath, 'The Years of Plenty and the Years of Famine: A Political Business Cycle?' *Kyklos*, 28 (1975) 400–3.

7. U. Ben-Hanan and B. Temkin, 'The Overloaded Juggler: The Electoral-Economic-Cycle in Israel, 1951–1984', in A. Arian and M. Shamir (eds), *The Elections in Israel – 1984* (Jerusalem: Jerusalem Academic Press, 1986) pp. 15–35; D. Levi, 'Electoral Economics and Business Cycles in Israel' (in Hebrew), *The Economic Quarterly* (January 1984), 865–73; G. Doron and B. Tamir, 'The Electoral Cycle: A Political Economic Perspective', *Crossroads* (Spring 1993) 141–63.

8. On the first point see Doron and Tamir (1983) 142; and J. Alt and A. K. Chrystal, *Political Economics* (Berkeley, CA: University of California Press, 1983). On the later points, see C. Frey, S. Bruno and F. Schneiderk, 'An Empirical Study of Politico-Economic Interaction in the United States', *Review of Economics and Statistics*, 60 (1978) 174–83.

9. Ben-Hanan and Temken (1986) p. 23,

10. On 'popular culture' see Eisenstadt (1967); on 'business orientation' see Y. Shapiro, *The Democracy in Israel* (in Hebrew) (Ramath-Gan: Massada,

1977); on 'economic affairs' see A. Arian, *Politics and Government in Israel* (in Hebrew) (Tel-Aviv: Zmora-Biton, 1985), especially chapter 3; on 'democratic basis' see Y. Aharoni, *The Political Economy of Israel* (in Hebrew) (Tel-Aviv: Cherikover Publishing, 1991) pp. 127–31.

11. T. Ferguson, 'Party Realignment and American Industrial Structure: The Investment Theory of Political Parties in Historical Perspective', *Research in Political Economy*, 6 (1983) 1–82.

12. The potential significance of such conflicting developments is emphasized in S. Bichler and J. Nitzan, 'Military Spending and the Structure of the Israeli Economy', in J. Bowring (ed.), *Competition in a Dual Economy* (Princeton, NJ: Princeton University Press, 1996).

13. Ferguson (1983) 20–30.

14. It is, of course, true that no rigorous proof that meets the canons of a 'dynamic' explanation of a link between desires of the elites and voter decisions has ever been provided by 'elitist' theorists such as Ferguson (1983), Domhoff (1979) or D. Abraham, *The Collapse of the Weimar Republic: Economy and Crisis* (Princeton, NJ : Princeton University Press, 1981). Nevertheless, the growing number of 'structural' studies showing domination of the media by business elites are highly suggestive of the possibility that such elites can exert significant impact on voting decisions. A short survey on the recent 'elitist' studies will be found in Domhoff (1990) ch 1.

15. M. Kalecki, 'Political Aspects of Full Employment' (1943) article is reprinted in Michael Kalecki (ed.), *Selected Essays on the Dynamics of the Capitalist Economy: 1933–1970* (Cambridge: Cambridge University Press, 1971).

16. Ibid., p. 144.

17. J. Steindl, 'Stagnation Theory and Stagnation Policy', *Cambridge Journal of Economics*, 3 (March 1979), 1–14.

18. See Steindl (1979) p. 8 on 'political trends'. The literature dealing with these trends is summarized in J. B. Foster, John Bellamy, *The Theory of Monopoly Capitalism: An Elaboration of Marxian Political Economy* (New York: Monthly Review Press, 1984) pp. 140–6.

19. On the doctrine of 'overloaded government' see S. P. Huntington, 'The Crisis of Democracy: The United States', in M. Crozier, S. P. Huntington and J. Watanuki (eds), *The Crisis of Democracy* (New York: New York University Press, 1975). For a critique of that doctrine, see C. Crouch, 'The State, Capital and Liberal Democracy', in C. Crouch (ed.), *State and Economy in Contemporary Capitalism* (London: Croom Helm, 1979) pp. 15–54, but especially pp. 14–16.

20. A. Arian and S. H. Barnes, 'The Dominant Party System: Neglected Model of Democratic Stability', *Journal of Politics*, 36 (1974) 592–614.

21. There is no space in this study for a full description of the development of the Israeli power elite. A more detailed account of its origins and development can be found in S. Frenkel and S. Bichler, *The Rich Families: Israel's Aristocracy of Finance* (in Hebrew) (Tel Aviv: Cherikover Publishing, 1984). It is important to note that this subject has not yet been systematically studied by Israeli social scientists.

22. The literature on core firms in the modern economy is examined and summarized in Bowring (1996). Additional data on the Israeli core corporations are found in R. Rowley, S. Bichler and J. Nitzan, 'Some Aspects of

Aggregate Concentration in the Israeli Economy, 1964–1986', Working Paper Series, Department of Economics (Montreal, Canada: McGill University, July 1988).

23. A. Aharoni, *Structure and Performance in the Israeli Economy* (in Hebrew) (Tel Aziz: Chrikover Publishing, 1976) especially chapter 7.

24. M. Shalev, *Labor and the Political Economy in Israel* (Oxford: Oxford University Press, 1992) see chapter 5.

25. See N. E. Farjoun's 1980 study on 'Palestinian Workers in Israel – A Reserve Army of Labour', *Khamsin*, 7 (1980) 107–43.

26. S. Bichler, 'The Political Economy of Military Spending' (in Hebrew), Unpublished PhD dissertation (Jerusalem: The Hebrew University, 1991). The relationship between inflation and the distribution of income and assets in Israel is examined in E. Alexander, 'The Inflationary Effect of the Income Redistribution Process during Inflation: An Income Redistribution Model of Stagflation and The Case of Israel and France', Working Paper (Los Angeles: University of California, 1978).

27. This particularly affected the assets of the core conglomerates: according to the report of the commission of inquiry dealing with the 1983 collapse of the stock market, shares of the three largest banks, which accounted for 7 percent of the aggregate value of all financial assets in 1973, rose to 44 percent of that total by 1982. See M. Bejski, V. Ziller, Z. Hirsh, M. Sarnat and D. Friedman, 'Report of the Commission of Inquiry into the Regulation of Banking Shares' (in Hebrew) (Jerusalem: The Government Printer, 1986), starting on p. 61. Data on stock market capitalization are from Bank of Israel annual reports (1974) 445; (1983) 282. The GNP figures are taken from the Central Bureau of Statistics, *National Accounts 1972–1985*, 166.

28. Rowley et al. (1989).

29. See for example National Insurance Institute, *Annual Survey* (Jerusalem: Bureau of Research and Planning), mainly for the years 1987–91. On the effects of military spending see Bichler (1991); and A. Halperin, 'Does Military Technology Affect Economic Growth?' Working Paper Submitted to the International Conference on 'Technology and Strategy: Future Trends' (Tel Aviv: The Jaffe Center for Strategic Studies, Tel-Aviv University, 1987).

30. For a critical review of economic data in Israel, see Bichler (1991) chapter 4.

31. The profits of the 'big economy' combine the net profits of Israel's five largest conglomerates: the Leumi group, Hapoalim group, IDB, Koor, and Clal. The data are based on the companies' consolidated reports and are expressed in constant prices. A detailed analysis of the financial performance of the big economy is given in Rowley et al. (1988).

32. The impact of military spending on the profits of the 'big economy' and on the process of aggregate concentration in Israel are analyzed in Bichler and Nitzan (1996).

33. The data are based on reports from the *National Accounts* of the Central Bureau of Statistics, for various years. For discussion of the feasibility of this data, see E. Berglas, 'Defense and Economy: Israeli Experience', Discussion Paper 83.01 (Jerusalem: The Maurice Falk Institute of Economic Research, 1983). In Israel there is no systematic data on the distribution of contract awards; nevertheless we can assume the bulk of domestic military contracts

flows to the big economy (as many unofficial indicators suggest); see, for instance, Bichler and Nitzan (1994).

34. A. Cockburn and L. Cockburn, *Dangerous Liaison: The Inside Story of the U.S.–Israeli Covert Relationship* (Toronto: Stoddart Publishing, 1991).

35. M. Gazit 'Israeli Arms Purchases from the US', Policy Oriented Papers 8, The Leonard Davis Institute for International Relations (Jerusalem: The Hebrew University, 1993).

36. Data on the rate of unemployment is based on the *Statistical Abstract of Israel*, various years, chapters on 'Labor and Wages'. The average real wage is computed by dividing the 'average monthly wage per employee post' (before taxes) by the annual CPI.

37. Unemployment rose continuously from 2.3 percent in 1979 – with the exception of some token pre-election decreases – to almost 12 percent in 1992. The trend in real wages was steadily upward from 1977 to 1988 (with the exception of 1985, the year of 'stabilization policy'). This trend was reversed between 1989 and 1992, when real wages decreased at an annual rate of 6.5 percent.

38. This resembles in some sense the claim by D. Gold, 'The Rise and Fall of the Keynesian Coalition', *Kapitalistate*, 6 (Fall 1977) 129–61, that, after the Second World War, there emerged in the US a 'Keynesian coalition' among the big economy, the large labor unions and the government to prevent stagnation via increases in military spending.

39. See, for example, Arian (1977); Shapiro (1980).

40. It is interesting to note that, while domestic military spending has declined in the last two years, military imports (supported by American grants) have not. If this continues, the Israeli contractors will eventually be forced to transform themselves into subsidiaries of their American counterparts (Tediran, one of the leading contractors, became in the last decade a considerable subcontractor of American arms suppliers). Readers should also refer to Emma Murphy's chapter in volume I.

41. L. Andoni, 'Redefining Oslo: Negotiating the Hebron Protocol', *Journal of Palestine Studies*, XXVI (Spring 1997) 17–29.

Epilog

J. W. Wright, Jr.

The chapters in this edition, and in its companion volumes, attempt to fill a gap in literature about trade economic factors and their effects on Middle East diplomacy. We have complained throughout of a lacking policy vision, certainly throughout the whole of the Clinton administration. And yet until recently few scholars have delved into socio-economic or political-economic analysis of the Peace Process, leaving an absence of clear information on which clearer economic policies could be formed. These issues are critical and by not studying them we are obliged to share the blame for the US's poor policy vision during the Peace Process.

It seems to me that we have a greater interest now than ever before in illustrating, through continuing research and contextual dialog, that the Peace Process has not only been politically divisive, but also commercially inefficient and economically ineffective. Moreover, we must recognize that as Israeli business interests in the West Bank and Gaza decline, there are fewer incentives for the private sector to exert its influences toward promoting peace and/or for retooling its industries. And, as the Palestinian economic environment spirals downward, it is less likely that foreign firms and/or people from the Diaspora will invest or form joint ventures. Pragmatically speaking, the real opportunities for external investment lie in the Gulf states. However, credibility losses within the PA have formed real disincentives for Gulf investment in Palestine. A similar situation exists in Egypt. By the same token, Israeli regimes have not done much to promote investor confidence or to prove that Gulf money would be safe or joint ventures fair.

The result is little collective commercial interest in supporting the Peace Process. Unless this situation changes economic decline and aid dependency will frame future peace talks, leaving negotiators with continually weakening political and economic structures to work around. So if there has been poor policy vision in the region it not only emanates from a lack of government initiative, but also from a lack of interest from globalization's commercial sectors. Because of the disincentives they face, these potential investors are disinterested in Palestine, and probably with good reason from a corporate point of view. If economic dominance was implied by Shimon Peres' coinage of the 'new Middle East' – whether we fear that vision or support it – then it is necessary that we better consider in our research and policy advice broader commercial and economic diplomatics that could support peace.

Moreover, we must recognize that the very structure of peace is paralyzing the process. The governing structures built into the processes' pacts, protocols, and agreements are so biased that they make further economic decline inevitable. Is there any wisdom in building economic and political institutions and structures that are by their design impediments to peace? Surely not. How can a pragmatic, much less a sustainable, peace be built with all of these economic and political impediments in place? Not easily. None of the scenarios presented in this volume or its two predecessors indicate much legitimacy, ideology, or long-term planning on the part of the American, Arab or Israeli negotiating teams. Rather, the evidence presented in these volumes indicates that corporate interests and personal political agendas – not real intentions for peace – seem to have ruled the day throughout the Clinton Administration's attempts to broker peace. It is this critical structural flaw that has led to so many crucial failures in the pursuit of Middle East peace. We should therefore put or energies into identifying, analyzing and correcting this situation during the George W. Bush Administration.

Index